# THE CHURCH AND
## MAN'S STRUGGLE FOR UNITY

## BLANDFORD HISTORY SERIES
(General Editor R. W. Harris)

### PROBLEMS OF HISTORY

### HISTORY OF EUROPE SERIES

### THE HISTORY OF ENGLAND SERIES

# The Church and Man's Struggle For Unity

**HERBERT WADDAMS**

*Canon of Canterbury*

**BLANDFORD PRESS**

**LONDON**

First published in 1968
© 1968 Blandford Press Ltd.,
167 High Holborn, London W.C.1
SBN 713 7048 02

*Printed in Great Britain by*
*Richard Clay (The Chaucer Press), Ltd.,*
*Bungay, Suffolk*

# CONTENTS

# Acknowledgments

Acknowledgment is due to the following for their kind permission to reproduce illustrations:

Byzantine Institute, Inc., Washington: No. 21
Cambridge University Press Ltd.: No. 8
Camera Press Ltd.: Nos. 9, 19
Church Information Office: Nos. 35, 36
Elsevier, Amsterdam (from *Atlas of the Early Christian Church*):
    Nos. 6, 15
Gallerie Vaticane, Rome: Nos. 1, 2, 3, 4
Italian State Tourist Office: Nos. 11, 20
Jordan Tourist Authority: No. 10
Koninklijke Bibliotheek, The Hague: No. 26
Kunsthistorisch Institut, Nijmegen: No. 5
Novosti Press Agency: Nos. 13, 22, 25, 28, 33
Paul Popper Ltd.: Nos. 32, 34
Radio Times Hulton Picture Library: Nos. 7, 12, 24, 27, 29
Royal Greek Embassy: Nos. 14, 16, 17, 18
Uitgeverij W. ten Have N.V., Amsterdam: No. 31

# List of Illustrations

(*between pages* 84 *and* 85)

xi

# A Note on Terminology

THE titles which churches adopt for themselves are not always accepted by others, for the titles themselves may involve implicit claims which other churches reject. The most obvious example is the title 'Catholic', if used exclusively of those churches which accept obedience to the Pope as alone justifying the adjective. There are a number of small churches which have the word 'catholic' as part of their own titles, and other churches, such as those of the Anglican Communion, dispute the right of Roman Catholics to the exclusive use of the description 'catholic'. It is not surprising that there is this opposition to the exclusive use of the word from the side of non-Roman churches which habitually use the creed in the form of stating their belief in one, holy, *catholic* and apostolic church.

It will therefore be the rule in this book to use the words 'Roman Catholic' to denote the church of which the Pope of Rome is the head. It is necessary at this point to specify 'Pope of Rome', since there are other bishops whose official description includes that of 'Pope', e.g. the Patriarch of Alexandria. The word 'pope' derives, of course, from the word for father, and a derivative of it is used as the normal form of address to priests in some parts of the world. But there are other churches which, though subject to the Pope (of Rome —normally this will be the meaning of the word), cannot strictly be defined as 'Roman Catholic' without confusion. These are the churches which are in full communion with Rome and which recognise the Pope as the head of the church, but follow a rite other than the Roman rite. These churches are most easily referred to by their distinguishing rite as Armenian Catholic, Greek Catholic and so on.

The churches with eastern rites which are in communion with Rome almost all correspond to churches of which originally they themselves were part, churches of Eastern Christendom usually called 'Eastern Orthodox' or just 'Orthodox'. It might seem that there is as much objection to a group of churches claiming an exclusive use of the word 'orthodox' as there is to 'catholic' for Roman Catholics. And in principle this is sound. Nevertheless, 'Orthodox' is a convenient and generally accepted designation for those churches of Eastern Christendom which form one family of churches recognising the Ecumenical Patriarch of Constantinople as their chief bishop, though only as first among equals.

There is another group of eastern churches which have been regarded as technically heretical, and which are separated from the Eastern Orthodox. These churches fall into two parts: (*a*) the so-called Monophysite churches, Armenian, Syrian, Egyptian (Coptic), Ethiopian; and (*b*) the so-called Nestorian Church, whose official title is 'The Church of the East', usually known as Assyrian. For a long time this group of churches has been known as the 'Lesser Eastern Churches', a descriptive title which more or less corresponds to their size, although some 'Orthodox' churches are smaller than some 'Lesser Eastern' churches. In recent years efforts have been made to find some other description which would be sufficiently distinctive and at the same time avoid the use of the word 'lesser', which in some quarters was thought to be condescending. But in fact no generally agreed description has been found, and most new proposals have objections. 'Ancient Oriental Churches' has been one suggested description, but the acceptance of this seems to depend on the implicit assumption that 'ancient' means something different from 'old' and that 'oriental' means something different from 'eastern'. It would be difficult to sustain this theory, and if the title merely means 'old eastern churches' it is confusing, as those churches are certainly not as old as the 'Orthodox' churches and both are equally 'eastern'. Another title suggested for them has been 'Non-Chalcedonian Churches' (or even 'Meta-Chalcedonian Churches'), on the ground that these churches rejected the findings of the Council of Chalcedon in A.D. 451. But, although accurate from a historical point of view, the title is clumsy and is totally obscure for the vast majority of Christians in the world and in those churches themselves. Moreover, some of the members of the churches in question would maintain that, whatever their historical attitude had been, they do not in fact reject the doctrinal teaching of the Council of Chalcedon. In this book, therefore, we shall use the title 'Lesser Eastern Churches' as being less open to objection than its alternatives.

The Anglican Communion is a family of churches which is in full communion with the Archbishop of Canterbury and recognises him to be the chief bishop so long as it is understood to be a position of honour only. 'Anglican' strictly means 'English' and, although most

Anglican churches throughout the world can trace back their ancestry to England, it is no longer possible to regard them as English. But no better name has been found, although a recent Archbishop of Canterbury (Dr. Fisher) offered a prize to anyone who could find a better title. We shall continue to use 'Anglican' in this sense. The titles of the various churches of this group differ considerably, and few of them have 'Anglican' included in them. In the United States of America the full title of the Anglican church is the 'Protestant Episcopal Church of the United States of America', and the church is normally referred to as 'episcopal' or 'episcopalian'.

Many Lutheran churches have the word 'Lutheran' in their official descriptions, and there no particular problems arise, but there are important exceptions. In the case of Calvinist churches, however, it is common to refer to them as 'Reformed' (with a capital letter) or 'Presbyterian'. The adjective 'reformed' therefore means Calvinist when used with a capital letter, but when used without a capital it merely carries its normal adjectival meaning or may be used to describe any church which has been developed under the influence of the Reformation.

# 1

## The First Christian Communities

### Introductory

MANY people, perhaps most, read into history what they want to read out of it: they interpret historical events and movements in the way which best fits in with their own outlooks and beliefs. This habit is common in dealing with secular history, and it is even more common with religious history. The words 'secular' and 'religious' here are not used in any exclusive sense. Indeed, it will be one of the purposes of this book to show that what is usually considered to be religious is always mixed with non-religious elements. There is no such thing in history as the exclusively religious or the exclusively secular. The two adjectives are used here as a convenient means of distinguishing different approaches to history.

In this sense, 'secular' history is the province of the general historian and is an all-inclusive term, whereas religious history is one aspect of a wider subject or, more accurately, it is general history seen from the point of view of the religious beliefs and practices of men. Because men's motives are mixed the history is likewise mixed. But when men come to read and interpret the history of the past they are more likely to be affected by their religious attitudes than by their other prejudices when dealing with historical topics. A religious attitude in a historian is not necessarily that of the particular religious body to which he belongs: it may equally well be, and often is, an agnostic or atheistic approach, which may be just as 'religious' as that of the most fanatical believer.

The subject of this book is affected by the interplay of religious ideas and institutions with secular life, and, whatever may be one's personal preferences, there can be no doubt that religious motifs have been important and influential in the development of men's

5

ideas and actions. But often the religious outlooks themselves have been deeply affected by non-religious elements which have not always been recognised. In this study we are concerned with the history of Christian unity and division, with the causes and effects of Christian bodies sometimes cooperating, sometimes at deadly enmity among themselves. Though a comparatively narrow field of history, it is one of considerable importance.

It is impossible for anyone to see the strong movements today[1] towards Christian unity in perspective without some idea of the background which has produced the present pattern. For the most part we are familiar with small patches of history which we have learnt in our earlier school days and which concern our own countries and the churches which are found in them. But this is not enough now, for in this, as in everything else, we move on a world stage and need to have a world-wide framework into which to fit our present-day picture. The history of the relations of Christian churches with one another is an essential prerequisite for a right perspective in assessing contemporary movements.

At one time 'Christendom' was a word which described the whole civilised world, but this has long ceased to be the case. Even that part of the world which is sometimes called Christian has largely ceased to be so in any conscious sense, even though its outlooks and thinking are deeply influenced by a Christian past and by Christian presuppositions. The world of the second half of the twentieth century is one in which all mankind is brought into close contact. Although it is not yet a political or social unity, mankind as such has to be the unit of men's thoughts. In other words, the whole world has to be taken into consideration when seriously examining any human question, even a question which at first sight seems to be confined to one region or one country.

The spread of a sense of unity among Christians is an unconscious recognition of the fact of human solidarity in all parts of the world. We use the word 'unconscious' because, in this as in many other aspects of religious life, those who participate in the ecumenical movement often look at it in exclusively religious terms. Such a view is inadequate, even from a religious standpoint rightly understood. It is a besetting temptation for Christians to assume that God teaches them only through religious means. But from a true Christian point of view this is an improper attitude, for it carries with it the implication that God can do his work only through religious or ecclesiastical persons or institutions. A mere glimpse at history shows how false such an idea is.

Modern ecumenical movements, therefore, can be seen as springing from various roots, and one of them certainly is the need for Christians to react to developments in the world which are changing the relationship of men and nations to one another. And it may fairly be claimed that the ecumenical reaction is in many ways a pioneering movement, ahead of most thinking in other fields. There can always be found enlightened minds who have read the signs of the times and have prophesied to their contemporaries, trying to persuade them to see the truth. But the ecumenical movement is a practical experiment in producing a new consciousness of world-wide unity which is of considerable significance.

Attempts towards unity in Christian history may be seen in a wider perspective as part of men's perennial struggle to bring unity out of division. The study of man's past reveals an ebb and flow of human relations in which a succession of changing factors has produced an ever-moving series of problems. The Christian Church has never been able to escape the imperatives of its own Gospel towards unity, in spite of the failures and betrayals in which it has been involved.

Historically the Christian religion has been responsible for division as well as for unity. The purpose of this book is to examine in broad outline the main developments of division and unity in connection with the Christian churches, so as to provide a world setting for understanding the activities of the churches, and especially the ecumenical movement in its present form. In pursuing this task an attempt will be made to look at historical events in as dispassionate a light as possible. History without interpretation is impossible. Our aim must be to try to see developments in Christian history in as broad a perspective as possible, and to interpret them in relation to events which are not specifically religious.

It is certainly the case that the divisions which now form the raw material for the ecumenical movement's work are widespread geographically, that they have arisen during the course of history and in some cases date back to the earliest years of the Church. They are not now localised as they once were, for the emigration of the modern world has carried members of churches of the Middle East into living contact with churches from the West, not only in North America but also in countries of migration such as Australia and New Zealand.

There can be no doubt that, just as Christian influences have affected the general course of history, so influences from outside the Christian Church have had considerable effects on the developments of the Christian bodies themselves. It is important to try to identify some of these influences. For one result of doing so is to indicate that the differences which resulted in division were not concerned solely with the high principles used as rallying cries at the time, but that they reflected other desires, political, racial, regional or national. When this is clearly perceived it becomes evident that the differences between the bodies concerned may be easier to cure than was at first thought, since the external conditions which helped to produce splits have long ago ceased to have any relevance.

On the other hand, once a division has occurred, there is a powerful tendency for it to harden, as it becomes more and more identified with and related to social or political conditions. The human tendency to seek security in social and political life causes men to use religious motives to strengthen what they find to be a convenient political or social structure, and vice versa. The one interacts constantly on the other. Geographical or other factors may have the result of preserving the peculiarities of a church by isolating it completely from the rest of the world, as was the case with the Assyrian Church of the East up to the First World War. It is to the examination of such factors that we intend to give our attention.

At first sight the relevance of schismatic events of the fifth century would not appear to have much to do with the present. But all historians know that the present is joined to the past by living links, and that it is only by some understanding of that past that the present can be rightly understood. Church relations in North America which, for example, are concerned with Armenians living there in considerable numbers, cannot be understood or handled without some knowledge of the history of the Armenian Church and nation from about the year A.D. 300 onwards. Or, again, in South Africa the solidarity of the Boers and their distinctive culture has been closely bound up with their Dutch Calvinist form of Christianity.

A book such as this, specifically aimed at dealing with the divisions and relations among Christians, cannot and ought not to try to reproduce a general history of the bodies concerned, for this would merely repeat what is available elsewhere in reliable and readable form. Nor in one volume could a book cover in detail even this restricted subject. It can only hope to give a general survey, an outline, which will enable readers to put the subject into perspective and go on to read in detail those parts of it about which he desires to be better informed. As a recent distinguished writer has said, it is possible to write some books only if there is 'a resolute determination to omit'.[2]

## The Earliest Years

From the beginning Christianity contained within itself powerful forces tending towards unity. Its message was one which brought people together in recognition of a loving act of God which was to be exhibited in their own lives by their loving relationship to one another (John 15:12–17 and elsewhere). But there is ample evidence to show that the ideals of brotherly love and unity, although they were often impressively displayed, were marred by attitudes and actions which fell far short of them. But, whenever division and strife were found, there was never any doubt in the minds of the Christians concerned that this state of affairs was contrary to the basic teaching of their faith and to the desire of their founder and head, Jesus himself.

The story of the relations of Christians to one another has many parallels with other movements. It would be rash to claim that Christians behaved much better than other groups with high ideals, yet their beliefs and message contained within themselves a dynamic which carried their religion through much opposition to a triumphant conclusion, when looked at from a worldly point of view. It began as a despised sect in an unimportant province of the Roman Empire, and in less than three centuries was accepted as the official religion of the Empire, which had tried on more than one occasion to stamp it out of existence.

The New Testament is the main source of our knowledge of the first events of the Christian Church. All the documents emanate from Christians themselves, and are to be evaluated in that light. They cannot be expected to provide the detached and judicious summing up of an outside observer. They are something more valuable, for they are the self-exposure of a living community in its formative years. There has been much debate as to the reliability of the gospel accounts of the life of Jesus, but all are agreed that in the four gospels we have a picture of what the early Church believed Jesus to have taught and done. The earliest documents of the New Testament are the letters of Paul, written for the guidance, teaching or exhortation of newly formed groups of Christians in various towns round the Mediterranean Sea. They reflect clearly the problems of unity which beset Christians at a very early stage.

In order to follow the relevant facts in the early life of the Church, one must be aware of certain governing attitudes in the lives of the early Christians. Perhaps the most important of these was the conviction that the world was to come to an early end with the triumphant return of Jesus as Messiah and the establishment of his reign over the earth. This belief was their form of the Jewish expectation of the coming of the Messiah, and it is clear that it was based on sayings of Jesus himself, though they may possibly have been misunderstood. There are passages attributed to Jesus in the New Testament which may refer either to the future collapse of Jerusalem or to the end of the world.

The early Christians therefore thought themselves to be living in an interim state, the short period which would elapse between the final disappearance of Jesus from the earth and his return as victor. This had the effect of making organisation appear to be unnecessary, except as a temporary measure. Men do not give their sustained attention to long-term organisational plans if they think that they are not going to be of any use. It was, therefore, some time before Christians began to face the fact that the return of Christ was not going to occur in the near future. And, as it began to be accepted, Christians saw the need to turn what had been envisaged as temporary groups of local Christians into permanent centres of Christian life.

Jerusalem occupied the centre of the religious consciousness of the Jews: it summed up the history and the hopes of the Jewish race and religion, and it was not only an earthly national and religious centre to which all Jews looked but also a symbol of the future reign of God. Its destruction in A.D. 70 shattered this attitude. Until then Christians, being for the most part Jews in the early years, continued to look to Jerusalem as the centre of their own religious life, a point of view borne out by the fact that the first council of the Christian Church was held in Jerusalem (Acts 15) and that it was apparently presided over by James, the Lord's brother, who seems to have remained there and been generally 'in charge'.

*Early Organisation*

These two factors, the fall of Jerusalem and the postponement of the end, meant that it became necessary to organise the growing church on a long-term basis, and at the same time this had to be done without depending on Jerusalem as a centre. The problems of doing this, and at the same time establishing the unity of groups of Christians with one another, brought out the opportunities and the difficulties which were to be repeated in one form or another during the succeeding centuries.

Christians were men with the same temptations as everyone else, and, in spite of their strong inner drive towards unity, failures of temperament and judgment were clearly evident. St. Paul set up many of the first groups in towns which he visited during his journeys round the Mediterranean, but he soon found that it was necessary to keep some sort of supervision over them, and by letter and personal visit to correct tendencies which were causing division. If we examine the situation then, or in any century thereafter, we find that there were three main areas in which division was apt to show itself. They were not separate from one another, and all were sometimes present in some measure. The first was the area of belief; the second, that of organisation; the third, that of forms of worship and religious practice.

The spread of Christianity through the Roman world made it necessary for Christians to justify the beliefs which they proclaimed. The preaching of the resurrection, which was the earliest form which the gospel took, soon needed explanation, especially as Christians came into contact later with the learned world. In the first place Jesus was preached as the man chosen by God, whose approval had been sealed through his rising from the grave after crucifixion. He was shown to have fulfilled the prophecies of the Old Testament in an unexpected way, and in a way which could be made to appeal to the religious Jew who was looking for a new and deeper message. But contact with Greek thought made quite different demands on Christians, and in working out the implications of the Christian faith there was evidently much scope for differences of opinion and for speculation.

Quarrels within groups of Christians were reflected in the first of Paul's letters to Corinth, where he mentions cliques which were rivals to one another, each claiming the name of some Christian leader. 'I have been told, my brothers, by Chloe's people that there are quarrels among you. What I mean is this: each of you is saying, "I am Paul's man", or "I am for Apollos"; "I follow Cephas", or "I am Christ's" ' (1 Cor. 1:11). The difficulties about belief can be shown in an early stage from his letter to the Galatians (1:9): 'I now repeat what I have said before: if anyone preaches a gospel at variance with the gospel you received, let him be outcast!' At a very early date these divisive tendencies were beginning to show themselves.

The organisation of the small local churches in the first century seems to have been fluid, and to have varied from place to place. There has long been dispute among scholars as to whether bishops were an essential part of the early structure of the Church, and the consensus of opinion is that they were not, at least in the sense in which we think of bishops today. It is quite clear that the apostles had an authority greater than that of others, and that they used this authority in disciplinary ways, as we have already seen in the case of Paul. Eventually the apostles died or were martyred, and when this occurred their authority does not seem to have been clearly passed on to other people: the leaders of the churches in the large cities assumed a certain weight of authority, though this could not be completely identified with the kind of authority associated with an apostle. For the apostles derived their particular status from the fact that they were eye-witnesses of the risen Lord and had been chosen by him. Paul's membership of the apostolic band seems to have come from his vision of Jesus on the way to Damascus when he was converted to the faith, but also from the general acceptance of his pre-eminence as a preacher of the gospel.

The authority of the apostles was shown in the Council of Jerusalem already mentioned. In their deliberations they were joined by the elders, though only the apostles are reported as speakers. The council had been called together to try to resolve the first serious conflict of the growing Church, which concerned the obligation to keep the law of Moses. There was a difference of opinion as to whether newly converted Christians, who were not already Jews, should be required to submit to circumcision and to keep the Mosaic law. Never has a decision been accompanied by weightier consequences, for the council's ruling meant that Christianity became a world-wide religion instead of remaining a Jewish sect. It is interesting too to note that the pattern of deciding such serious questions by a council of those in authority has continued throughout the centuries, the latest example being that of the second Vatican Council in Rome from 1962 to 1965.

The early Church was not free from rivalry and disputes, even among its most eminent members. The Acts of the Apostles relates a rather unedifying squabble between Paul and John Mark (Acts 15:38) because the latter had not done all that he should have done in Pamphylia, though Barnabas seemed to bear no grudge about it. No doubt Paul was a difficult character, and was not in the habit of mincing his words. It has often been a feature of men with the drive and ability of Paul to be aggressive in their actions and outspoken in criticising others. He tells in his letter to the Galatians (2:14) how he opposed Peter to the face over the same matter which had occupied the attention of the Council of Jerusalem, namely the tension between Christians who were insisting on the Mosaic law and non-Jews who had joined them without accepting the law of Moses. 'When I saw that their conduct did not square with the truth of the Gospel,' wrote Paul, 'I said to Cephas (Peter) before the whole congregation, "If you, a Jew born and bred, live like a Gentile, and not like a Jew, how can you insist that Gentiles must live like Jews?" '

The carrying of the Christian gospel from place to place depended on a number of different factors. Its spread was much facilitated by the great system of communications which the Roman Empire had built. It has been stated with good reason that travel in the area of the Empire was swifter and safer then than at any time until the middle of the nineteenth century, and more widespread than it was until a later date still. Within the Empire there was an immense traffic for many purposes, especially administration, armed forces and trade. The Jews were dispersed everywhere and had set up their own colonies in every town of importance. There was therefore a ready-made network for the spread of new ideas, perfectly adapted for the dissemination of a vigorous and lively religious movement such as Christianity.

Although we know many of the outstanding pioneers such as Paul, the spread of the gospel must have depended on the activities of ordinary Christians as they went from place to place. Traders and slaves were mentioned as carriers of the message, and it was through the Jewish communities that Christianity first penetrated into many towns. In the great cities of the Empire and eastern Mediterranean—

Rome, Antioch and Jerusalem—Christians came to have substantial congregations, which were afterwards to play an important rôle in the Church's life as a whole. Christianity thus began as a religion of the towns, and its subsequent development reflects this fact. It was from the towns that the countryside was eventually covered, and the early form of organisation was based on the *metropolis.*

### Presbyters and Bishops

Evidence for the early organisation of local churches is scanty, but the most likely course was the establishment in most small Christian communities of leaders, called presbyters or elders. No doubt in the smaller groups one presbyter might be sufficient for the group, but, as Christians became more numerous in the larger towns, more than one was needed, either in the large gatherings or in different groups in the same locality. When this occurred one of the presbyters was elevated, either by appointment or election, to be president among the rest. From this arrangement developed a system of 'bishops', a title which generically means overseer or supervisor, though it is impossible to decide from the evidence now available at what stage elder became bishop. It is likely that in some places the two offices were indistinguishable for a period at least.

But, whatever may have been the exact course of development, it is plain at the beginning of the second century that the office of bishop was more or less established. Ignatius, Bishop of Antioch, was martyred in about the year 115. His letters show the great importance being placed on agreement with the bishop as a bond of unity among all Christians. In his letter to the Trallians he wrote: 'Be on your guard against such men (sc. docetic heretics). And this will be your case if you are not self-assertive and if you are inseparable from Jesus Christ and from the bishop and the institutions of the Apostles. He who is within the sanctuary is pure: he who is outside is not pure; that is, he who acts independently of bishop and presbytery and deacons. Such a man is not pure in his conscience.'[3]

There seems little doubt that the early Christian churches came to the notice of the Roman authorities mainly through being a disturbing element within the important Jewish minority. This minority was both numerous and influential. Its numbers have been calculated as high as 7 per cent of the population, and its penetration into all ranks of society, even the most exalted, is sufficiently shown by the Emperor Nero's marriage to a Jewish wife, Poppaea, in A.D. 62. A reference by Suetonius to the expulsion of the Jews in A.D. 52 probably refers to troubles between them and the Christians. For he writes that they were 'continually making disturbances at the instigation of Chrestus'.[4] At all events, Christians were sufficiently identifiable as a distinct group by the year A.D. 64 when they suffered the first major persecution under Nero, who tried to put on them the blame for the great fire in Rome of that summer. An account of this persecution is to be found in the *Annals* of Tacitus. According to this, 'an immense multitude was convicted, not so much on the charge of arson as because of hatred of the human race'.[5] This 'hatred' seems to have referred to the unwillingness of Christians to conform to the pagan society of the day. It was this persecution which used Christians as objects of the cruellest public amusement, the effect of which in the end was rather to arouse pity for the victims than to gratify the public.

## Christian Worship

There is no need to pursue in detail the development of the life of Christians or the relations which they had to the society of their day. The hostility of the Roman authorities to men who would not fit in with the social and religious demands of the community in which they lived must have had the effect of strengthening the young organisation by making it necessary for Christians to depend on one another's practical help in such a situation, and also to conceal as far as possible those practices which the authorities found obnoxious. Christian meetings, whether for worship or discussion, had to take place behind closed doors, and this in turn aroused more suspicion as to their behaviour in the minds of those who were not admitted to them.

From the first there seem to have been regular weekly gatherings for worship, and the first day of the week, being the day of the Lord's resurrection, began to take the place of the Jewish sabbath. References in the New Testament show this development. At Troas the Christians came together on the first day of the week to break bread, that is, either to share table fellowship or to remember their Lord by repeating the actions by which he solemnly instituted the Lord's Supper just before his death. The regular repetition of this service in response to the instructions of Jesus to do it in memory of himself was soon regarded as an interim central rite in which all Christians naturally engaged. In writing his first letter to the Christians at Corinth, Paul said that the purpose of breaking and eating the bread and of drinking the wine was to 'show the Lord's death till he comes' (1 Cor. 11:26). Christians met in one another's houses in order to take part in this rite, and, as the first day of the week was not free from normal work, such meetings had to take place either in the early morning or in the evening. There was often also a common meal, called *agapē* or love-feast.

The importance of this service from the beginning of the Christian Church has never been lost, and, whereas the service of the Holy Communion has been a great creative force for unity, it has also been the centre of violent disagreement and dispute. (It has a number of titles which all refer to the same basic act of worship—the Lord's Supper, the Mass, the Eucharist, the Liturgy, etc.) The differences of conviction have been concerned with every aspect of it—its meaning, its language, its ceremonial, its frequency, the use of leavened or unleavened bread—all have figured in Christian division and continue to do so. This is specially ironic, as the sacramental rite was, above all, intended to express unity—of Christians with their Lord and of Christians with one another.

In the first century of the Christian era the form of the Holy Communion was fluid and variable. The evidence suggests that, although the words of institution which Jesus used at the Last Supper formed the centre of all such services, they were enclosed in a prayer which was often extempore and mainly consisted of a giving of thanks. (Hence the title 'Eucharist' from the Greek word for 'thank'.) There were other elements included in Christian worship which were taken over from the Jewish worship, with which the earliest Christians were familiar—the reading of the sacred books, the singing of chants, sermons and prayers: these were gradually adapted more and more to Christian use, and were no doubt accompanied by the reading of such documents as letters sent by Paul to one or other of the local churches. Ecstatic utterances by some of those present also marked these gatherings. This form of witness to the power of the Spirit had already begun to cause trouble during the New Testament period, for Paul found it necessary to write to the Corinthian Christians (1 Cor. 14) to prevent the practice from getting out of hand. While he recognised the legitimacy of ecstatic utterance ('speaking with tongues'), he tried to play down its importance and made it clear that it was to be considered less useful than speaking in a language which people could understand without the need of an interpreter.

## Stresses and Strains

Paul's first letter to the Corinthians provides in miniature a picture of the tendencies which could, and often did, become divisive within the growing communities. They arose partly through the natural imperfections of men and women and partly because of habits of mind or influences from elsewhere which unconsciously affected them in their outlooks.

We have already noted that the tension between Jewish Christians and others created a crisis over the question as to whether Gentiles who joined the Christian Church were bound to keep the provisions of the Mosaic law. This was decided in the negative at the Jerusalem Council. But, in spite of this decision, there remained groups which refused to accept it and which continued to be composed of Jewish Christians only, continuing to obey the Jewish law. So far as we know, these Christians did not differ from others in their general beliefs, but preferred to separate themselves into their own communities, being known as 'Nazarenes'. (This word is used in two senses in the New Testament, namely (a) someone from Nazareth, and (b) a general term for the early Christians following the man from Nazareth. A similar word is still used in Arabic for Christian.) There is no evidence in the New Testament for the existence of the Nazarenes as a sect, but they appear in the fourth century and must have existed from the earliest days. In this case we see a simple influence on Christians of their earlier religious upbringing, almost certainly mixed with the national feeling which was associated with the Jewish race and religion. It was a form of identification which will be seen on many other occasions throughout history. No doubt it was due to deep psychological urges which resisted any action that seemed to involve a loss of identity. The Nazarene Christians were willing to accept the additional insights of the teaching of the gospel, but not at the cost of cutting themselves off from those practices which to them had hitherto been identified with their own personal self-consciousness.

Another sect, called the Ebionites, sprang out of the religious ferment east of the Jordan, which also continued to follow the requirements of the Mosaic law, but they adopted beliefs which fell outside those generally held by the Christian Church. In their practice and beliefs they were the typical products of a temperament to be found in the area of their origin. They were ascetics and regarded Jesus as the embodiment of a divine teacher who had often appeared on the earth. In this sect we see the start of another kind of division which arose from a difference of interpretation of the meaning and person of Jesus. The Ebionites were perhaps the first example of the mixture of Christianity with eastern religious elements prone to magic and superstition: they seem to have originated at the end of the first century.

In the first century, too, we can discern other divisive tendencies which later became more formidable in the main stream of church life. The New Testament itself, for example, provides some evidence of the danger of docetic teaching, that is, teaching which regarded the life and suffering of Jesus as mere outward appearance, a sort of puppet show put on by God for the benefit of his people. The epistles of John twice refer to those who denied that Jesus Christ had come in the flesh (1 John. 4:1–3; 2 John 7).

Nero's persecution of Christians did not continue for long, and the Church's experience of persecution was intermittent. The attitude of the Roman authorities was generally tolerant of other religions than that of the State, but the Christians' unwillingness to offer incense to the Emperor brought their loyalty into question. The Emperor Domitian instituted a persecution in A.D. 95, and the social separation of Christians from their fellows, together with their condemnation of the popular licentiousness of the time, produced resentment on which official action could rely for some support. Trajan, whose reign as Emperor began in A.D. 98, would not allow complete toleration for Christians, but he did not want to pursue an attack against them with any great vigour, as is shown by his letter to Pliny:[6] 'They (sc. Christians) are not to be sought out; if they are informed against, and the charge is proved, they are to be punished, with this reservation— that if anyone denies that he is a Christian, and actually proves it, that is by worshipping our gods, he shall be pardoned as a result of the recantation, however suspect he may have been with respect to his past.'

At the end of the first century we find the Christian Chu
an organisational unity which would strengthen its positic
its members together. To this trend a number of differen
were contributing. The situation in the Empire was fav
inter-communication between them; there was a common language,
Greek, spoken everywhere; the Jewish dispersion offered a starting-
point for Christian communities to be established in all the main
towns—over forty centres were recorded in the first century.

The postponement of the messianic return, which had been
confidently expected at an early date, altered the perspective of
Christians who, as a result, now began making plans for a long period
instead of a short one. There was no agreement as to the proximity
of the second coming, but it became clear to all that it might not be in
the immediate future. This was probably the strongest single motive
in permanent organisation.

Long-term arrangements necessitated a recognised form of
authority within the Church, and, if we remember the great travel
throughout the Empire, it is evident that such an authority had to be
one generally recognised by Christians coming from outside the locality. The apostles had such authority, and at the turn of the century
this authority can be seen to have largely passed to the bishops,
who henceforth played the central rôle in this regard.

The same pressures also encouraged greater uniformity in ways of
worship, especially in the Eucharist, which was the service common
to all Christians, by which they were distinguished in their practice
from other religious groups. So long as Christian worship was
conducted in Greek, uniformity was not so important, any more than
it is in Free Church assemblies today. But fixed forms tend to affect
liturgical life in a body which has a large geographical spread and
needs to welcome people from a distance.

At this time only the first signs of differing beliefs had appeared,
but enough to sound the notes of what was to be a growing problem
through the subsequent centuries, as Christian teaching came openly
into contact with the learning of the world of the time. Up to the end
of the century it had been nurtured in what was largely a Jewish
environment and way of thought. It had indeed opened its doors
to the non-Jewish convert, but there had as yet been no need to
grapple with philosophical systems based on quite different ways of
thinking. Christian teaching had been a stumbling block for the Jews

and foolishness to the Greeks (1 Cor. 1:23), but it had not yet tried to come to grips with the intellectual world of its day.

[1] Known in recent years as the ecumenical movement.
[2] Stephen Neill, *A History of Christian Missions*, London, Penguin Books, 1964, Preface.
[3] Henry Bettenson, *The Early Christian Fathers*, Oxford University Press, 1956, p. 60.
[4] Henry Bettenson, *Documents of the Christian Church*, Oxford, 1946, p. 3.
[5] *Ibid.*, p. 2.
[6] *Ibid.*, p. 6.

# 2

## The Church Spreads Through the Empire

### Facing Contemporary Thought

IN the second century the growth of the Christian Church began to bring it out of the shadows and expose it more to the light of history. Its strength lay in the eastern provinces of the Roman Empire, and the local churches of the West were few and far between. Rome, as the capital, was naturally a centre of importance. St. Paul's letter to the Christians at Rome, and his own trial and the events connected with it, showed a vigorous group of Christians established there. The early tradition of the martyrdom in Rome of St. Peter and St. Paul added to the importance of a place which would probably in any case have become the leading Christian settlement. The destruction of Jerusalem in A.D. 70 left a vacuum which Rome naturally filled, for, with the disappearance of the centre to which Christians would naturally look for religious reasons, especially those with Jewish connections, the capital of the Empire would most conveniently take its place. This development would depend not so much on the proximity of Rome to the largest numbers of Christian centres, for it was in fact a considerable distance from them, but on the fact that lines of communication all went to Rome. Parallels are easily seen in the modern world, where, for example, in the United States of America New York is the centre for many national organisations, although it is geographically on the north-eastern edge of an immense country.

The distribution of Christian churches in the second century showed the vast majority of them recorded in Asia Minor. Of rather more than a hundred which are known there were but six in Italy and four in the rest of western Europe. There was a larger total than this—seven or eight—in North Africa in the vicinity of Carthage, and

Cyrene and Egypt also had their churches, Alexandria being particularly important. It cannot, of course, be concluded that there were not other centres too, but there is no doubt that the distribution of Christians followed the recorded pattern.

## Problems of Authority

As the Church spread and the Apostles were martyred or died, an alternative system of authority needed to be established, as we have already seen. It was in the second century that the system of bishops became visible everywhere, and by the middle of the century everyone accepted the episcopal system without question, and assumed that it had always been in operation and that it derived directly from the apostles themselves. But the evidence for this simple view is not convincing beyond the clear fact that the apostles began by having supreme authority in the Church and that, after a period of uncertainty, the bishops of the second century were seen to have acquired it. The question of succession became of importance. Just as local churches claimed, whenever possible, to have been founded by an apostle, so the bishops claimed to have derived their authority from the apostles, and tried to establish the fact by naming the succession.

Apostolic succession has been a fruitful bone of contention throughout Church history, especially since the Reformation. It still remains a matter of difference between the churches which regard themselves as faithful to the traditional order of the early Church and the subsequent centuries on the one hand, and on the other those Christians who claim that the episcopal office and system cannot be established from the New Testament, to which alone they appeal as authoritative. There are several different senses which the term 'apostolic succession' can bear. In modern usage it is most commonly used to mean an unbroken line of ordination by the laying-on-of-hands from the apostles to the bishops who succeeded, and thence without interruption to the bishops of the present day. In viewing apostolic succession in this light, many Christians believe that this method is the only means by which the authority, and therefore the charisma (or spiritual power) of Christian ordination can fully be transmitted. Without such uninterrupted consecration a Christian ministry, they think, cannot claim the full authority of the catholic church, and such a ministry is the only form of ministry which can ever be universally recognised by all Christians as fully authentic.

But there are other forms of 'apostolic succession'. There is the succession of teaching by which the true form of the Christian faith has been handed down from teacher to teacher without a break and without falsifying or watering down the truth of the gospel. And this is closely connected with the third meaning, namely the succession of bishops in office. The interpretation of the relative importance of these aspects of succession belongs to later controversies, and there is no evidence that there was any exact thought about the relative importance of these elements in the first centuries, but merely the valuing of succession as a guarantee of unbroken reliable teaching. That, at least, seems to have been the point of view of Irenaeus writing towards the end of the century. Irenaeus lived from about A.D. 130 to A.D. 200 and was Bishop of Lyons. His main work was written to confound heretical views, and in the course of it he claimed that the succession of bishops from the apostles was a proof of the soundness of orthodox views. He said that the succession could easily be established, and, as it would be wearisome to trace it in all sees, he would take one example, the see of Rome. 'For this church has a position of leadership and authority; and therefore every church, that is, the faithful everywhere must needs agree with the church at Rome; for in her the apostolic tradition has ever been preserved by the faithful from all parts of the world.'

Irenaeus then goes on to give the list of bishops of Rome, saying that after founding and building the church the apostles Peter and Paul 'handed over to Linus the office of bishop'. He was succeeded by Anacletus, Clement, Euarestes, Sixtus, Telesphorus, Hyginus, Pius, Anicetus, Soter and then Eleutherus the holder at the time. 'In this order and succession the Apostolic tradition has come down to our time.'[1] It is likely that Irenaeus derived his list from an earlier list compiled by Hegesippus to which the historian Eusebius refers.[2]

### Bishop of Rome

This extract brings to our attention another enduring ecclesiastical controversy, namely the position of Peter, so often termed the first Bishop of Rome, and the claims which have been associated with that see. Although in the passage quoted, Peter with Paul is referred to as the founder of the church at Rome, he is not said to have been the first bishop, but with Paul to have established Linus in that office.

Moreover, the word 'founder' seems to be more honorific than accurate so far as the Christian community at Rome is concerned, since from Paul's letter to the Romans, written before he went there, it would seem fairly certain that there had been no apostolic visitor before him.

But it is not the task of this book to try to solve a question which continues to cause controversy among partisans. The question of the exact authority of the see of Rome in early times must remain a matter of conjecture, since the evidence is not conclusive either way. If it were, there would be no more room for dispute. Historians must weigh the evidence that is available and conclude from it what is the most likely explanation, carefully avoiding the pernicious habit of reading back into one period of history ideas which arose only at a later period.

What is significant at this early date is that we find already the material for subsequent controversies which have been the occasion or excuse for division among Christians. The three main groups are already provided with their raw material to produce: (a) the Roman Catholic claim for supremacy of the bishops of Rome over the whole Church; or (b) the claim that it is the episcopal office as such in unbroken succession which is the essential feature of the Church's hierarchy; or (c) that neither of these is necessary, but that some other pattern ought to be followed from what can be deduced from the writings of the New Testament itself.

During the second century there was no New Testament as such, for that collection of books known as the 'Canon of the New Testament' had not yet been fixed. The four Gospels and the letters of Paul were in general circulation during the first half of the century, but only the Old Testament books were formally recognised as Scripture. Towards the end of the century, between 170 and 220, the Gospels and Pauline Epistles came to be put on the same level as the books of the Old Testament, but other writings were also used and given different value in different churches. The exact point at which the other New Testament books were decided is not known, and the earliest complete list of them is not found until 369 in the writing of Athanasius. The fixing of the Canon was of great importance as providing an authoritative source of guidance on the true faith, both for the nurture of Christians themselves and for the rejection of false doctrine.

## Gnosticism and Montanism

The second century also saw Christians engaged in serious dispute with other forms of belief, and in particular upholding the true content of their own gospel against tendencies to distort it. As Christianity came into contact with other eastern religious outlooks it was attacked for its supposed inadequacies. In particular, it had to fight against what are known as Gnostic heresies. Most of the teaching of the Gnostics held that there was a complete dichotomy between matter, which was evil, and spirit, which was good, and that the idea that God could or would identify himself with material man was an impossible thought. They attempted therefore to make a gradation of powers between God and Jesus. It was an attempt to correct what appeared to those thinkers to be an absurd naïveté in the Christian message.

The influence of Gnostic thought upon Christianity was the direct effect of its contact with other religions, and in rejecting its views Christians were struggling not only against those outside their own church but against many within it who had adopted these ideas. Gnosticism is a term which covers a whole range of varying theories, and one of its key concepts was that salvation came through *gnosis*, the knowledge which was acquired only by the sophisticated. Its teaching was to be found in the great Christian centres, but by the end of the second century its adherents had been dissipated into a number of separate sects.

Against the teaching of the Gnostics the main writers were Irenaeus, Tertullian (flourishing about A.D. 200), and Hippolytus (*c.* 170–236). Tertullian came from North Africa, being born at Carthage about the middle of the century. His appearance is the first sign of the importance which the Church of North Africa was to have in succeeding years: its growth was a tribute to the vigour of the Church in putting down roots in new areas of the world.

The Gnostic threat shows one kind of difficulty which the unity of Christians had to face and overcome: it did so in the only possible way. The heretics formed sects of their own, separate from the main body of the faithful, and in course of time died out.

But another sort of problem arose in the second century which, like heresy, was to be repeated again and again in subsequent church history, and this was demonstrated by the schismatic movement known as Montanism, named after its leader Montanus. Montanus himself was a fanatic and a heretic, but the movement itself was not so much concerned to propagate false doctrines as to try to restore what it thought to be the proper purity and strictness of Christian practice. It is of interest to see that what might be called a puritan reaction to laxity is to be found as early as the middle of the second century, in conditions which often led to suffering and hardship for Christians in dealings with the State. It would seem to indicate that in a number of places the Christian life faced no particular hazards, which had resulted in a rather easy-going attitude towards its demands. Perhaps the relations of some Christians with pagan neighbours, and perhaps the Gnostic dangers which followed, were the cause of the Montanists' insistence on an exclusive attitude towards non-Christians. The followers of the movement evidently felt acutely the dangers of becoming tainted with secularism, and against this imposed a strict church discipline on themselves. They revived the habit of prophesying, some of which got out of hand, and stressed the rights of the laity against the hierarchy.

The same tendencies which we see in Montanism crop up again and again in Christian history and often led to schism and heresy. They sprang from temperamental reasons, and from the need for men to be whole-hearted about their religion, reacting against slackness and laxity. But the emphasis on spiritual inspiration, which was often confused with or accompanied by strong emotional experiences, frequently led to views which were unbalanced and ultimately undermined the truth of the gospel. The New Testament itself in the Gospels stressed an element of severity and suffering which can never be banished from the full Christian life, and it was to these elements that movements such as Montanism looked for their justification. The Montanists also showed themselves to be millenarian, that is, believers in a future millennium before the final judgment in which Christ will reign on the earth.

### Sacraments

In the second century a clearer picture began to emerge of Christian worship and cult. Two main ceremonies formed the basis of Christian religious practice and membership of the Church—Baptism, with its associated rites, and the Eucharist. Disputes continue today about the exact nature of the Last Supper, whether it was a Passover meal or a ceremony of some other kind, and the documents which are relevant to the second century seem to show that there was never a generally agreed attitude as to its nature or to the nature of the Eucharist which depended upon it. We see how from very early time the rites of the early Church carried within themselves the seeds of disagreement and divergence. 'Christians in all ages have placed a great variety of interpretations upon the Eucharist, convinced of its real connexion with the risen Lord and not concerned to tie themselves to any one theory of its origin or origins,' writes a recent commentator. 'The process began early. The Emmaus story (Luke 24:13-31) emphasizes fellowship with the risen and invisible Lord. Melito's *Homily on the Pasch* illustrates the Passover tradition; the *Didache* introduces the theme of the unity of all mankind represented by the bread which "was scattered upon the mountain". Unanimity is perhaps no more desirable than it is probable.'[3] Melito, Bishop of Sardis, died about A.D. 190, and the date of the document called the *Didache* is thought either to be the beginning of the second century or possibly about A.D. 170.

Baptism, too, shows minor differences in the rite in different places, though the general pattern is the same everywhere. The exact method of performing it would naturally differ from place to place; the common features include preparation, fasting and vigils beforehand, renunciation, and exorcism by anointing with oil, the triple immersion in the water as a response to the confession of the baptismal faith, followed by a further anointing. The laying on of the hands of the bishop with prayer was probably followed by a third anointing by him, and the candidate was then received by the company of the brethren with the kiss of peace and then partook in his first Eucharist.

It was in connection with baptism that the use of a creed first arose, for an essential part of the rite was the public confession of the Christian faith by the candidate. But in the early times there was no question of a creed in the form which we know today, which may be called a declaratory creed. On the other hand there was a series of questions put to the candidate at the culminating point of the baptism —an interrogatory creed—in response to which he said 'I believe' and was plunged three times beneath the water.[4] The later forms of the developed creed were associated after the fourth century with training the new candidates in the faith during their catechumenate, before they were baptised and became full members of the Church.

Nevertheless, the need for expressing this belief in some sort of form became clear as the Church developed, and later the acceptance of creeds became of vital importance in the struggle to maintain the unity and the purity of the Church and its teaching.

In the early practice of the Church the bishop was the centre of the ministry, being himself the celebrant of the Eucharist in the place where he lived. According to Hippolytus, at the weekly celebration of the Eucharist the bishop communicated all the people with the broken bread and the cups were managed by the presbyters and deacons.[5] The form used was still in process of development and probably varied from region to region. It had many connections with Jewish practice, as is only to be expected in view of its origin, but the teaching connected with it was still vague and far removed from the subtleties which later doctrine was to attach to the eucharistic action. 'The language is far indeed from being precise; but it establishes the fact that in the year 150 it was the common teaching that the elements were to be received as the flesh and blood of Christ, after they had been blessed by the word of the prayer, or better perhaps, the "prayer of the word, that is from him".'[6]

Apart from the light which he has thrown on the worship of his time, Hippolytus is an interesting character, since he figured in the first active schism in one of the main sees of the Church, that of Rome. He was a bitter opponent of Callistus, whom he despised for his origins as a slave, and eventually they were both rivals for the bishopric of Rome itself. Since Callistus eventually became victorious, Hippolytus is named as an anti-Pope, and this name reveals him as a rival claimant. The two were rivals in theology as well as in personal status. Eventually Hippolytus was exiled but is thought to have been reconciled to his opponents before he died, after continuing to oppose the successors of Callistus as well. The persecution under the Emperor Maximin (235–8) had the ironic result of exiling Hippolytus to Sardinia with the opposing Bishop of Rome, Pontianus, and it was perhaps through this enforced proximity that the quarrels were put aside. It is somewhat illogical that in spite of this hostility and also in spite of suspicions of heretical tendencies in his writings he was added to the list of saints of the Church.

*Date of Easter*

Another source of division during this century was the controversy over what is called *quartodecimanism*, which, deriving from the Latin word for 14th, concerned the date on which Easter ought to be kept. It arose from the early custom of always celebrating Easter on the Jewish date Nisan 14, whichever day of the week it happened to be, rather than on the following Sunday. Asia Minor was the centre of this practice, and it was claimed that it derived from John the Apostle. In Rome the other habit prevailed, and when Victor became Pope (189–198) he determined to suppress the quartodeciman practice. He tried to secure this unanimity of practice first by ordering synods to be held throughout the Christian world. In a council which he called in Rome he threatened to excommunicate bishops of Asia Minor if they did not give up their practice, and he actually did so. However, it appears that this action did not break communion between Rome and the churches of Asia Minor, and the conclusion is drawn that the sentence was not put into effect or perhaps withdrawn. The action aroused criticism for its undue severity from such eminent church leaders as Irenaeus.

This particular controversy shows another field in which divergence could easily take place, and it is of interest to observe that in the Christian world of the twentieth century there are still differing dates on which Easter is kept, the eastern and western parts of the Christian world basing their calculations on different systems. The result is that sometimes they coincide, but they may differ from one another by as much as six weeks. In course of time other discrepancies in the dates of feasts also appeared, as will be seen later.

Of these events in the developing Church we may note two tendencies which were to militate against that unity which the Church professed and has constantly tried to pursue. The *quartodeciman* affair showed a praiseworthy desire on the part of Victor to secure that all Christians should celebrate Easter, their main feast, on the same day. No one would dispute that this was a desirable aim. But the way he went about it undid much if not all of the good, for he tried to impose it by excommunicating those who disagreed with him. This is an extreme form of ecclesiastical force, and a penalty which should be reserved only for matters of extreme gravity, offences which are universally recognised as a betrayal of the heart of the

Christian faith itself. It is a sign of the inadequate understanding of the spiritual importance of unity that excommunication should be used to try to establish an administrative unity which did not touch the essential matters of the faith at all. Victor's example would, alas, be followed by too many of his successors, both at Rome and elsewhere. It was the mark of the administrator, over-anxious to see everything tidy and with no loose ends, and determined to use his power to impose his own solution on others before they were ready to accept it of their own free will.

The case of Hippolytus versus Callistus, which carried us into the third century, revealed another source of tension, or at least it may have indicated such a source, namely that arising from different social status. Whereas Hippolytus probably came from the higher levels of society, Callistus was born a slave, and his rise to influence added fuel to the fire of the opposition of Hippolytus. The latter depicted his rival in a most unfavourable light, and his attitude has been summed up as follows: 'This man, who was despised by Hippolytus as a slave, an adventurer and a criminal, became his hated rival in the Roman church; the patron of the opposite school of theology; and finally his rival as bishop. The theological divisions which were the ostensible and very real cause of this grave schism obviously had their social and political and personal antecedents. There were, as there always are, some non-theological factors involved.'[7]

### Growing Strength Meets Persecution

An attempt to follow the developments of relations between groups of Christians may easily lead to the impression that the history of these events is mainly a story of failure to exhibit the Christian unity which the principles of the Christian religion required among its adherents. And the events can be interpreted in this way. But to do this would be to ignore the starting-point and the proportions of the problem. Christianity began within a unity which was provided by the Jewish religion and the common idealism of its first proponents. That unity had a character which derived its strength from its narrowness: it sprang from the close fellowship of a Jewish religious outlook combined with a still smaller intensity of common life centred around Jesus. This character could only last for a relatively short time if the message of the Christian gospel was to be carried into wider circles.

The problem which faced the growing Church was how to put into practice the principles of unity which lay at the heart of the Christian message when the ready-made structure of unity in which it was first received no longer had any validity. There were some who could see Christian unity only in terms of the unity which originally clothed it, and the result of their outlook was the perpetuation of Christian Jewish sects and enclaves, which in time simply disappeared. Meanwhile, with its rapid expansion, the Christian communities were faced with the question of how they could unify disparate elements from all parts of the Roman world. The background of these elements was as varied as the Empire itself, from religious, social and intellectual points of view. Moreover, different regions were marked by different traditions, so that geographical differences carried with them outlooks which had their own peculiar emphases in doctrine and in philosophical approach.

The modern student is apt to assume that the Church is a very old institution, and to picture himself as standing at the end of a long historical development on which he is looking back. Evidently there is truth in this way of looking at things. Yet it is equally possible, and some would say more realistic, to see the Christian Church as a young institution which is still, in the twentieth century, struggling with the early formative years. This point of view has been expressed by a writer as follows: 'The history of the Church has to be seen in the light of evolution, and in evolutionary terms its two thousand years of existence can measure no more than its early childhood; but the miracle of Pentecost reversed the tide of evolution itself, for from this moment, and at first very slowly, it could be seen that the Church's destiny was to rebuild mankind in the image and unity of Christ. The scattering of the nations represented by the Tower of Babel, when men's tongues became confused, was annulled at Pentecost, when each understood his fellow, though speaking unknown tongues. The convergence of humanity upon itself had already begun.'[8] Whether one accepts Professor Zaehner's interpretation or not, the growth and development of the Church can be seen, quite reasonably, in this light. It would certainly appear to be true that the development of Christian unity is, historically speaking, a process which began with the Christian faith itself and is still in process of completion. This is probably a better way of seeing things, in providing a sense of perspective which is more in accordance with actual events.

The main source for the early history of the Christian Church is the historian Eusebius. He lived from about A.D. 260 to 340 and wrote an ecclesiastical history in ten books. Somewhere about the year A.D. 315 he became Bishop of Caesarea, and throughout his life he played an important part in church affairs. His lifetime spanned the period during which the Church moved from being a persecuted minority into being the official religion of the Roman Empire; and Eusebius himself was present at the first General Council of the Church at Nicaea in A.D. 325. He was therefore in an excellent position to chronicle the events of his own time.

Although Eusebius did not have the critical standards of historians today, he is much more reliable as a historian than many of his contemporaries. He accepted a number of stories which were inaccurate and can be shown to be impossible in the form in which he retails them, but he distinguished clearly between the material which he presented and his own views and opinions. As so much recorded history depends upon him, the views of a modern historian about him may be quoted: 'His mind moved along well-defined lines. His detestation of heresy was balanced by his glorification of martyrdom. His admiration for Constantine was excessive but sincere. His style is wretched. But he is faithful. He never invents. There are no imaginary narratives or speeches. He uses sources which he generally identifies, and in so doing he is the forerunner of the modern historian; nobody before him seems to have done it. His methods of quotation are not always as exact as we might wish. Sometimes his extracts seem to have been reproduced in part only or to be imperfect in some way; and in these cases he may have relied on notes that he made, or trusted in some assistant who had not quite grasped his instructions. Nevertheless, we are able to a very considerable extent to make use, through him, of original documents which no longer exist; and, as we can check the accuracy of his quotations in those instances where the originals do exist, we are able to get a good idea of his standards of fidelity, which must be regarded as high.

'It is evident what, without Eusebius, we would not be able to construct a history of early Christianity at all.'[9]

## Doctrine Takes Shape

The beginning of the century in which Eusebius was born saw the expansion of Christianity in the intellectual centres of the Empire, such as Alexandria, and its attempts to come to grips with the current Greek philosophies. In undertaking this task, which was indispensable if the Christian faith were to speak to the great majority of the intelligent members of the Roman world, the leaders of Christian thought found themselves faced with the necessity of translating into Greek thought the concepts and message of Christianity, which up to that time had been largely presented in terms of the Jewish messianic hope and in religious ideas which derived from the Jewish religion. Moreover, it is always necessary to bear in mind that Jesus himself in his teaching assumed religious and historical ideas which are never specifically mentioned, just because they were the common coin of Jewish religious thought at that time.

But, although Alexandria was the most important centre of learning, it was not alone in becoming a centre of Christian writing and teaching. Rome continued to be an influential centre in this respect, and during the third century the influence of Carthage (near the modern Tunis) in North Africa became great. Further to the east Antioch had from the beginning played an influential rôle in Christian thought, and during this century Edessa was growing in its importance as a centre for the expansion and thought of Christianity further to the east still, especially in Persia, where a great church grew and later disappeared, almost independently of the rest of Christendom.

The relevance of these various centres to our subject arises from the fact that the differences of emphasis and outlook which are found among them, when exaggerated, gave rise to fierce struggles of doctrine and to consequent division. Christian belief and teaching were not yet formed in any defined sense, and attempts to relate them to current thought inevitably involved speculative theories and explanations, some of which could not withstand close examination. There was, indeed, no other way of reaching an agreed truth except by the public exchange of ideas among thinkers. Such an exchange was bound to be a process of intellectual trial and error with all the attendant risks of misunderstanding and stress.

The fourth and fifth centuries were pre-eminently those of doctrinal dispute and definition in the Church; and we can see the germs of those disputes gradually taking shape in the developing schools of Alexandria, Antioch, Carthage, Rome and Edessa. These centres did not all develop equally at the same time, and in the third century Alexandria was of particular importance for the growth of Christian thought. Clement was the first of its famous teachers. He was head of the catechetical school there from 190 until about 202, when he was forced to flee by the persecution under Septimus Severus, which was particularly aimed at catechumens and at the prevention of conversions to the Christian faith. This persecution produced martyrs in Alexandria itself, Perpetua and Felicitas in Carthage; and Irenaeus, the great Bishop of Lyons in South Gaul may himself have been martyred.

The third century saw a number of other persecutions which produced their own problems. These took place mostly in the first half of the century, and varied in intensity. At other times toleration was the normal condition of affairs. Christians periodically suffered severe persecution, but had long periods of quiet during which their numbers increased and their organisation was gradually established. After the reign of Septimus Severus, which ended in 211, there was peace for the Church until that of Maximinus (Thrax) who succeeded to the throne in 235 and began a fierce persecution, together with an attempt to encourage popular dislike of the Christians. This action, however, was mainly confined to the beginning of his reign. Decius, who succeeded him in 249, ordered that all should sacrifice to the State gods on pain of death: he endeavoured systematically to root out Christianity, which he regarded as a threat to the State. Persecution was continued under Gallus, his successor, causing many Christians to abandon their religion. These pressures and consequent apostasy were the cause of tension and schism within the Church, and raised problems of the conditions on which those who had denied their faith could be readmitted when the persecution had ceased. After Gallus, Valerian (253–260) continued a policy of attack, mainly concentrated on the leaders of the Church, both clergy and laity, many of whom were executed. But the end of his reign saw the beginning of a long period of peace. Diocletian became Emperor in 284, and for most of his reign there was no effort to harry the Christian Church, though in 303, two years before he died, he launched the last severe persecution which the early Church was to undergo. Some of the effects of these experiences we shall examine below.

## Organisational Growth

Earlier we referred to the establishment of bishops as the rulers of the Church. In the second and third centuries the episcopate became the key structure of the Church, through which its unity was to be safeguarded. The problems of unity which arose varied as the Church grew. The earliest aim was to keep unity within the small Christian units established by the preaching of the first missionaries, and here the bishop became the centre round which this unity was created. In the letters of Ignatius (died *c.* 107) it is clear that only those who rallied round the bishop were to be considered faithful Christians. But, as the number of Christians became greater and the bishops more static, their areas of influence came to be more defined, so that the authority of a bishop became restricted to one particular area. When this occurred the next problem of unity naturally arose, namely, how to keep different bishops and their dioceses in unity with one another.

To meet this next stage a process of federation took place, which has been summarised in these words: '1. It had been found convenient to restrict any given Bishop's authority normally to a certain sphere, but yet he retained his right as a Bishop of the universal Church. 2. Conversely, his neighbouring Bishops had agreed normally not to interfere with him in his own sphere, but yet they retained their right to interfere in case of necessity. 3. Occasions were bound to arise when it would be necessary for neighbouring Bishops to intervene, e.g. when a Bishop died, or in case of disputes, therefore it was convenient to federate the Bishops of any neighbourhood into a formal group.'[10]

The natural boundaries to follow in such a development were those of the civil administration, just as in the present day this is frequently the way in which churches organise themselves. The first bishops were almost always in towns where the earliest Christian congregations were first established, and they naturally came to exercise authority over those towns and over the neighbouring countryside, which for the most part was evangelised from the town centres. When it came to forming larger units the civil province again provided a natural unit, and the very word 'province' has survived in the organisation of the Church to the present day, even when it has disappeared from civil use. Originally the word 'metropolis' seems to have meant a mother-city, and the bishop came to be known as a 'metropolitan' because he was the bishop of such a city. This use of the term is to be found in the Orthodox Church of Greece at the present day. But the general use of the title 'metropolitan' came to be restricted to the bishop who was the chief bishop of a province. This is the present use in England, and the Orthodox Church of Russia restricts the title to sees of special importance. As provinces became better organised, the metropolitan bishop came to acquire powers connected with problems of vacant dioceses, and it was to him that members of dioceses in the province naturally turned in cases where there were disputes. After the recognition by the Empire of the Christian faith the position of bishops became much more important.

The Church as a whole, therefore, consisted of a collection of provinces, and again the problem of relations between these units had to be dealt with. A still larger unit came to be set up, called a patriarchate, in which the Patriarch was the chief bishop of a collection of provinces. Rome was no doubt the most important of these, and although we are anticipating subsequent developments, the other four most important patriarchates came to be Constantinople, Alexandria, Antioch and Jerusalem. The organisation of the Church did not to come to be completely fixed until, having been recognised by the State, it was free to settle its arrangements in agreement with the civil authorities without threat of hostile interference.

## Schools of Teaching

If we return to the different emphases of teaching which were growing up during the third century the characteristics of the catechetical school of Alexandria might be summarised as being an attempt to reconcile the teaching of the Christian gospel, tied as it was to the Old Testament and the Jewish religious outlook, to the Greek way of thinking and to its philosophical methods. In order to do this the Alexandrian teachers adopted methods of interpreting the Old Testament which to us seem extravagant, to say the least. They did not invent the method, which is to be found in the Palestinian Rabbinical schools, but they developed it and carried it to an extreme length. It was based on the conviction that in the Old Testament—quite apart from the facts recorded—God had provided an account which prefigured later events and which could be interpreted to show this by means of the allegorical method. The Alexandrian school found such an allegorical meaning in almost every line of the Old Testament and sometimes dispensed altogether with any literal sense. Clement and Origen were the Alexandrian teachers most famous for this approach.

The Alexandrian teachers were particularly influenced by Platonic ideas, and the effect of Origen's writing on later theologians there was immense. His power of thought and energy were vast. 'He has been called the first great scholar of the Church, the first great preacher, the first great devotional writer, the first great commentator, the first great dogmatist.'[11] Some of these titles may be disputed, but the fact that they have been applied to Origen is tribute to his remarkable personality and work.

But for the purposes of our study the important thing to notice about the development of Alexandrian thought is that it came to give certain emphases which became characteristic of Alexandrian thinkers in subsequent centuries, and which differed from other Christian schools such as Antioch. The Alexandrian writers stressed particularly the transcendence of God, and in the growth of Christian doctrine about the Godhead they emphasised especially the Godhead of all three persons of the Trinity. During the third century this discussion had not reached its climax, but the early forms of Alexandrian thought foreshadowed later developments. So great was the emphasis on this last point that Origen himself is generally thought to have fallen into the error of tritheism. The theology put a strong stress on the divinity of Christ, which came out later in disputes about the nature of the person of Christ. We are not here concerned with the history of Christian doctrine, but the main differences in emphasis will later be important for understanding the divisions which appeared within the Church.

The tendency of theology at Antioch was different and often opposed to that of Alexandria, being Aristotelian and historical rather than Platonic and mystical. It adopted a more critical attitude towards the Bible, distinguishing between the value of different books and concentrating on trying to discover the intention of the writer rather than on some hidden allegorical meaning. The Antioch theologians objected strongly to the tendency of Alexandria to weaken the teaching of the unity of God by undue stress on the three Persons of the Trinity. Paul of Samosata, Bishop of Antioch from about 260 to 268, when he was adjudged heretical, showed in his theology a typical Antiochene emphasis, in holding that Christ was a man only and that he differed only in degree from the prophets. He was the precursor of later heretics, such as Nestorius, whose followers created a permanent schism from the main body of the Church.

Paul of Samosata was a man who brought out the problems of unity which the Church had to meet in the middle of the third century. He himself seems to have been an unattractive character, conceited and self-opinionated, whose morals were not above question. Eusebius accused him of improper relations with spiritual sisters called *subintroductae* (VII. 30). He was one of the most important people in Antioch and comported himself as such, having had a successful financial career under the government before being elected bishop. After giving some details about him the great Roman Catholic historian Mgr. Louis Duchesne wrote: 'However, as he was very indulgent to the weaknesses of the clergy, his worldliness would have been forgiven him, if he had not taken up theology. This proved his ruin.'[12]

Other bishops intervened, and more than one council was held to consider his views. Eusebius reports (VII. 29): 'In Aurelian's day a final synod of an exceedingly large number of bishops was assembled, and the leader of the heresy at Antioch, being unmasked and now clearly condemned of heteredoxy by all, was excommunicated from the Catholic Church under heaven.' In this incident we see how, in the interests of unity of belief, other bishops could act against another of their number when he was guilty of departing from the proper teaching of the Church. But, although excommunicated, Paul refused to give up his position as bishop, and an appeal had to be made to the Emperor Aurelian, whose intervention established the new Bishop Domnus, who was himself the son of Paul's predecessor as Bishop of Antioch.

Problems of unity arising from false teaching were accompanied by problems arising from the persecutions. North Africa produced two outstanding writers in this century, Tertullian and Cyprian. The former was a lawyer ordained in middle life at Carthage, who died about 220. He wrote a large number of distinguished apologetic works, mostly in Latin, and was the first Christian theologian to write in this language. In reaction against the laxity of Christians in Rome Tertullian associated himself with the schismatic and puritanical Montanist movement, but this association did not diminish the value of his writings, which were in most respects perfectly in accord with the general teaching of the Church. Cyprian gained much of his knowledge of Christianity from Tertullian's writings, and was made Bishop of Carthage in 248, two years after his conversion. The Decian persecution broke out only a few months later, and many Christians lapsed by sacrificing to the State gods. There was also a brisk trade in false certificates, which were sold to Christians, stating that they had sacrificed to idols when in fact they had not done so (called *libelli pacis*).

When the persecution ended many of the lapsed were readmitted on easy terms, a practice which Cyprian strongly opposed. Suitable penances, more severe for those who had actually sacrificed than for those who had merely bought a certificate, were imposed and advocated by Cyprian, whose views, taking a middle way between a rigorist and lax attitude, eventually prevailed.

In Rome the difference of opinion gave rise to a schism headed by Novatian, its most accomplished theologian, who advocated a rigorist position. He began a schism in 251 which persisted for several centuries.

Cyprian was involved in a dispute as to whether those who had been baptised by schismatics ought to be rebaptised on entry into the Church. He engaged in a fierce correspondence with Stephen, Bishop of Rome, on the point, and was supported by three councils of African bishops in his view that the sacraments of the Church could not be administered by those who were not members of it. Rome held the position that anyone could validly baptise. The principles behind this difference appear again and again in subsequent church history and are still today a cause of misunderstanding among different groups of Christians.

The second half of the third century is scarce in recorded historical events, but during this century the Christian faith was being spread in more eastern centres, such as Armenia and Edessa. In Edessa (now Urfa) a Christian centre had been established from early times, and although the legend recounted by Eusebius of correspondence between King Abgar of Edessa and Jesus is clearly unsound, there is evidence in it of Christianity at Edessa at an early date. The church there, which was destroyed by flood in 201, is the earliest known Christian building. Edessa was the centre of Syriac-speaking Christianity, and the tendencies of this part of the Christian world were later to cause difficulties. It later became the home for extreme views which originated in Antioch. Syriac is a language which is allied to the Aramaic spoken in Palestine at the time of Jesus, and the Syrian outlook was more direct and simple than that of the Greek-speaking theologians.

Although it is impossible to establish the truth or otherwise of the tradition that the Church in Armenia was founded by St. Thaddaeus and St. Bartholomew, there is virtual certainty that it was steadily growing during the second and third centuries. The martyrology of the Church contains the names of early martyrs, and there are also traditions of early bishops, though nothing is known about them. But the fact that this country was the first to adopt Christianity as the official religion of its people certainly testifies to the spread of the Christian Church at an earlier date as well as to the labours of St. Gregory the Illuminator, who was at work at the end of the third century, and who had been consecrated bishop by the Metropolitan of Caesarea in 294. From the first, Armenia was conscious of itself as a separate nation, and the adoption of the Christian faith by its king, Tiridates III, in 301 shows that at that time it had its own national consciousness, which has persisted throughout the centuries to the present day. Living on the borders of the Roman and Persian Empires, the Armenians were a buffer state, constantly subject to attack by the great powers on either side of them: it was in such political circumstances that their national identity was forged, and their religious outlook became inextricably fused with their national feeling and aspirations. They led the rest of the world in making Christianity their official religion, and in doing so they set the pattern for the whole Empire to follow more than a decade later.

[1] Henry Bettenson, *The Early Christian Fathers*, Oxford, 1956, pp. 124–5.
[2] *Ecclesiastical History*, iv, 22.
[3] A. R. C. Leaney, 'What was the Lord's Supper?' *Theology*, February 1967.
[4] On this question see J. N. D. Kelly, *Early Christian Creeds*, London, 1952.
[5] Philip Carrington, *The Early Christian Church*, II, Cambridge, 1957, p. 340.
[6] Carrington, *op. cit.*, p. 345.
[7] Carrington, *op. cit.*, II, p. 376.
[8] R. C. Zaehner, *The Convergent Spirit*. London, Routledge and Kegan Paul, 1963, p. 185.
[9] Carrington, *op. cit.*, II, p. 487.
[10] Walter Howard Frere, *Alcuin Club Collections*, XXXV, Oxford, 1940.
[11] Henry Bettenson, *The Early Christian Fathers*, Oxford, 1956, p. 27.
[12] *The Early History of the Church*, I, 341, London, John Murray, 1957.

# 3

## A Christian Empire

### Christianity, the Official Religion of the State

BY chance Britain witnessed the event which was to produce a dramatic change in the position of Christianity at the beginning of the fourth century. In the year 306 Constantius Chlorus, the chief Emperor in the West, died at York, and his son Constantine was acclaimed as his successor by the troops of that northern headquarters. During the next eighteen years he became master of the whole Empire, East and West, and Christianity was established as its sole official religion. For the unity of the Christian Church this change brought entirely different conditions, and, while from an organisational point of view it added greatly to the elements tending to uniformity and discipline, at the same time it introduced a range of motives and pressures which weakened the growth of the spiritual unity on which outward conformity must be built if it is to be more than a shell.

The motives of Constantine in becoming Christian must to some extent remain a matter of speculation, but there is no reason to suppose that Constantine's conversion was other than sincere. The fact that he did not accept baptism until near his death was a natural, and not uncommon, reaction to the rigorous attitude taken by the Church to post-baptismal sin, and reflected a common desire to remain on the safe side of forgiveness. It seems likely that Constantine genuinely believed the God of the Christians to be on his side, and finding him, as he thought, a successful ally, was encouraged in the simple belief that he had adopted.

But, whatever may have been his reasons for establishing Christianity as the religion of the Empire, once it had been done, then unity of religion became an interest of the State itself. It would be absurd to suppose that any ruler of the time could view the religious activities of his subjects other than in the light of their usefulness to the stability of the Empire he governed. For Constantine, therefore, it became a matter of importance for the Christian Church to be a means of stabilising the Empire under his own general direction. This did not mean that he considered himself qualified to solve disputes concerning the churches, still less that he had any pretensions to understand or decide theological issues. No doubt he approached such matters on a strictly practical basis.

### Donatist Schism

From the beginning of his reign, when still sharing the government of the Empire with Licinius, he discovered serious tensions within the Church. The most serious was the schism arising from the persecution by Diocletian, for this persecution had left the Church seriously weakened, not so much by loss of numbers as from internal dispute, and it is probable that Constantine was taken by surprise by what is known as the Donatist schism.[1] He was also unprepared to deal with the serious doctrinal troubles which were soon to break out.

The persecution under Diocletian had caused numbers of Christians to abandon their faith, to hand over sacred books and vessels, and in other ways to betray their Christian loyalties. When the time came for peace—and with official recognition this time it was peace with honour—it is not surprising that those who were the first to give way to pressure were the first to wish to mount the band-wagon when the danger was past. In Carthage a critical question arose about the new bishop, Caecilian, who was said to have been consecrated by a man who had given up the Scriptures to the persecutors. A rival bishop was consecrated by other African bishops, Donatus, after whom the schism is named, being his successor. The seriousness of the division was a measure of the high feelings which were aroused by the question of the reconciliation of those who had defected: a similar difficulty had arisen sixty years earlier with the Novatian schism after the persecution of Decius.

In the case of the Donatist split we find the religious issue made more serious by nationalist considerations. Constantine, who at that time was ruling in the West alone, tried to find a solution by referring it to a commission of bishops, of whom the most important was Miltiades, Bishop of Rome. He does not seem to have done this with any idea of recognising the authority of Rome over others. The Donatists had asked for arbitrators to be appointed, and Constantine had acceded to their request. Three other assessors were chosen to sit with Miltiades, but the Pope, apparently by his own decision, added another fifteen Italian bishops to the gathering, and by doing so made it much more like a church synod than it had been, either in appearance or in intention. This group of bishops decided against the Donatists' claim. At this point it seems that the Donatists, who were dissatisfied with a decision which went against them, appealed to African sentiment against it. They claimed that St. Cyprian, a former Bishop of Carthage, took their view, and the dispute was complicated by this 'nationalist' feeling.

Constantine tried again to settle the matter, in the second place by calling a council, which met at Arles in the year 314. This method of settling disputes had ecclesiastical precedents, and it was the first occasion of his reign on which Constantine resorted to a method which was to be more and more important as time went on. The council at Arles decided against the Donatists for the second time, and in one of its clauses upheld the validity of ordinations, even if they had been performed by those who had been branded as traitors to the Church.

*Church and State*

A most significant development followed, for in accepting the decision of the council Constantine proceeded to use the power of the State to try to root out those who dissented from it. He was not particularly successful and some traces of the Donatist schism lasted until the seventh century. For the first time we see the power of the State being used to persecute those who will not conform to the decisions made by orthodox Christian authority. It set a pattern which was to be followed with deplorable results through many centuries of Christian history, and which has not altogether ceased even today. From the Christian point of view it could hardly be squared with the gospel which the Church was supposed to be preaching. And even from the lowest motives of calculation it was a bad policy, for if orthodox authorities have the right to persecute their opponents it is hard to deny the same right to heterodox or anti-Christian powers.

But at that time the use of the power of the civil government to promote the religion of which it approved was taken for granted. Just as the worship of the old gods was supported by the civil arm, so any religious system which the State wished to promote would enjoy the same support. There was no real alternative before Christians in the situation which then prevailed. The Church as such made no conscious choice of one course rather than the other: it was the State which decided. Even if there had been a choice, it is unhappily probable that each side in a dispute would have welcomed support which would give it the victory. Nevertheless, the adoption of this policy for the Christian Church was to prove one of the most serious obstacles to the discovery in practice of that unity which its nature required, and it was to blind the eyes of many generations to the fact that an imposed unity was no true unity at all, if measured by the standards of the gospel of Jesus.

The nationalism which we have noted as creeping into the Donatist schism was a small sign of much greater difficulty to follow. The larger the unit of religion, the more likely there are to be variations within it, and when Christianity became coterminous with the Empire the stresses and strains of the civil state were imported into and became mixed with religious differences. As has already been seen, national churches, such as the Church of Armenia, were growing on the frontiers of the Empire: they expressed themselves in difference of language. The Christianisation of Armenia was accompanied by the reduction of its language to writing, and different parts of the Empire began to exhibit the same trend. The unity of the Greek language, which had been a mark of the Empire a century and more before, was giving way to distinct language groups. Rome itself had abandoned Greek for Latin, and the middle of the third century had seen the first Christian apologist writing in Latin—Tertullian. This distinction of language was to cause strains between different parts of the Christian world which retained the same doctrine, owing to the difference of nuance in Latin and Greek.

It was from the middle of the third century that we see the rise of monasticism in Egypt, later to spread throughout the Christian world. The official acceptance of Christianity gave the growing movement an additional fillip when the Church added to its members large numbers of nominal Christians, who inevitably lowered the level of Christian life. Monks in Egypt, and later in Constantinople and elsewhere, were to take a leading part in the controversies about doctrine which were to mark Christian life for several centuries to come. In Egypt they also encouraged the use of the Coptic tongue in the settlements outside the towns, thus contributing to the growth of a Coptic church consciousness which was to frustrate unity later on.

## The Arian Heresy

But the controversy which agitated Christendom during the entire stretch of the fourth century was that surrounding the person and teaching of Arius, and is known as Arianism. Official approval of the Christian Church had the effect of releasing obstacles to the free discussion of its tenets, and by the year 300 many Christian doctrines had not yet been adequately discussed or worked out. The process of reaching agreed conclusions on obscure theological matters, such as the doctrine of the Godhead or the person of Jesus Christ, inevitably involved public controversy as a means of examining, accepting or discarding speculations on the subject. Moreover, the whole process of discussion became of intense interest to the populace at large, and Arius himself showed a distinct flair for publicity by writing popular songs giving expression to his own theories.

It would be tedious to trace the details of the controversy, and would need considerably more space than is at our disposal, though the general course of events needs to be noticed. Arius himself was ordained deacon by Peter, 'Pope' of Alexandria, whose martyrdom marked the end of the Diocletian persecution.[2] He was, however, excommunicated as a member of a schism which originated in Alexandria, known as the Melitian schism from its originator, who objected to the easy terms for the return of the lapsed which Peter allowed during a lull in the persecution some years before his own death. The Melitians identified themselves with the views of Arius and were bitter enemies of orthodox teachers such as Athanasius.

The essence of the Arian point of view was a refusal to accept the term *homoousios* (being of one substance) to describe the relations of God the Son to God the Father. This word was established as the test of orthodoxy by the first 'General Council' of the Christian Church ever held, that of Nicaea in 325. It was called by the Emperor for the express purpose of dealing with the heresy of Arius, who held the Son to be inferior to the Father, and, although its decision has been described as being reached by a snap vote, it settled this central doctrine of the faith for all subsequent centuries in the words of the

Nicene Creed. Some emperors were orthodox in their views and supported Athanasius, whereas some were Arian or semi-Arian and supported his opponents. It was during the reign of a pro-Arian emperor that the phrase *Athanasius contra mundum* came to be used. One of the emperors, Julian, ever afterwards termed 'the Apostate', tried to revive heathenism during his reign from 361 to 363.

Constantine himself, who began by supporting the orthodox conclusions of Nicaea, later vacillated and in the last part of his life supported the Arians. Gibbon summarises his attitude as follows (II. xxi): 'The ecclesiastical government of Constantine cannot be justified from the reproach of levity and weakness. But the credulous monarch, unskilled in the stratagems of theological warfare, might be deceived by the modest and specious professions of the heretics, whose sentiments he never perfectly understood; and, while he protected Arius, and persecuted Athanasius, he still considered the Council of Nicaea as the bulwark of the Christian faith and the peculiar glory of his own reign.' The final establishment of the orthodox doctrine against Arianism was achieved in the second General Council of 381, held at Constantinople under the Emperor Theodosius I. The creed, known as the Nicene Creed or sometimes as the Niceno–Constantinopolitan Creed, is so called as being the expression of the belief of the Church as expressed in those two councils of the whole Church. It may be noticed in passing that, although there were no delegates from the western church at the Council of Constantinople, it has been universally recognised as ranking as a 'General Council' of the whole Church.

## General Councils

The authority of 'General Councils' plays an important rôle in the subsequent history of church unity, and although such councils are not universally regarded as infallible, they are accepted by the majority of Christians as having more claim on their obedience than any other identifiable decision-making body. Roman Catholics came later to endow the Pope with almost limitless claims on their obedience, but they, too, recognise the authority of the councils. The Church of England cautiously included a statement in the Thirty-nine Articles of Religion that such councils 'may err, and sometimes have erred, even in things pertaining unto God', but carefully refrained from identifying the errant decisions. The purpose of the article

(No. XXI) would seem to be to reserve the right to criticise any detail which later seemed unacceptable. But even when the authority of General Councils is admitted, the question still remains as to how many of these councils are to be reckoned as binding. Anglicans have for the most part accepted the first four without question, but there seems no reason why they should not be deemed to accept the first six or seven. The first seven are of particular importance, since it is these, and these alone, which are regarded as binding by the Eastern Orthodox Church, to whom they are known as 'Ecumenical Councils'.[3] The Roman Catholic Church recognises these seven councils but also many more, the most recent of which was Vatican II, which concluded in 1965.

It will be observed that three of these councils were held at Constantinople, the capital city of the Empire. When Constantine became the sole ruler of the imperial dominions he decided in 324 to found a new capital city on the shores of the Bosphorus, and did so in 330. Here there was already a Greek city with the name of Byzantium, and his new capital was built on that site and named after himself Constantinople. The present Turkish name of the city, Istanbul, is a corrupted form of Constantinople.

The siting of the centre of the Empire's administration at the junction of Europe and Asia was immensely important: the ramifications of this decision affected the whole subsequent course of world history, the relations between the western and eastern parts of the Empire and the religious developments of the future. Hereafter no aspect of life would be unaffected: economic, political, theological, ecclesiastical and cultural developments were directly influenced by the fact that the centre of the Empire was in the East, and that it was within the framework of a Greek-speaking culture and form of thought that the centre of civilisation was placed.

The future of Christianity in the Persian Empire was seriously jeopardised by Constantine's attempts to strengthen the Christian cause. Among them he made a public declaration that all Christians everywhere were under his protection. In Persian eyes this at once linked their Christian subjects with the country's political enemies, and suggested that they might be a 'fifth column' within their own gates. The resiting of the imperial capital at Byzantium reinforced the threat posed by the Roman Empire. Under Persian rule the Christians enjoyed a semi-independent status as a *millet*, that is, a community identified by its religion and allowed to administer its own affairs (see also p. 204). The misguided declaration of Constantine gave an opportunity to religious opponents within the Persian Empire to attack the Christians on the grounds of their political unreliability.

There were Christian leaders who extravagantly praised Constantine and regarded him not only as heaven-sent, which might be excused as a result of a belief in divine providence, but also as heavenly inspired, for which it is more difficult to find reasonable justification. Eusebius, the historian, was a fervent admirer of his and wrote *Vita Constantini*, which has been described as 'merely an extravagant and unqualified panegyric upon every act of Constantine'.[4] No doubt such attitudes derived partly from the simple process of transferring the old forms of adulation for the emperors to the new Christian occupants of the throne. With this natural transfer went, it seems, something of the semi-religious attributes which the emperors had claimed for themselves and received in the past. From a Christian point of view there is nothing to be said for such an idolatrous attitude, and it resulted in a position for the Emperor, for which the term Caesaro-papism has been coined. It reflected an attitude which can be traced into modern times in Russia, and which has even left its mark on the modern Russian Communist State.

Caesaro-papism is a term which can bear different emphases. It can mean the complete control of a monarch over the Church, so that in effect the Church is in bondage to a lay power. Or it can describe an attitude in the popular mind which attributes to the ruler semi-divine authority side by side with the authority to be found in the ecclesiastical structure and hierarchs. There is no doubt that the attitude of eastern Christians towards the Emperor was less inclined to assert the independence of the Church as such than was the West. This was probably in part simply a reflection of the fact that there was a Christian ruler in the East, whereas it was not long before the West was battling with barbarian invaders whose leaders were evidently not to be accorded rights over the Church. This difference in outlook is the beginning of a gradually widening gap between the eastern and western halves of Christendom.

*Problems of Language*

The difference of language, already mentioned, was an important element in widening the gulf between Christians in both parts of the Empire. The problems which arose can be illustrated by a simple example taken from the debate about the Arian heresy. The orthodox word for the relation of the Son to the Father was, as we have seen, *homoousios*, making use of the Greek word *ousia* meaning essence. The orthodox doctrine of the Trinity, as it was eventually adopted in Greek, spoke of one essence (*ousia*) and three persons (*hupostaseis*). In Latin the equivalent terms were one substance (*substantia*) and three persons (*personae*). The difficulty is that linguistically the Greek word *hupostasis* is equivalent to the Latin word *substantia*: both mean 'that which stands under'. But in the Greek and Latin forms of the doctrine they refer to different parts of the formulation, the Greek word referring to the distinctions within the Trinity and the Latin to the underlying unity. It is not surprising, therefore, that such confusions led to misunderstanding, for it was only too easy for the Latins, for example, to think that the Greeks were advocating belief in three different substances, which appeared to them to be a form of tritheism, though there was indeed a difference of theological outlook underlying their approaches.[5] A similar misunderstanding arose in Aramaic and affected the attitude of those who were later called Nestorians.

Although the debates seem to a twentieth-century mind somewhat unreal, they were in fact of great importance, and the subjects with which they dealt are still relevant in the presentation of the Christian faith today. Certainly discussion could not today be carried on in the thought-forms of the fourth and fifth centuries; nevertheless, it is right that we should understand the general relevance of the themes which were debated. They dealt with the character and authority of the life and teaching of Christ, and covered the vital question as to whether in Christ men were to see the direct action of God mediated to them by God himself. For it is only when this is established that the Christian experience and teaching of the possibility of the reconciliation of man with God, and of man's fulfilment in a life of unity with God can be firmly held. If the life of Christ is anything less than a substantial and reliable expression of God's love in human terms, it can hardly carry conviction as a means of bringing fulfilment to men. Similarly, in the fifth-century controversies about the person of Christ himself the issue was whether men could see in Christ not only the means by which God had intervened to bring them a knowledge of his love but also a real identification of God with human nature, with man, which did not make that human nature unreal. Unless Jesus Christ were true man, he could not be deemed to be truly one of us; unless he were true God, he could not be the full expression of God's saving action.

During the fourth and fifth centuries the Church was trying to put into words its own experiences of God, of Christ, and of the working in its own life of the Holy Spirit. The heresies which arose during the course of the years fall into the categories which these three divisions represent. They were heresies of the nature of God—Trinitarian heresies arising from the consideration of the nature of God in himself. Orthodox belief was concerned to safeguard the basic Christian teaching of a God of love whenever it spoke of the Godhead itself, though we should not fall into the vulgar error of supposing that the definitions which were eventually accepted were meant to be descriptions of the whole of the life and character of God. There were also Christological heresies, such as Apollinarianism, and there were heresies about the Holy Spirit, such as that of Macedonius, both of which were condemned at the first Council of Constantinople (381).

Great Christian teachers arose in the fourth century, the most influential of whom was St. Augustine of Hippo in North Africa, born soon after the middle of the century, and dying in 430. He was not baptised until 387, and his influence was mainly exercised in the following century. To him we must give more detailed attention, since in subsequent centuries he became a court of appeal for Christians who wished to reform the Church, and his influence on Luther was particularly great.

## Theological Debates and Councils

The furious enmities which differences of doctrine aroused in past centuries seem to many today to be unreal. Yet passionate partisanship in Christian doctrine is still to be found, and indeed it is a measure of the importance of the subject, for it is only when men think it to be vitally relevant that they care deeply enough to engage their whole energies in a doctrinal dispute. What marks the second half of the twentieth century is a conviction that the issues must be dealt with by liberal discussion. It may indeed be because there is no longer any chance of using methods of political pressure, academic censure, or economic threat, that Christian disputants have perforce to confine themselves to methods which are more in accord with what they teach. It is not long since in England every kind of weapon was thought suitable to try to silence one's theological adversaries, as the disputes of the nineteenth century show clearly enough. The attempt to oust men from their university posts or to withdraw their degrees on what now appear to be absurdly narrow grounds was a matter of course, and political influences were not absent from what on the surface appeared to be church struggles.

In fact, it has been taken for granted for 1,500 years that in the quarrels arising from different theological points of view 'anything goes'. It was certainly the case in the fourth and fifth centuries that the disputes which raged round the doctrines of the Trinity or the person of Christ were affected not only by the political situation of the Empire and the personal views of the emperors but also by the personal ambitions of prelates and theologians. The battle raged backwards and forwards, now one party and now another being in command of the great sees of Christendom. In a number of sees, such as Alexandria, there were for a period of years rival bishops, representing parties for or against the latest council, who replaced one another according as the fortunes of their side improved in the battle. Athanasius, for example, was Bishop of Alexandria from 328 until his death in 373, but no less than five times he was driven out of the see to be replaced by an opponent. The power to remove him was exercised by the State according to the policy or theological opinions (which were often the same thing) of the Emperor.

## Augustine of Hippo

In the midst of the debates of the fourth and fifth centuries the great St. Augustine was to lay the foundations of Latin theology by his works, of which the *Confessions* and *The City of God* have become classics. He was undoubtedly the most influential single theologian in the history of Christian thought, for much of what he wrote was formative for subsequent generations in the West. But not all of his teaching was healthy, and it may even be considered a tribute to his extraordinary range that out of it can be taken such a variety of insights, even though some of them have to be corrected. But it must be admitted that those views which have been inadequate have carried many Christians into further mistakes.

Augustine's attitudes were governed by two main experiences of his life. The first was his own early life and attachment to Manichaeism, a religious theory which held that there were two principles in the world, one of evil and one of good, both of them ultimate. When he became a Christian, Augustine laid the firm foundation for a rejection of Manichaeism and introduced the concept of evil as a privation of good. But his personal attitude to life carried with it a suggestion that the things of the flesh were in themselves tainted with evil to such an extent as to require a negative view of them. In his teaching, especially that against the Pelagians, he stressed the importance of concupiscence as the origin of sin, due to the fact that, as a consequence of the Fall, the senses were no longer subject to reason in man. His teaching was immensely influential in encouraging a negative attitude towards the sexual powers and activities.

The second aspect was his opposition to the Pelagian view that men were free to choose and achieve the good, unaffected by Adam's fall, a point of view which makes the grace or help of God an optional extra in men's lives, said to be the typical British heresy. Pelagius, the originator of the heresy, was a British or an Irish monk who came to Rome at the turn of the fourth and fifth centuries. He later went to Africa, where he met the full opposition of Augustine. The controversy was conducted in terms of Adam's fall, and assumed the historical accuracy of the first chapters of Genesis, but the substance of the debate was of importance to the whole religious life.

Augustine was also concerned in the Donatist controversy, and this caused him to write extensively on the subject of the validity of sacraments and the action of those who celebrated them while cut off from the main body of the Church. Here we find a different emphasis from that of Cyprian. The latter put his main stress on the importance of the minister of the sacrament (whatever the sacrament was) being himself in full communion with the Church, and therefore properly authorised by his unity with the authoritative body to celebrate the sacrament on its behalf. Augustine, on the other hand, put the emphasis on the innate character of the minister which he had received in his own ordination, which bestowed on him a power which he could exercise, whether at the time he was in full communion with the rest of the Church or not. This theory had a disastrous effect in subsequent ages, since it was generally accepted by the Church in the West. Its practical effect was to cut the sacraments off from the Church, within which alone they can have their full meaning. It has led to the appearance of small and unauthorised groups arising from the exercise of the powers of ordination by those who had no authority except their own for consecrating bishops or ordaining priests.

One effect has been the appearance all over the world of men who claim to have been validly consecrated bishop by some other bishop or bishops. They are known technically as *episcopi vagantes*, wandering bishops. Some of them have been morally respectable, but not all. In most cases such bishops have had very small congregations, made up of a small group of people whom they have been able to attract. The magnetic possibility of becoming a bishop has for some men proved such a powerful attraction that they have been unable to resist the temptation of securing consecration by irregular means. According to the Augustinian theory, their consecration has been irregular but valid.[6]

But more important in the history of Christian theology were Augustine's views of the fall, of grace, of sin, and of free will. In some of these subjects he fell into exaggerations which have now been repudiated by most Christians, but which have been the source of stresses in theological disputes throughout the centuries. They were exceptionally important during the Reformation period, and influenced Calvin and Luther strongly. To Augustine the fall had made man incapable of righteousness, to all intent totally depraved and unable to originate any good thing. This had some fearsome consequences, such as the consignment of all unbaptised children to everlasting perdition. From time to time he showed himself completely predestinarian, and maintained that men are saved exclusively by the unmerited *fiat* of God. There were other less extreme elements in his writing, in which he taught that man suffered only from a certain serious deprivation and that he could still do moral acts of his own choice, even though he needed the grace of God to be saved.

It would be absurd to suggest that the complexities and richness of Augustine's thought can be summed up in a few words. As a writer of a great book on Augustine has said, we may be misled by systems which claim his name, and what is known as Augustinianism is largely a 'cruel travesty' of his best thought.[7] But in a study such as ours we have to pick out those aspects which are chiefly relevant to

C

our own topic, and we therefore inevitably see larger than life the exaggerations which were later to cause tension and division.

Augustine opened up for Christian theology in the West a vast range of practical and theoretical studies which were later to form the subject of theology for his successors, and it has been justly noted that without his 'massive intellect and deep spiritual perception Western theology would never have taken the shape in which it is familiar to us'.[8]

Augustine was laying the foundations of western Christian theology at the moment when decisive events were forcing apart eastern and western Christendom. From 323, when Constantine defeated Licinius, the Empire had been ruled by a single Emperor with his seat at Constantinople. But from the year 395 the rule was divided between Honorius in the West and Arcadius in the East, and this unity was broken. In 410 the Christian world was shocked to hear that Rome had been taken by the Goth, Alaric, and sacked. It was this event which was the immediate cause of Augustine's writing *The City of God*. The success of the Goths was a long step towards the split between the two parts of Christendom, since the struggles of the West effectively isolated it from the normal life of the rest of the Empire. The ineffectiveness of the Imperial Government was also a most important element in the growth of the responsibilities and influence of the Roman see. The position of Rome was recognised in the Christian world as one of primacy, but it was the only one of the great Christian sees to be found in the western part of the Empire, and to those living in Constantinople its conquest would have appeared important though distant.

Meanwhile in the rest of the Church controversies continued to agitate the minds of laymen as well as ecclesiastics. At the Council of Constantinople in 381 the capital see had been given the second place after Rome. The third canon of the council read: 'That the Bishop of Constantinople have the prerogative of honour next after the Bishop of Rome: for Constantinople is New Rome.'[9] With the disappearance of old Rome from the scene of ordinary church life the position of Constantinople grew and was consolidated as the chief see of the capital city of the remaining Christian Empire.

## Nestorians and Monophysites

During the fifth century two heresies arose which were to issue in schisms still in being today, although recent signs have indicated possibilities of healing them. The heresies in question are known as Nestorianism and Monophysitism: the expounder of the former was Nestorius, Patriarch of Constantinople from 428 until his deposition by the Council of Ephesus in 431. It is a matter of curiosity that the doctrines attached to men's names do not by any means necessarily represent the views which they themselves held, and there is doubt as to whether Nestorius actually believed the doctrines which were condemned under the name of Nestorianism. The heresy held that there were two persons in Christ, and objected to the use of the word *theotokos* as applied to the Virgin Mary. The word *theotokos* means literally 'God-bearing' and, because of the recognition of the divinity of Christ, refers to the Virgin Mary as Mother of Jesus. The word became the badge of orthodox belief, although it was clearly open to theological misunderstanding, the Latin equivalent 'Mother of God' even more so.

Nestorius was much influenced by the theology of Antioch, which traditionally stressed the humanity of Christ and concentrated attention on the historical life of Jesus. It laid emphasis on the importance of the moral life among Christians, and in some ways was sympathetic to the Pelagian approach. Because of the close contacts between Antioch and Edessa, this theological approach was particularly influential among the East Syrian Christians and those of Persia. Its outlook thus became identified with certain regions, the churches of which found it easy to bring together their particular theological views with their regional political and linguistic sense of identity.

It should be noted that what was heretical in Greek appeared orthodox in Aramaic, the language of the East Syrians. It therefore seemed to them a positive advantage to adopt a form of theology which, while adhering to the true tradition, at the same time showed their independence of the Christians of the Byzantine Empire.

A similar process occurred with those churches affected by the Alexandrian outlook, which, in contrast with that of Antioch and often at loggerheads with it, stressed the unity of Christ to such an extent as to do away with the distinction between the two natures and hold that there was only one nature in Christ—hence the term (*monos* = one, *phusis* = nature) Monophysite. The chief protagonist of this point of view was Eutyches, an Archimandrite (literally ruler of a monastery) of Constantinople, who was condemned by the Council of Chalcedon in 451.

Associated with the Alexandrian point of view were the churches of West Syria and Egypt, together with that of Armenia. Here again the conscious espousal of a particular doctrine was accompanied by resentment against the Greek-speaking organisation of the Empire and the identification of Constantinople and the Greek-speaking churches with that hegemony. At Ephesus in 431 there were no western representatives present, and Nestorius's opponent Cyril of Alexandria proceeded with the council and condemned him before even the arrival of the delegates from Syria. At Chalcedon all the members were eastern bishops with the exception of two papal legates and two bishops from Africa.

## The Great Sees

The bishops at Chalcedon, besides dealing with doctrine, also passed canons settling the status of the great sees. Jerusalem was raised to patriarchal rank, and thus became one of the five patriarchates, which ranked in this order: Rome, Constantinople, Alexandria, Antioch, Jerusalem. Canon XXVIII of the council gave this rank to Constantinople and included the following sentences: 'For the Fathers properly gave the Primacy to the throne of the elder Rome, because that was the imperial city. And the 150 most religious Bishops, being moved with the same intention, gave equal privileges to the most holy throne of new Rome, judging with reason that the city which was honoured with the sovereignty and senate, and which enjoyed equal privileges with the elder royal Rome, should also be magnified like her in ecclesiastical matters, being the second after her.' This canon Rome refused to accept. The wording is by no means clear, and the 'equal privileges' would naturally provoke a hostile reaction from the see of Rome, which had been given by the Council of Sardica in 343 the right to hear appeals. One of the pretexts for the refusal was a supposed anxiety on the part of Rome to protect the rights of the other patriarchates, sc. Alexandria and Antioch, which were of older foundation than Constantinople. It also refused for some time to recognise the see of Jerusalem as a patriarchate, but eventually agreed to do so.[10]

The second half of this same Canon XXVIII gave to Constantinople the right to ordain the Metropolitans of 'the Pontic, and Asian, and Thracian dioceses who are amongst the barbarians'. This statement of jurisdiction seems to have referred to specific areas at the time of the Council. But since that time Patriarchs of Constantinople have claimed the right to jurisdiction over Eastern Orthodox Christians living in any area of the world which lies outside the boundaries of a recognised Orthodox Church. This claim, still upheld in the twentieth century, has met with the vigorous opposition of other Orthodox Churches, who claim jurisdiction over their own people abroad. There has thus arisen out of this canon not only tension between the eastern and western halves of Christendom but also tension among the Orthodox Churches themselves. The result has been the existence in non-Orthodox countries of the West of a number of Orthodox jurisdictions organised independently of one another, and in some cases distinctly hostile to one another. The claim of the Oecumenical Patriarchs has thus offended their own Orthodox brethren, and it is worth noting that it also implies that Christian countries in the West which have their own churches fully organised under their own hierarchies are to be considered not as fellow-Christians but as 'barbarians', for certainly Canon XXVIII gives the Patriarch extra jurisdiction only in the dioceses which are 'amongst the barbarians'.

During the fourth century the practice of the monastic life spread from Egypt into Palestine, where a large number of establishments were set up. The monks lived in various stages of isolation: some of them were hermits; some of them lived in a *lavra* which provided for individual cells grouped round a centre to which they came for certain occasions of worship; or they might live a common life in a *coenobium*. They earned their meagre substance by simple work, such as the making of rush-baskets, and emerged from their cells or caves only at weekly intervals. It strikes a modern reader as strange to find a number of bishops who so much wished to spend their life in solitude and prayer that they abandoned their dioceses, if they got the chance, and disappeared anonymously into some desert place, often pretending to be laymen. The disputes on theological topics were reflected in the desert, and the situation for many years had the appearance of a field of war where the monastic towers and buildings were strongholds of one party or the other. In the end the Chalcedonian monks triumphed in Palestine, but not without vicissitudes.[11]

## East and West Move Apart

In the situation developing in the fifth century the West found itself cut off from the cultural life of the Empire. The ravages of the barbarians destroyed the old educational institutions, and the intellectual life of the laity almost came to an end. Whereas in the East the laymen took a prominent and vigorous part in theological and philosophical studies and discussions, in the West intellectual life and educated persons came more and more to be confined to the clergy. There were also different emphases of outlook, some of which have already been noted. The West on the whole was practical and down to earth, interested in legal matters: in short it was heir to the qualities shown by the Romans at their best. The East was far more interested in philosophical speculation, and was also much attached to its own habits of cult and worship. So far as religious practice was concerned, the liturgy in the East was in the language of the people, or at least in a language which the people could more or less understand, whereas in the West it was in Latin, which none of the people understood. The result was that the affairs of the Church in the West became more and more concentrated in the hands of the clergy, who at the same time were increasing in importance in civil as well as ecclesiastical matters.

Out of a situation such as this it easily occurred that the Christians of the East came to see themselves as the lineal descendants of original Christianity. True, they recognised the status of the patriarchate of Rome and its services to orthodox faith, but they could hardly take seriously a form of religious practice which was harried by the barbarian invaders and constantly under attack or pressure from them, especially as it was unfamiliar. It is in the Byzantine Empire that we first find an attitude of mind, still to be found within the Eastern Orthodox forms of Christianity, that Orthodoxy, and some think Greek Orthodoxy, can alone claim to be the authentic heir of the Christianity of the early Church.

This was put succinctly by Dean Stanley in 1857 in his deservedly well-known Lectures on the History of the Eastern Church:

'The Greek Church reminds us of the time when the tongue, not of

Rome, but of Greece, was the sacred language of Christendom. It was a striking remark of the Emperor Napoleon, that the introduction of Christianity was, in a certain sense, the triumph of Greece over Rome; the last and most signal instance of the maxim of Horace, "Graecia capta ferum victorem cepit." (When Greece had been enslaved she made a slave of her rough conqueror.) The early Roman Church was but a colony of Greek Christians or Grecised Jews. The earliest Fathers of the Western Church, Clemens, Irenaeus, Hermas, Hippolytus, wrote in Greek. The early Popes were not Italians but Greeks. The name of "Pope" is not Latin but Greek—the common and now despised name of every pastor in the Eastern Church. It is true that this Grecian colour was in part an accidental consequence of the wide diffusion of the Greek language by Alexander's conquests through the East, and was thus a sign not so much of the Hellenic, as of the Hebrew and Oriental character of the early Christian communities. But the advantage thus given to the Byzantine Church has never been lost or forgotten. It is a perpetual witness that she is the mother and Rome the daughter. It is her privilege to claim a direct continuity of speech with the earliest times, to boast of reading the whole code of Scripture, old as well as new, in the language in which it was read and spoken by the Apostles. The humblest peasant who reads his Septuagint or Greek Testament in his own mother tongue, on the hills of Boeotia, may proudly feel that he has an access to the original oracles of divine truth, which Pope and Cardinal reach by a barbarous and imperfect translation; that he has a key of knowledge, which in the West is only to be found in the hands of the learned classes.'[12]

One may perhaps doubt whether there are in fact many peasants reading the Septuagint on the hills of Boeotia—or reading anything else. And, in spite of the disclaimer, many Greek-speaking Christians do in fact identify Christianity with Hellenism. But taking into account the romantic flights of the passage just quoted, it represents exceptionally well the feeling which is to be discovered among Orthodox Christians as a whole, and especially among those who belong to the Greek tradition. It explains much of the trouble which was later to arise between East and West, for they resisted claims of power and jurisdiction which became more and more characteristic of the Roman papacy as time went on. Here were the seeds of serious future tension.

This tension can be seen in its first manifestation of division with the publication by the Emperor Zeno in 482 of his *Henoticon*, an attempt to bring together the warring factions after Chalcedon, and to end the political dangers of the schism which had occurred. The document had the support of the Patriarchs of Constantinople and Alexandria, and it tried to create a basis for unity through the omission of any reference to the two natures of Christ or to the formulations of Chalcedon. It was widely accepted in the East, but immediately met the firm opposition of Pope Simplicius, who excommunicated the Patriarchs of Constantinople and Alexandria and the Emperor himself. A breach was thus caused between East and West which lasted from 484 until 518. It was then healed because the Emperor Justin I for political reasons wished to have the friendship of Rome and exercised pressure on the then Patriarch to remove the offending Patriarch Acacius and his successors from the official diptychs.[13]

---

[1] T. M. Parker, *Christianity and the State in the Light of History*, London, A. & C. Black, 1955, p. 48.

[2] Derwas Chitty, *The Desert a City*, Oxford, Blackwell, 1966, p. 1.

[3] The first seven councils with their dates were: Nicaea I 325; Constantinople I 381; Ephesus 431; Chalcedon 451; Constantinople II 553; Constantinople III 680/1; Nicaea II 787. The word 'ecumenical' is sometimes spelt 'oecumenical' in accordance with the original Greek spelling, but the shorter form is now becoming more and more used and is therefore adopted in this book.

[4] Parker, *op. cit.*, p. 59.

[5] T. M. Kelly, *Early Christian Doctrines*, London, A. & C. Black, 1958, p. 136.

[6] H. R. T. Brandreth, *Episcopi Vagantes and the Anglican Church*, London, S.P.C.K., 1961: Peter F. Anson, *Bishops at Large*, London, Faber & Faber, 1964.

[7] John Burnaby, *Amor Dei*, London, Hodder & Stoughton, 1960, p. 231.

[8] *Oxford Dictionary of the Christian Church*, London, 1957, p. 107.

[9] *Canons of the First Four Councils*, Oxford, 1869.

[10] Runciman, *The Eastern Schism*, Oxford, 1955, p. 15.

[11] Derwas Chitty, *op. cit.*

[12] Everyman Edition, p. 65.

[13] Runciman, *op. cit.*, p. 16. The diptychs were the tablets on which the names of the living and dead were written and read out for prayer during the liturgy. The presence of a name on the diptychs meant that the person was in communion with the church: its absence meant his excommunication.

# 4

## National and Regional Churches

### Lesser Eastern Churches

*The Assyrian Church*

IT will be well first to refer to various titles which have been applied to this church, which today exists only in small remnants in the Middle East and in the United States. Its own proper title is 'The Church of the East', a phrase which recalls the great days of its earlier history of which hardly a trace remains. Its members are sometimes called 'Nestorians' for reasons which we shall presently see. They are also called 'East Syrians', a geographical name, and Dean Stanley[1] called them Chaldaeans. But the word Chaldaean is now normally reserved for that branch of the Assyrian Church which is in communion with the Roman Pope, and it is this use which we shall follow.

The Christian faith spread into the area east of Edessa in the second century at the latest. These districts formed part of the Parthian Empire from the second century B.C. until the third A.D., occupying a substantial part of the former great Persian Empire. But about A.D. 224 another Persian Empire was established under the Sassanian dynasty, which remained in existence until 651, when it was finally vanquished by the Arabs. The religion of Persia was Zoroastrianism, which was sometimes enforced by the power of the State, but for a large part of the Sassanian period Christians were able to live and prosper in the Persian dominions.

In the areas of Persia the language of Christians was Aramaic or its later form Syriac. Their religious outlook differed, as we have seen, from the Christian attitudes associated both with the Greek and the Latin tongues. The evidence available for the history of the early developments is scanty, but it seems probable that with the condemnation of Nestorius and Nestorianism by the Council of Ephesus in 431 numbers of Christians who regarded themselves as sympathetic to Nestorius moved further east, out of reach of the pressures of the imperial forces which wished to enforce the orthodoxy of Ephesus. The Persian rulers were in a constant state of tension with the Empire, which they were usually either attacking or resisting. Their earliest attitude to Christians was hostile, since they regarded them as representatives of the official religion of an enemy empire.

When, however, Christians sympathetic to Nestorius began to move into Persia as a means of escaping the enmity of the imperial authorities Persian national policy was able to take a different view of them and to see them as useful allies against their political opponents. When the Persian policy was governed by Zoroastrian religious considerations the Christians suffered, but, in spite of this hostility, the church began to grow, and it became one of the most powerful and missionary-minded churches in the Christian world.

With the coming of the Arabs the church continued to flourish, for the first waves of Arab invasions followed a policy of tolerance towards Christians and Jews, regarding both religions as 'religions of the book'. The church continued as a separate millet under the Arabs, and enjoyed a period of expansion during the seventh and eighth centuries. It survived until the end of the fourteenth century, when calamity overtook it after the capture and the sacking by Timour of Baghdad, Damascus and Aleppo. He initiated a policy of fearful persecution and succeeded in destroying the church except for the remnants which managed to escape to the mountains of Kurdistan, where they survived until modern times in small isolated communities. There they were engaged in constant warfare with the Kurds, who massacred four thousand of them in 1843. They formed small compact mountain units, and maintained their religious customs under a patriarchate which descended from uncle to nephew.

In its prosperity the Church of Persia was a great missionary church under its patriarch at Seleucia-Ctesiphon. It spread the Christian faith across Asia, establishing itself in China, where inscriptions of the year A.D. 781 refer to the arrival of Christian missionaries in 635. It flourished there, it seems, until the dissolution of all monasteries by the Emperor Wu Tsung in 845.[2] At the time of its mission to

China the Church of Persia is thought to have included as many as two hundred dioceses.[3]

In the year 1886 Archbishop Benson of Canterbury, hearing of this small and isolated Christian community, decided to send a mission of help to it. The mission had no intention of trying to convert the Assyrians from their ancient form of Christianity; on the contrary, it was aimed exclusively at rendering them assistance in education and training of their clergy. One consequence of this ecclesiastical action, quite unforeseen and unintended, was that on the outbreak of the First World War the Assyrians joined forces with the British against their age-old enemy the Turks. Being mountaineers, they proved excellent fighters, and were not troubled with some of the inhibitions which British soldiers had. They proved a useful aid to the victorious allies. A series of pressures and calamities resulted in the emigration of the whole nation to Baghdad at the end of that war, where with complete confidence they appealed to the British Government to find them new homes or to set them up in their old ones.

The story after that time was one of deplorable indecision and muddle by the authorities concerned, whether British or international. A few devoted British friends tried for years to get justice for the nation, but with singularly little success, and some of the schemes which were tried were doomed to failure from the start. A fearful massacre of Assyrians took place at Simel in Iraq in 1932, and the position of those who remained became more and more difficult. They were largely held together by the fact that at its large air base outside Baghdad (Habbaniyah) the British Air Force employed Assyrians in the 'levies' on which the security and safe running of the base depended.

In the Second World War, when Rashid Ali rose against the British and tried to capture the air base, the Assyrians kept the Iraqi Army at bay and saved that important centre for the allied cause. This and other earlier incidents did not increase their popularity among the Iraqi people. Nevertheless, the Iraqi authorities have since supported plans to settle them in the country.

The present situation is that the Assyrians, who still maintain their ancient beliefs and worship, are scattered in various centres, the major parts being in Iraq, Syria, and Iran, with a colony which has emigrated to the United States and an old-established group in South India. The present Patriarch, who was consecrated in 1920 at the age of twelve, lives in the United States and does his best to shepherd his flock, though he has difficulty in entering some of the countries where they live.

The Assyrians provide a good example of the way in which religion and nationality can become so intertwined that they are impossible to separate. We shall later see other examples, but it is worth noting here that this sort of unity, we might even call it 'confusion', is characteristic of many Christians in Europe and the Near East: it is to be found in a less crude form in England and Scotland, and, although it is a testimony to the way in which the particular form of Christianity has been integrated into the lives of its followers, it may make it difficult to come to decisions on Christian grounds rather than on those of national prejudice or interest. Whether the latter-day Assyrians are Nestorians may be questioned. Indeed, it is unlikely that the question would have any identifiable meaning for most of them, who are not skilled in ordinary literary ability, still less in theological problems. Moreover, although it is thought that the Assyrians did not accept the Councils of Ephesus and Chalcedon, there is evidence that it did in fact accept the latter council, for it is referred to in the local Council of Mar Aba in A.D. 540. Its failure to accept Ephesus may have been due to the fact that it did not get told of the council, and, even if it had been notified, the main decisions of the council were taken, as we have earlier observed, before the arrival of the Syrian delegates. It is therefore not at all clear at what point communion with the main body of the church could be considered to have ceased. From the answers to questions submitted to the bishops of the church before the First World War, it seems clear that they no longer held a doctrine which would be thought unorthodox, either with regard to the person of Christ or with regard to the Virgin Mary.

The unhappy events which caused so much suffering to the Assyrian Church and nation since the First World War brought this church for the first time since the early centuries into living contact with the rest of the Christian world. It has been befriended by the Church of England, which admits members of the Church of the East to communion at its services; it is a member of the World Council of Churches, and it may be hoped that its relations with other churches will become as close as possible without losing what is valuable in its own distinctive tradition.

*The Chaldaeans* are those Christians, originally belonging to the Assyrian Church, who broke away and submitted to the Pope. The split seems to have originated from a dispute about the succession to the patriarchate in the year 1551. A large group, reacting against the customary practice of electing the former Patriarch's nephew, elected another. Being unable to find the required three bishops to consecrate him, they appealed to the Pope, who undertook the consecration and thus secured the oversight of the Chaldaean Catholicos (or Patriarch) and his people.

Since coming into the Roman ambit, the Chaldaean Church has adopted a number of western practices which originally were not included in their religious habits, e.g. forms for the sacraments of penance and anointing of the sick. Other aspects of western influence have in some cases been removed from their service books in accordance with the policy of the Roman Catholic Church to encourage and retain the original traditions of the various non-Roman rites, so far as possible without uncharacteristic additions. The branch of the church in Malabar in South India has been much affected in its worship by contact with the Portuguese.[4] The largest number of Chaldaeans is to be found in Iraq, and their head, the Patriarch of Babylon, resides at Mosul.

## The Armenian Church

The Armenian nation occupied territory which was a key area between Asia and Europe. It lay in the expanding funnel of land which opened into India and the East, and commanded the two land entries into Europe, one over the Caucasus to the east and the other through Asia Minor to the Bosphorus to the west. During the Christian era it found itself sandwiched between the Empire of Parthia or Persia to its east and the Roman Empire to the west. The inevitable consequence was that it became a battle-ground for control by both of these two powers, and, being itself a relatively minor power, enjoyed little complete independence. Nevertheless, it had a national identity of its own and often enjoyed relative independence, which varied according to the policies of the powers in question.

Into the political situation were injected religious elements too. Armenia was the first country ever officially to adopt Christianity as the State religion, under King Tiridates III, probably in 301. Its great missionary was St. Gregory the Illuminator, and the church is sometimes erroneously termed 'Gregorian' on this account. The Armenians had their own language and were never culturally 'overcome' by neighbouring peoples. An Armenian alphabet was composed in 404 and the Bible translated into the language by 433.[5] These were important influences in welding together the Armenian Church and nation.

The Armenian Church is classed among those called 'monophysite', for while it accepted the decrees of the Council of Ephesus against Nestorius in 431, it did not accept those of the Council of Chalcedon twenty years later. It has been a common mistake in Christian history to suppose that, if a church did not accept the decrees of a council, it must therefore believe the contrary. But this is far from evident, especially when one takes into consideration the various strands which led to such action or lack of it. In the case of the Armenian Church, it was impossible for delegates to go to Chalcedon, even if they knew of the council, because at that time the nation, with church leaders at its head, was engaged in a deadly struggle to prevent the Persians from imposing the Zoroastrian religion upon its members. Religion and nationality combined to resist the enforcement of this policy, though the Armenians were defeated in the critical battle. This battle, that of Averayr, was fought in the very year in which the Council of Chalcedon was held. Because of its internal problems, questions of interpretation of doctrine did not come to be considered by the Armenian Church until the beginning of the following century.

It is also necessary to remember that after the Council of Chalcedon a protracted struggle took place as to whether or not the decrees were to be generally accepted. And, although its decisions have been and are explained in an orthodox manner, and indeed they have *become* orthodoxy, they could be and were easily interpreted in a manner which was distinctly unorthodox, especially when seen in the light of partial information. There is no evidence that the Church of Armenia either wanted or intended to make a break with the bulk of Christendom, but by the time it came seriously to take account of theological matters, divisions were already forming on the periphery of the Empire.

A recent study has maintained that it is wrong to suppose that the decisions of Armenia against Chalcedon were due entirely to political reasons.[6] The first official decision taken against Chalcedon occurred at the Council of Dowin in 506/8, and it was reiterated in succeeding centuries. But whatever the formulations which were accepted or rejected, the conclusion of the study is that both the churches which accept and those which reject Chalcedon are in fact expressing the same incarnational faith in different ways.[7] Certainly the rapprochement recently between the two groups of churches seems to indicate that the differences between them on doctrinal points are more apparent than real.

It is not without significance that the form of Christian faith which the Armenians treasured was distinct from that of other Christians to whom they were neighbours. In the Persian Empire the Christians were attached to Nestorius, and especially to his great teacher Theodore of Mopsuestia (c. 350–428), and, if not heretical, at least they adopted an emphasis which was different from the rest of Christendom. In the Roman Empire, on the other hand, the Christians accepted Chalcedon, which Armenia rejected. There seems here to be some unconscious inclination to use its religious outlook to help identify and hold together the nation itself. Certainly church and nation are more closely identified than in any other Christian church of comparable size. The church and nation have undergone terrible sufferings, and without this identification it could hardly have survived as a conscious entity. It is impossible to measure the part which national consciousness played in religious attitudes, but it would be surprising, in view of the evidence of history, if it were not one of significance.

During the Middle Ages the Armenian Church came into closer contact with Christians of the West, especially through the crusades. There was a series of discussions which had church unity as one of its aims, but which also reflected the desire for dominion on the part of the Pope and for useful alliances on the part of the Armenians. Later more active proselytisation was undertaken by the Roman Catholic Church, resulting in the formation of a community of Catholics of the Armenian rite. These Armenians were persuaded to change their allegiance under powerful propaganda financed from Rome and supported by the French within the Ottoman Empire. The present numbers of Armenian Catholics are estimated at a little over 50,000, compared to more than 3,600,000 members of the Church of Armenia.

The Armenians suffered fearful decimation from massacres under the Turkish yoke from 1894 onwards. No less than 600,000 of them are calculated to have perished during the persecutions and deportations of 1915, a large number of bishops being among those killed. The present organisation of the Armenian Church has four chief centres. The Supreme Catholicos resides at Etchmiadzin in Soviet Armenia: he is universally recognised as the chief bishop. Another Catholicos, who is independent in ecclesiastical administration, lives in the Lebanon outside Beirut and has the title Catholicos of Cis (Cilicia). There are also two Patriarchs, one in Jerusalem and one in Istanbul.

## The Syrian Church

The Syrian Orthodox Church (the official title) belongs also to the group of churches commonly termed 'monophysite'. It is also known as the Jacobite Church, and is sometimes referred to as West Syrian. The name 'Jacobite' was an unfriendly epithet first recorded as being used by the second Council of Nicaea in 787. It derived from Jacob Baradaeus (490–577), who was the organiser of the church, making it in some sense the national church of the West Syrians. 'Baradaeus' was a nick-name meaning 'dressed in rags', for he habitually travelled about the country dressed as a beggar. Jacob was consecrated bishop with the support of the Empress Theodora, who favoured Monophysitism, and he spent many years travelling about Syria, ordaining priests and consecrating bishops. In this way a minority of dissident church members was turned into an organised and self-conscious community, opposed to Chalcedon.[8]

Although historians must note the other varying strands of influence which together caused division and unity among Christians, the power of ideas should not be underestimated. Theological opinions firmly held must be ranked among these ideas, though it is impossible in the nature of the case to make any accurate measurement of them. But individuals were certainly governed by their convictions about truth, and the Empress Theodora is a case in point. She was a woman of remarkable intellect and ability, exercising considerable influence on her husband the Emperor Justinian I. It was probably because of her views that he came to favour the Monophysite groups and tried to satisfy them, even at the expense of the decisions of Chalcedon. The Monophysite point of view, holding that there was only one nature in Christ, was close to the emphasis which was common in the school of Alexandria, and opposed to that of Antioch, where the Nestorian teaching of two persons in Christ was an exaggerated form of the approach of that school. Justinian's efforts to placate the Monophysites led to the holding of the fifth Ecumenical Council.

Jacob was the means by which a rival Monophysite organisation was created in Syria in opposition to those who accepted Chalcedon and its decrees. He showed such zeal and effectiveness that by the end of his labours there was not a single orthodox see which did not have its rival Monophysite bishop with clergy under him. The head of this Jacobite church was called, like his orthodox opposite number, Patriarch of Antioch. In his lifetime Jacob is said to have consecrated two Patriarchs of Antioch and eighty-nine other bishops.[9] The church even spread to Persia, and in the twelfth century counted a hundred bishops in Syria, Asia Minor and Cyprus, as well as eighteen sees in the East.

Throughout the Middle Ages the church continued to exist, but gradually diminished until today it is small, and probably does not number more than 200,000 members. During the crusades the Syrians were brought into close touch with Latin Christians from the West, and their general hostility to the Greeks arising from their past history had the effect of helping to create friendly relations with the Latins. In the seventeenth century a large number of Syrian Christians seceded to the Roman Catholic Church. Under the Pope there is a church of the Syrian rite which consists of those who have been won from the Jacobites and their descendants. The Syrian Christians use Syriac as their liturgical language.

## Malabar

Of particular interest is the ancient settlement of Christians in south-west India on the Malabar coast. Their tradition claims that their church was founded by St. Thomas the Apostle, but there is no convincing evidence to substantiate this. Nevertheless, there is clear evidence that there were connections between Syria and India in the first century A.D. 'India' is a word which in ancient times might cover almost any place south and east of Parthia or Persia. An ancient legend dating from the third century connected the names of St. Thomas and a King Gundaphorus, a story generally regarded as unreliable. But at the end of the nineteenth century excavations in the Punjab made it clear that Gundaphorus was an historical person, a king of Indo-Parthia, who lived in the first century. There is much evidence of travel between India and the Mediterranean area at that date.

An aspect of the Christian communities in Malabar especially relevant to our subject is the way in which they changed their allegiance for various practical reasons, and were therefore supposed to have changed their beliefs. It is often found to be the case that the doctrines which any one group of Christians is assumed to have adopted are identified by the jurisdiction under which they find themselves. But this is an unreliable guide, for the simple reason that the beliefs and practices of people are not easily switched from one pattern to another except over a prolonged period, apart from some violent upheaval. In the struggles between the Papacy and the Orthodox churches to gain jurisdiction over Christians in eastern Europe an experienced observer remarked that the people themselves did not care to which jurisdiction they belonged, so long as they had a priest for their church and village who did his duty and was not given to drunkenness or other immoral habits. The course of history for the Christians of South India, although to the outside observer it appears changeable, probably affected the everyday life of the church members very little.

When the Christian Church of Malabar first reached the light of history it was closely related to the Church of Persia, and it seems probable that much of the evangelistic work was done by that church, which in other ways showed such missionary zeal. The Indian Christians had bishops consecrated by the Persian Church, which was technically Nestorian in doctrine. There is nothing to show whether or not the general beliefs which they adopted were Nestorian or not, but it may be surmised that the violent controversies over these matters which marked the main body of the Church did not occur to the same extent in South India. Merely from a geographical point of view Christians lived in a clearly defined area, bounded on one side by the mountains and on the other by the sea. The connection with Persia continued until the end of the thirteenth century, and there remains a small church today in Malabar which continues to belong to the Church of the East, and to be subject to Mar Shimun, Patriarch of the Assyrian Church.

The coming of the Portuguese to India radically changed the situation in Malabar. But before that date there were already contacts between the Pope and Malabar, for in 1330 a bishop, Jordanus, was sent with a papal bull to the Christians at Quilon. But from the end of the fifteenth century the Portuguese commanded the seas, and in 1542 Francis Xavier landed in Goa. He began a great campaign of conversion supported by the civil authorities. But he did not succeed in breaking the resistance of the Malabar Christians, whom he tried to bring under the jurisdiction of the Pope. It was the arrival of Archbishop Menezes in 1592, with less scruples as to his methods, who eventually broke most of the resistance, and at a synod at Diamper in 1599 most of the Syrian Christians submitted to Rome. Some congregations, said to number thirty-two, refused submission, while eighty-four accepted Roman rule.

What were the thirty-two congregations to do? They now had no bishops, since the Portuguese authorities would permit no contacts with Persia, to which they had previously looked for consecration. To meet the emergency twelve priests joined together to consecrate an Archdeacon Thomas to the episcopate. This was irregular, and from the Latin point of view invalid. It was only when the Dutch captured Cochin in 1663 that connections with the outside ecclesiastical world became possible. The Dutch, being Protestants, had no reason to prevent a consecration, and two years later a bishop named Mar Gregorius arrived from Jerusalem. (The title 'Mar' is commonly used for bishops in the Lesser Eastern Churches: it means 'lord'.) He was welcomed by the people and invited to consecrate their nominee as bishop, which he did. But Gregorius was a bishop of the Jacobite Church, and this group of Malabar Christians in consequence found themselves part of that Church, theoretically Monophysites, whereas earlier they had been theoretically Nestorians.

It is clear from this succession of incidents that the great churches of west and east were ready to indulge in empire-building by persuading other bodies of Christians to come to them for ordination, which was the sign of submission to the church from which it was received. Until comparatively recently among the Syrians in South India one group was attached to the Syrian Orthodox Church in the Middle East, but it was faced by a rival group, which did not differ in teaching, but claimed independence for the local church. The two parties were known as the patriarchal and catholicos parties, and the division between them has been healed since the Second World War. In the nineteenth century, as the result of the influence of English missionaries who were anxious to purify the supposed corruptions of the eastern churches, an additional schism was caused by those who split from the rest of the Syrian South Indian groups on the grounds that they should exclude from the liturgy such unreformed elements as prayers for the dead and invocation of the saints. No doubt the fact that the Church Missionary Society representatives were English, and therefore associated with the British raj, added to the weight of their influence, quite apart from purely theological considerations. This church is known as the Mar Thoma Church.

We therefore find in miniature in South India the main divisions of Christendom, reproduced in this group of ancient Syrian Christians, who even within a close similarity of rite are divided in their allegiance among Rome, Jacobites, Assyrians and a reformed section as well. Other rites have, of course, been introduced into the area since then, as has occurred all over the world, Latins, Orthodox, Anglicans and other kinds of Protestants.

*The Coptic Church*

The word 'copt' is a form of the pre-Arabic word 'Egypt', and therefore means a member of the Church of Egypt. But its use has come to be confined to a member of the Egyptian Church which is separated from the bulk of orthodox Christendom, and is reckoned to be among the Monophysite churches. Alexandria was the second most important centre of culture and learning in the Roman Empire, and it early became a place of importance for Christian teaching. Its tradition maintains that the see of Alexandria was founded by St. Mark, though there is no convincing evidence to substantiate the claim.

The gradual division between the Church of Egypt and the rest of Christendom seems to have arisen primarily as a consequence of two differing elements within that church. Lower Egypt, with its centre Alexandria, was predominantly Greek-speaking and therefore closely linked with the orthodoxy of Greek-speaking Byzantium. The rest of the Church of Egypt was Coptic-speaking and consisted of Upper Egypt and the monasteries of that area. There were also social and financial differences which tended to keep these two groups apart. The Greek-speaking Christians were for the most part either imperial officials or people in some way connected with the court and the ruling classes, and therefore in the upper income brackets, to use a modern phrase. The Coptic-speaking Christians were the natives of the country, mainly employed in the agricultural economy of the country districts.

In the second half of the fifth century and in the following century the Christians of Egypt were engaged, like the rest of Christendom, in debates about the Monophysite heresy, and, as occurred elsewhere, the fortunes of the battle swayed this way and that. When orthodoxy was in the ascendant there was an orthodox Patriarch of Alexandria who threw all the Monophysites out of their offices and installed orthodox officials in their place. When their rivals secured power the same thing happened in reverse. Both sides claimed to represent the true faith of Christendom and regarded their opponents as heretics. The vast majority of Egyptian Christians gradually formed themselves into a group on the Monophysite side, and the orthodox side became more and more exclusively identified with those who spoke Greek. The difference in the language of their services helped to deepen the division. The gradual identification of orthodoxy with official Byzantine policy gave rise to the name 'Melkite', which was applied to those who were on the king's side, and meant 'king's men'. It is well to remember that this Greek group was in fact an occupying power imposed on a subject race, not often popular with those whom it rules. This use of the word 'Melkite' needs to be noticed, since it is now used only for the Uniate Church, now under Rome, of Syrians and Egyptians: it is one of the most important of the Uniate churches.

Had the Byzantine authorities frankly recognised the existence of two churches in Egypt from the start, it would have avoided much mutual recrimination and even persecution, but such a concept was quite impossible in the ideas of the time. No one imagined that there could be more than one Christian bishop in one place, and all efforts were therefore directed to ensuring that the party one supported should have possession of the see.[10] In the ins and outs of the Patriarchs of Antioch, historians always mention Timothy the Cat, no doubt because of his picturesque title, who reigned in Alexandria on behalf of the Monophysites from 457 to 460 and again in 475. Soon after the Acacian Schism (484–519) began, which divided the eastern and western parts of Christendom, and during this period Egypt was an important centre for all who were promoting Monophysite views.

Such was the general situation until the arrival of the Arabs in 639.

Like all foreign occupiers, they were glad to encourage those tendencies which were hostile to the interests of their chief enemy, and the Copts were natural allies against the Empire. It is said that their hatred of the Roman Empire was so great that the Copts welcomed the Arabs as liberators. If this was so, it was certainly not the last time that a similar situation would arise, and in consequence they became the recognised Christian community in Egypt. In their turn the Copts were able to drive out the Melkites from the seats of power, and although a small community seems to have continued to survive, the orthodox Melkites almost disappeared from Egypt at this time. For more than seventy years from 655 there was no Melkite Patriarch of Alexandria.

Egypt remained under some form of Muslim domination for more than twelve centuries. During this long period Christians suffered incredible oppression and persecution, the refinement of cruelty and torture to which they were subjected being unsurpassed. It is surprising that the church managed to survive at all. One element in their survival was that the Copts were better educated and more capable than their Muslim fellow countrymen, and therefore were usefully employed in clerical and professional positions. Hidden help could often be given even in serious crises, and employers would sometimes protect their own employees in times of persecution.

But the troubles which the Copts had to endure and the exactions which they had to undergo left the Church in an extremely weak position, often given to corruption and bribery as a result of having to resort to such measures in order to secure its own existence. Under Muslim rule, moreover, the penalty for leaving Islam was death. Those Christians who had given way to threats or torture by embracing Islam could never return without forfeiting their lives.

In modern times many other churches have come to Egypt in company with traders and foreign residents. Protestant missionaries have been among them as well as Roman Catholic missionaries. These have often spent their energy in trying to convert Copts rather than Muslims, and the Coptic Church was further weakened by their efforts. At the present day it numbers about a million members. In recent years it has come into contact with Christian churches outside the country for the first time on any scale.

Roman Catholic efforts to gain over the Copts began in the fourteenth and fifteenth centuries, but they had little success. In the seventeenth century the efforts of the Franciscans succeeded to the extent of forming a small community of converted Copts, and things continued thus until the nineteenth century, when further access was possible: in 1895 the Pope established two dioceses, and a third has been added since. As in the case of every eastern church, there is a corresponding church under the Pope, called the Coptic Catholic Church, with a Patriarch of Alexandria who resides in Cairo. It has about 80,000 members.

Our short survey has already revealed three Patriarchs of Alexandria—Greek Orthodox, Coptic, Coptic Catholic. This is an inevitable result of the policies of proselytisation of the churches. There are in fact even more, since there is a 'Melkite' Patriarch of Alexandria also—in the modern sense of Melkite, that is, a Uniate Patriarch. The same confusion is to be found in the other great sees of the East.

## The Ethiopian Church

Closely connected with the Coptic Church of Egypt was the Church of Ethiopia or Abyssinia. Although earlier claims are made, the first reliable history begins with a certain Frumentius, who as a result of a shipwreck was brought to the King of Axum, the capital of Ethiopia, and later became bishop there in the fourth century. He received the title, still used, of *Abuna*, meaning 'our father'. Throughout the centuries until recently the head of the Ethiopic Church was consecrated by the Coptic Patriarch of Alexandria and was always a Copt. Often he could not even speak the language of Ethiopia nor did he understand its church customs, which have peculiarities of their own. This dependence on Egypt continued until after the Second World War. On the return of the Emperor Haile Selassie to Ethiopia, an arrangement was agreed after protracted negotiations, not unaccompanied by other pressure, which secured to the Church of Ethiopia virtual independence while still maintaining the ancient connection with Egypt.

The language used in church services is Ge'ez, an ancient language of the country, no longer understood. The church was isolated from the rest of the Christian world for most of its history, and it developed customs and superstitions which are to be found nowhere else in the Christian world. Some of them seem to be Jewish, and tradition says that they come down from the time when the Queen of Sheba visited King Solomon. It is an interesting fact, which may be significant, that an Ethiopian expedition in 522 invaded Arabia at the request of Justinian and established there a Christian kingdom which survived until the time of Muhammad. Muhammad knew a good deal about Christianity from his travels and from people close to him, though his knowledge was imperfect. There was a militia in Mecca composed of Ethiopian mercenaries, and priests and monks were to be found in the markets of Arabia exercising their ministries.[11] He might perhaps have embraced Christianity himself had it not been for the disputes which he observed among Christians, especially the quarrels between the Monophysites and the Nestorians.

With European penetration, Roman Catholic missions attempted to convert Ethiopian Christians to their obedience, and eventually succeeded in establishing themselves in the country in the nineteenth century. They suffered considerable loss of influence by their identification with the Italian invaders and conquerors in the twentieth century, but have been suffered to remain after the restoration of Haile Selassie. There is a Uniate Ethiopic Catholic rite, with more than 150 priests belonging to it.

The number of churches belonging to the Ethiopic Church is rather more than 6,500, each of which must be served by a minimum of two priests and three deacons.[12] After the Second World War the Church of Ethiopia began to play a part in world Christianity and to make contacts with other churches belonging to the Monophysite group, as well as increasing its already close contacts with the Church of England, with which the Emperor had had especially cordial relations during his years of exile. Egypt in the mid-twentieth century has appeared more as part of the Arab world than of the world of Africa. In the growing independence and national consciousness of African states the Church of Ethiopia has begun to play a rôle as the only indigenous African church which has a continuous history from the earliest days of Christianity.

### The Uniate Churches

The Uniate churches are those churches of eastern rite which are in union with the Pope and under his jurisdiction. They are often referred to by a name which indicates their rite, followed by the word 'catholic'. Thus we meet the names 'Armenian Catholic', 'Coptic Catholic' or 'Greek Catholic'. But this does not cover all such churches, for example, the Chaldaeans (Uniate Assyrians) or

Maronites. Moreover, a title like 'Greek Catholic' may be used to cover any Uniate group of the Byzantine rite, whether the actual rite is in the Greek language or not. A list of the titles and their provenance is provided at the end of this chapter.

It is impossible to discuss any of the eastern churches and their relations with other Christian traditions without coming upon the problem of the Uniates. The name 'Uniate' is distasteful to some Roman Catholics, but, as a foremost expert on the subject has said, it seems a reasonable enough way of describing them.[13] All the Uniate churches except the Maronite correspond to churches independent of the Pope, and are the descendants ecclesiastically of the original groups. In almost all cases the Uniate groups are only a small minority of the total number of Christians of the rite in question.

Eastern liturgical rites normally commemorate in them the names of their church leaders, for whom the prayers of the people are asked. In this practice the group shows to what jurisdiction it belongs. When an eastern rite becomes Uniate the Pope and other authorities of the church displace the names of the eastern Patriarchs and Archbishops who would otherwise be mentioned. Where there is any doubt about the orthodoxy of phrases in the liturgy in the case of supposed heretical eastern rites, then the necessary amendments are also made in the Uniate services.

The various Uniate churches have been formed as the result of differing historical circumstances, which are noted in their place elsewhere. But it can be safely said that for the most part they have come into existence as the consequence of a deliberate proselytising activity on the part of the Roman Catholic Church. This fact makes the Uniate churches very unwelcome to the eastern churches, and they have provided a constant cause of irritation. In particular, the Orthodox dislike what seems to them to be the element of deceit involved in the Uniate method. At first sight this might appear unjustified, but in reality it is a serious matter. Large numbers of the Orthodox faithful in the Balkans and eastern Europe have consisted of peasants, for the most part unlettered and ignorant. They have had a long tradition of devotion to their church, which came to play an indispensable part in their daily lives. They were, and are, closely attached to their form of service, but apart from this they wanted to have a priest who was a good man and fulfilled his duties in a way which did credit to his profession. Beyond these simple attitudes they did not much care, or did not even know, of subtleties of jurisdiction. The difference in the eastern liturgy and that of the same liturgy when it was part of a Uniate church was so small as to be of no importance to the religious life of the average parishioner. They were content so long as their simple religious needs were met.

Ordinary parishioners could thus become pawns in the game of ecclesiastical power politics; and, without knowing anything about it, they could be changed from one church to another without noticeable interruption of their customary worship. In many of the manoeuvres in eastern Europe, for example, Roman Catholic expansion was ready to use political pressures as well as other means to persuade clergy to change their allegiance from an eastern authority to that of the Pope. The Orthodox churches not surprisingly saw in this sort of activity a means of deceiving simple people into abandoning the religion of their forefathers.

The tensions which the presence and activities of the Uniate churches create in Orthodox countries are still considerable, as recent statements have often revealed. On more than one occasion Orthodox Church leaders have described the Uniate churches as the biggest single factor in preventing better understanding between their churches and the Roman Catholics.

On the other hand, from the point of view of the Roman Catholic Church, the Uniate system is a thoroughly logical and good one. We do not attempt to defend all the methods by which Roman Catholics have tried to extend the Uniate churches. But in principle it introduces into the Roman Catholic Church a variety of rites, to which considerable importance is given, even though in numbers the adherents of these rites form only a small part of the whole church.

Were it not for the eastern rites of the Uniate churches, the Roman Catholic Church would be a church of one rite—the Roman rite. It is true that there are some variations within it, such as the Ambrosian rite in Milan or the Mozarabic rite in Spain, but both these variations belong to the Roman rite generically. If its worship were to be confined to the Roman rite and its variations it would be difficult for the Roman Church to claim, as it has done for centuries, that it was the only adequate expression on earth of the Catholic church, for it is evident that there has been a variety of rites from the beginning of the church's life. Its opponents could then have pointed to the restriction to the Roman rite as practical proof that the Bishop of Rome was merely the Patriarch of the West.

Moreover, the creation of Uniate churches made it possible for the Roman Pontiff to appoint Patriarchs of the great sees of the East who were subject to him, and could therefore be quoted as proof of his universal jurisdiction. It would have been illogical for the Pope to have claimed universal jurisdiction and not to have acted in accordance with such a claim by appointing to the other chief sees of Christendom. But such action set up rival Patriarchs against the ancient Patriarchs of the East, another fruitful cause of tension. Moreover, the number of Uniate rites corresponds to the number of differing eastern rites, which themselves produce rival claimants to the Orthodox patriarchal thrones, as has been noted elsewhere. For example, there is an Orthodox Patriarch of Alexandria, and a Coptic Patriarch of the same see. The Roman Church therefore found itself in an odd situation when it had distinct Uniate churches corresponding to these two churches, for it was more or less bound to create rival Patriarchs of its own for both the churches in question. This it did, but it obviously could not claim for each of its own Patriarchs that both of them were the true Patriarch of Alexandria. It therefore made them Patriarchs of the *rite* to which each belonged. So as to avoid too great a multiplication of Patriarchs, it sometimes combined them, making one person Patriarch of Alexandria, Antioch and Jerusalem in one case, or putting two of them together in another.

This method of proceeding entirely abandoned the ancient theory that there could only be one bishop in one place who was the bishop of the Catholic Church there. It is not unusual now to find that there are four or five bishops, all subject to Rome and therefore fully recognised by the Pope as Catholic, exercising jurisdiction in the same city, but each doing so over people of his own rite to which his authority is confined. This is not *ipso facto* a bad thing, but, whether bad or good, it is something of which many western Christians are quite ignorant, and which needs to be taken into account in considering efforts towards unity.

Historically there has been a strong tendency to insist in any church on uniformity of rite, which often became the badge of loyalty. From a religious point of view this had many disadvantages, as well as being of doubtful theological and liturgical propriety. The variety introduced into the Roman Catholic Church by Uniate rites has witnessed to an important principle of Christian unity, namely that variety of worship, language or ceremonial is no bar to the completest kind of Christian unity, even though jurisdictional control was an essential part of its organisation. It might be said that such variety is only tolerable where there is some jurisdictional central authority, and that without it there would be no chance of maintaining unity. But there is evidence in history for variations of rite, for example among the Orthodox, with which unity has been maintained without centralisation.

The Uniates have nurtured distinguished churchmen and theologians who have held with some reason that on their shoulders has fallen the maintenance of the true eastern traditions, which would otherwise have disappeared, owing to the parlous state in which some of the eastern churches found themselves under Moslem oppression. There is certainly a case to be made on these grounds. But the eastern churches may well reply that the same care which Rome took to protect their own Uniates might have been expended on upholding the rights of their eastern brethren, had Rome taken towards them an attitude of brotherly love instead of one of powerful hostility. But arguments about what might have been are bound to be sterile. As it was, the best of the Uniates were faithful to the good traditions of the eastern churches to which they corresponded in rite.

It ought not to be overlooked, moreover, that the Russian Orthodox Church has itself approved of a Uniate church in reverse in France, where there are Orthodox under the jurisdiction of the Patriarch of Moscow who are western in origin, and understand neither Old Slavonic nor Russian. They follow a Roman rite in French, but regard themselves as Orthodox. It is more difficult to justify such practices from an ecumenical point of view than those of the Roman Catholics, and indeed the action of the Church of Russia in this matter has gone far to weaken the case against the Uniates which most of the other Orthodox churches make.

## A List of Uniate Churches

The origin of Uniate groups is mentioned during the general historical survey, when appropriate, and the following details are provided for the purpose of general classification and reference.

*Byzantine Uniates.* This group comprises all those Uniates who use the Byzantine rite in some form or other. The Byzantine rite is that which originated in Byzantium, just as the Roman rite is that which originated in Rome. The Byzantine rite is to be found in a number of different languages: Old Slavonic for the Slav Churches (Russian, Serb, Bulgarian, Ruthenian), Rumanian, Greek, Arabic. The group which uses Arabic is now called Melkite or Melchite (though this name was originally used by the Copts for those Christians who were in communion with the Orthodox Patriarchate of Constantinople). These groups have been united with the Papacy at widely different points in history, and a very small proportion may have continued in union with Rome throughout the centuries, as, for example, some of the Italo-Greeks.

*Chaldaeans.* These are sometimes called Chaldees and represent the Assyrians who have united with Rome. The Uniate group therefore corresponds to an eastern church which is sometimes termed Nestorian.

*Coptic Catholics* have been separated from the ancient Church of Egypt and united to Rome.

*Syrian Catholics* are those from the Jacobites who are under the Pope.

*Abyssinian Catholics* constitute a small group from the Ethiopic Church.

*Malabar Uniates* are those originally belonging to the Syrian Orthodox Church of Malabar.

*Armenian Catholics* is a title which explains itself.

*Maronite Church* is a Uniate church *sui generis*, since it does not have an eastern counterpart. The Maronites consist of those who originally embraced the monothelite heresy (seventh century), and were united to Rome *en bloc* in the twelfth century.

[1] *Op. cit.*

[2] Stephen Neill, *A History of Christian Missions*, London, Penguin Books, 1964, p. 97.

[3] E. Molland, *Christendom*, London, Mowbray, 1959, p. 41.

[4] Irenée-Henri Dalmais, *The Eastern Liturgies*, London, 1960.

[5] Malachia Ormanian, *The Church of Armenia*, rev. English edition, London, Mowbray, 1955, p. 18.

[6] Karekin Sarkissian, *The Council of Chalcedon and the Armenian Church*, London, 1965.

[7] *Op. cit.*, p. 217.

[8] B. J. Kidd, *The Churches of Eastern Christendom*, London, Faith Press, 1927, p. 436.

[9] Kidd, *op. cit.*

[10] Adrian Fortescue, *The Lesser Eastern Churches*, London, Catholic Truth Society, 1913, p. 217.

[11] De Lacy O'Leary, *The Ethiopian Church*, London, S.P.C.K., 1936, p. 37.

[12] Douglas O'Hanlon, *Features of the Abyssinian Church*, London, 1946, p. 22.

[13] Adrian Fortescue, *The Uniate Eastern Churches*, London, 1923.

# 5

## East and West Diverge

### Theological Development in the East

THE first four Ecumenical Councils had taken place in the East, and the West from the beginning of the fifth century found itself under constant pressure from the invasions of the barbarians. Intellectual life was in the West very restricted, whereas the East was the continuing arena for theological debate and discussion. The discussions were matters of moment not only to the theologians but also to the emperors, who had views of their own and also wished to use unity of belief and practice as a means of holding the Empire together. The West had willy nilly been excluded from the general cultural and religious life of the Empire, and no doubt the educated classes of Byzantium thought western culture to be of little or no account. The Pope continued to play a part in the councils and official acts, and he did not omit to claim rights for his own see. On more than one occasion, for example at the Council of Chalcedon in 451, the Pope's contribution was of the greatest importance in establishing orthodoxy, the *Tome of Leo* on that occasion being accepted as the standard of orthodox teaching.

But the debate continued in the East with regard to the person of Christ, and, apart from the struggle for power between orthodoxy and Monophysitism, further aspects were debated as time went on. The situation which prevailed during the fifth and sixth centuries threw a clear light on the very wide powers which the emperor thought belonged to him in the matter of declaring doctrine, and the disputes which arose often took their origin from actions which the emperor had initiated. The greatest of all the Byzantine emperors was Justinian, who came to the throne in 527 and reigned until 565. For much of this time he was influenced by his wife, Theodora, who was distinctly partial to the Monophysite cause (see p. 68) and seems to have influenced her husband during the middle part of his reign to act in its favour. Justinian began his reign by using the imperial powers to insist on the orthodoxy of Chalcedon and to punish those who opposed it. But his attitude changed later. It is more than probable that his main motives were political rather than theological, since he was certainly very much aware of the hostility to Chalcedon of large numbers of his subjects in Egypt and Syria.

In 543 Justinian issued a condemnation of three writers associated with the Nestorian heresy in a document aimed against what have become known as *The Three Chapters* (*Capitula*). These had been accepted at Chalcedon, and the condemnation was meant to be a gesture of conciliation towards the defeated Monophysites. The emperor had some reason to suppose that such a statement would be accepted without trouble. In the same year on his own authority he had issued a long condemnation of Origenism, where Origen's doctrine strayed from the path of orthodoxy. This statement had been signed by all the five Patriarchs, apparently without any question or difficulty, although in character it was merely a State edict, and not a statement of the Church as such. But the condemnation of the Three Chapters raised a storm. The four eastern Patriarchs only signed under duress, with the condition that their agreement was valid only if the Pope also signed. Pope Vigilius refused, and was arrested and forcibly taken to Constantinople on the Emperor's orders. He arrived there in 547, and after some pressure agreed to sign. But this by no means brought the matter to an end, as there was open revolt by the North African bishops, who actually excommunicated the Pope, and in the West he found that his own people disowned the decision.

## Fifth Ecumenical Council

Vigilius therefore appealed to the Emperor to summon a council to decide the matter. The Emperor agreed, but immediately put the whole apparatus of State coercion into operation to make sure that the council came to the decision which he required. Opposition bishops in North Africa were arrested and replaced: the Patriarch of Alexandria was exiled and dismissed for refusing to accept the document prepared by the Emperor for signature. The council eventually took place at Constantinople in 553. Vigilius sent a document which

1 Burial vault, Catacomb of Calixtus, Rome, third century

2 *The Food of Life*, Catacomb of Priscilla, Rome

3 *The Living Water and Christ the Teacher*, Catacomb of Calixtus, Rome

4 Funeral meal chamber, Catacomb of Priscilla, Rome

**5** Constantine the Great (*c.* 288–337), coin *c.* 325

**7** Justinian (483–565)

**6** Anchorites' dwellings, Lebanon

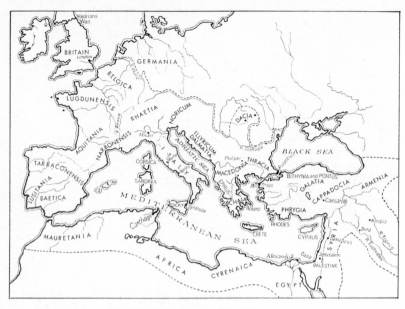

**8** The Roman Empire under Trajan (53–117)

**9** Corfu Island monasteries

**10** Abraham's tomb

**11** Pantheon, Rome, completed *c.* 120 as a pagan temple, later made a church

**12** St Sophia, Istanbul, founded 532

**13** Etchmiadzin, U.S.S.R., Armenian Church of the seventh century

**14** Mount Athos, the Holy Mountain, Greece

**15** Mar Saba, founded 492, south-east of Jerusalem

**16** Mount Athos, monks painting ikons

**17** Mount Athos, monastery of Simon Peter

**18** A monk on Mount Athos

**19** Canterbury Cathedral

**20** S. Maria Maggiore, Rome

**21** Fresco of the Resurrection, Parecclesion, Istanbul, *c*. 1320

**22** Ikon of the Trinity, by
Rublov (died 1430)

**23** Cyril Lukaris (1572–1638), Ecumenical Patriarch

**24** William Laud (1573–1645), Archbishop of Canterbury

**25** St Basil's Cathedral, Moscow

**26** St Paul's outside the walls, Rome, interior before the fire of 1823

**27** Baptism of Negroes on a French ship

28 Cathedral of the Assumption, Kremlin, Moscow

29 Funeral of Timotheos, Patriarch of Jerusalem, January 1956

30 Cyril Garbett, Archbishop of York; Christophoros, Patriarch of Alexandria, and others, Cairo, 1943

**31** World Council of Churches, 1948, first Presidents

**32** Pope John XXIII, died 1963

**33** Alexis, Patriarch of Moscow and All Russia, 1962

**34** Pope Paul VI on his visit to the Holy Land, 1964

**35** The Ecumenical Patriarch of Constantinople and the Archbishop of Canterbury, 1967

**36** The Patriarch of Rumania and the Archbishop of Canterbury at the tomb of the Unknown Warrior, 1966

never reached the council, and the Emperor presented instead the earlier statement which Vigilius had signed under pressure. The council confirmed the condemnations, and in the end Vigilius also consented to its decision. In making its decisions the council did in fact contribute to the positive development of doctrine. Vigilius died on his way back to Rome, and his supporter Pelagius arrived there as the Emperor's candidate for the vacant throne of the papacy. There was more than a little difficulty in persuading the West to accept the decisions of the council, and a schism occurred which established Aquileia as a patriarchal see, where a rival line of Patriarchs continued until the eleventh century.

The use of imperial power in this dispute illustrated only too well what was a common practice for centuries, namely the dismissal and appointment of Patriarchs at the will of the emperor, an example to be followed subsequently by the Ottoman rulers. It was already well established at the time of Justinian, and one has the impression that men took it more or less as a matter of course. It was a permanent feature of the uncertainty of ecclesiastical office that it should depend on the whim, the political advantages or the theological opinions of whoever happened to be the emperor. In comparing these events with the history of the West, it can be seen that the establishment of the power of the papacy against temporal rulers had much to be said for it.

It was during the middle period of Justinian's rule that the Syrian Monophysites were provided with their own hierarchy by the activities of Jacob Baradaens (see page 68). In the Byzantine east relations of State and Church, which grew closer over the early centuries after Constantine, had a deep influence on the outlook of all eastern Christians afterwards, and can be traced through subsequent centuries to the modern world. There was no distinction between Church and State such as grew up in the West. The Church as such was seen to be the spiritual side of the State, rather than a separate identifiable body. The best-known comparison, often used, was that of the body and soul: the State was the body, the Church was the soul. But such a point of view meant that there could be no organisational identity of the Church distinct from the State. All citizens belonged to the Church, and the Church was the State seen from a spiritual angle.

The other extreme has often been seen in the Christian West, where truth and its exposition had been confined to the ecclesiastical

D

organ as such, and where this concept became enshrined in its most extreme form in the doctrine of the infallibility of the Pope. In the East the acceptance of Christian doctrine and its guarantee as true did not depend on an ecclesiastical pronouncement. It did not even depend on an ecumenical council, but on such a council when it was recognised and accepted as ecumenical by the *consensus fidelium*, the general consent and agreement of the whole body of faithful people. Thus a council such as that of Ephesus in 449, known as the 'Robber Council', was rejected by the conscience of the Church. Writing of this period a modern Orthodox historian has said:[1] 'The abuse of power by the state was largely linked with the fact that a crystallization of the Church's experience and doctrine was going on within the Church itself, inevitably combined with divisions, disputes, and conflicts. But those who seemed on one day crushed by state absolutism were glorified on the next as saints, and the Empire itself was obliged to revere the heroism of their opposition and their indomitable freedom of spirit.'

Parallel to centralisation in the West, where the papacy was growing as an indispensable centre of Christian authority, there was also a centralisation in the East at Constantinople, which grew automatically out of its position at the administrative centre of the Empire. The twenty-eighth canon of the Council of Chalcedon formally recognised an inevitable development. Officials from all parts of the Empire came to the capital on business from necessity, and it naturally became the custom to call bishops together there to discuss some common problem. Out of such a convenience grew the patriarchal synods of the future. This was not necessarily a deliberate policy on the part of the Patriarchs of the capital city: many of them gave no sign of administrative ambition, though there must have been others who encouraged the tendency from motives of ambition. But it can hardly be doubted that the centralisation was an inevitable growth in the conditions of the Empire.

Justinian saw the Empire in the old terms, as one united territory under the control of the emperor at Constantinople. In furtherance of this ideal he mounted campaigns to free the West from the various forces by which it was being attacked. He reconquered Spain and Italy, though the rule of his subordinates did not increase the popularity of the Empire. But at the same time he was suffering from the inroads of enemies on the north, much nearer the centre of the

Empire. In the service of his ideal he wasted his resources in the West to no permanent advantage, and thus weakened the Empire's power to resist effectively elsewhere.

Reference to the reign of Justinian cannot omit a tribute to the greatest cathedral in Christendom, still standing today, the church of Holy Wisdom (Saint Sophia) in Constantinople. Used for centuries as a mosque, and still adorned with the minarets of another religion and containing few of its former interior adornments, it witnesses to a superb architectural vision, and remains a striking testimony to the place of the Christian faith in the great civilisation of the Roman Empire of Constantinople. Although Christianity had this central place, Justinian's theory of the State had no place for the Church as such, and this was the fatal flaw in the outlook which Justinian represented.[2]

The position of the Church and the growing power of the Patriarch of Constantinople in it was indicated by the assumption in the year 595 of the title 'Ecumenical Patriarch', which has been kept ever since. This produced strong protests from the Pope, who saw in it a claim to universal jurisdiction in direct conflict with his own. From his point of view the Pope may have been right to resist the claim, but there is little doubt that he exaggerated its significance to the Patriarch. To him the *oekumene* was the Empire as viewed from Constantinople, and the adoption of the title was merely a recognition of his situation as chief bishop of the Empire under the authority of Constantinople. But it was a further cause of strain between the Church in East and West.

In 619 a Persian fleet appeared opposite Constantinople and captured Chalcedon on the Asia Minor shore. At the same time there was pressure on the Empire from the north from invasions of Slavs. In 626 the capital was actually under siege from the Persians. The following years, however, saw the defeat of the Persian forces. But a much more serious threat appeared at the same time, as yet merely the size of a man's hand. Muhammad died in the year 632, having captured Mecca two years earlier, and Arab forces within the next few years conquered vast areas of the East.

From 590 onwards the Armenians were allied to the Persians against Constantinople, though the unity was by no means continuous or unbroken. Efforts were made to patch up ecclesiastical agreement with the Assyrians in 630, but although there was theoretical unity among some of the leaders, there was no permanent union among the people. In 635 the Arabs began to invade Syria, and five years later entered Egypt, where they were welcomed by the Coptic native Christians, who saw in them the likelihood of a more tolerant rule than that of their ecclesiastical opponents with the support of Constantinople.

### Sixth Ecumenical Council

Military threats to the Empire showed the Monophysite schism to be a great source of weakness. The Emperor and Patriarch at Constantinople therefore engaged on an enterprise to try to mollify the Monophysites by a new formula. In 638 the Emperor Heraclius published a document known as the *Ecthesis*. The Patriarch Cyrus invited Pope Honorius to concur with the document, which expressed what was known as the monothelite heresy, namely, that Christ had two natures but only one 'divine–human operation or will'. The Pope agreed to the formulation, apparently seeing no great significance in the language which was used. But his successor Martin in 649 repudiated it as being a form of Monophysitism in a disguised shape. This gave rise to a schism with the East which lasted until the next ecumenical council in 681. By this time Syria and Egypt were totally taken over by the Arabs, and the need to make concessions to the Monophysites no longer existed. The Sixth Ecumenical Council was called at Constantinople (the third in this city), and the Monothelites, including Honorius, were condemned. The acts of the council echo the language of that of Chalcedon: 'We also preach two natural wills in him and two natural operations, without division, without change, without separation, without confusion.'[3] This council is often referred to as the council 'in trullo' because it was held in a domed chamber called 'trullus'.

The condemnation of Pope Honorius at this council has been a weapon in the hands of those who have resisted the claims of the Pope to infallibility, since the Roman Church itself joined in the condemnation repudiating his action in accepting the *Ecthesis*. One great name in the Eastern Church, that of Maximus the Confessor, later canonised, stood out in opposition to the policy of the emperors to promote monothelitism: he died after persecution and exile for his faithfulness to the truth.

The relative position of the great sees of Christendom was radically changed by the Arab conquests, which brought under Muslim rule the eastern patriarchates of Alexandria, Antioch, and Jerusalem. Rome and Constantinople remained the only patriarchates outside Muslim control, and Rome was more and more engaged in defending its life and extending its powers in the West. The Christian Empire was left with only one patriarchate which was free, that in Constantinople, and it therefore inevitably acquired an immense increase of power and prestige, since it stood unrivalled by any other historic see in the Empire.

In the Lebanon a permanent legacy of the monothelite views was left in a community centred on Beit Marun, a monastery in the mountains. These Christians became known as 'Maronites', and they continued to hold their doctrines until 1181 when they joined the communion of Rome by coming under the Latin Patriarch of Antioch, a patriarchate which had resulted from the activities of the crusaders. They are said to have broken away from the Roman Communion for a time,[4] but from the end of the fifteenth century they have remained under the Pope as a Uniate church with its own liturgy. Its language was the Syriac tongue and its liturgy of an Antiochene type, but during the centuries their forms of worship have been much affected by Latin influences. (See also p. 81.)

*Seventh Ecumenical Council*

One more Ecumenical Council was to come. Although connected with the previous disputes, it centred on a new aspect of teaching which closely affected the practice of Christian worship, namely the use of images. The subject is known as the iconoclastic controversy from the Greek word *eikon*, which means 'a figure or likeness'. In eastern Christian use it means a picture painted on a flat surface, usually representing a saint or Jesus Christ: the word does not include three-dimensional images or carvings; or more accurately it does not include sculpture in the round, although it does cover bas-relief and other raised work on a flat surface. Those who wished to do away with icons were called iconoclasts, and those who wished to retain them iconodules. The controversy was one which concerned only the eastern part of the Empire, and was not reflected in the West. It was one more sign that the religious interests and outlooks of East and West were more and more independent of one another. The forms which the disputes took were governed by considerations which had little to do with religious issues. There were religious aspects to the controversy, and one result of the disputes was to bring a definite ruling as to the attitude of the Church to the way in which icons should be regarded. But it seems probable that the religious side of the argument was a convenient way of giving expression to rivalries which arose from political, social and economic factors.

At the beginning of the seventh century the practice of venerating icons was at its height. Not only were they to be found in church but they were commonly set up in the homes of the people as centres of religious devotion. In origin the veneration paid to icons was in some cases confused with that paid to relics, for representations of sacred figures were often placed over relics or thought to have come from direct contact with their origins. Thus one heard of 'icons not made with hands', likenesses imprinted on a cloth which had come into contact with a saint. The shroud of Turin is a western example of this kind of icon. Some of the saints, for example the Stylites or pillar saints, used to imprint their own images on clay, which were thought to have included elements from the saints' bodies. From this they became generally venerated as a means of coming into spiritual contact with the person represented on them.

The political parties in the capital, the Blues and the Greens, had already been identified in some measure with different sides in earlier theological disputes. The Blues had supported the Chalcedonians and the Greens the Monophysites. In the iconoclastic affair they took different sides again, and the religious issue thus became a means of expressing political rivalry. Moreover, the religious rivalry over the iconoclastic issue itself was to a certain degree unreal, as can be seen from the fact that one side gave in easily when the other came out on top: there was little deep-lying religious conscientious motivation. Other ecclesiastical and political aspects can also be seen. The iconoclastic side was allied to those who wished to see the monks subject to the discipline of the bishops, and also to a certain extent with those who wanted to see the Church more subject to the emperor. This explains why the monks were in the forefront of the battle against the iconoclasts, since the cause was that of their own independence against episcopal interference with their affairs.

'The acrimony and the duration of the controversy upon the Images only becomes intelligible if it was in reality also a struggle between two political factions and if it had its roots not in that complete fantasy "a Semitic horror of the image" but in sociological and there-fore ultimately in economic factors.'[5] The Emperor Leo III the Isaur-ian, who initiated the iconoclastic policy, does not seem himself to have been particularly enthusiastic about it; but he did recognise that it had the strong support of the army, most of which was recruited in the highlands of Asia Minor. In 726, nine years after his ascent to the throne (717), he issued orders that all icons should be destroyed, and it was this which provoked a dispute which was not finally settled until the year 843.

There were a number of councils in which the fortunes of the contestants swayed backwards and forwards. The bishops' prefer-ences were clearly exhibited in a council at Hiereia in 754 when 338 of them declared in favour of iconoclastic policy.

Two particularly powerful voices consistently opposed the policy. John of Damascus (Damascene), recognised as one of the foremost theological thinkers of the East, wrote continually against icono-clasm. His voice could not be silenced by the emperor, for he lived under the protection of the Muslims, and was free to express his opinions without hindrance. He died about 750. In Constantinople itself Theodore of the monastery of Studium (the Studite) was an implacable opponent of the iconoclastic emperors. He organised continual opposition in Constantinople until his death in 826.

The decisive council, which later came to be accepted as ecumeni-cal, was that of Nicaea in 787, ranking as the seventh Ecumeni-cal Council, completing those recognised in that category by the Christian East. Nevertheless, two further councils repudiated its findings in 815 and 830, and only at another council in Constant-inople in 843 was iconoclasm finally defeated. Since that time the first Sunday in Lent has been celebrated each year in the Orthodox churches as the Feast of Orthodoxy to commemorate the triumph.

The decisions of the council of 787 distinguished between the respect which can properly be given to representations of Christ and the Virgin Mary and the worship which can only be accorded to God. The icons may rightly be paid 'the tribute of an embrace and a reverence of honour, not the actual worship which is according to our faith, and which is proper only to the divine nature'.

Although the dispute was not reproduced in the West, it attracted the attention of the Pope, who from the start denounced the icono-clasts. The West refused to accept iconoclasm and rebelled against the emperor's decrees. The emperor replied by confiscating part of the papal lands and putting dioceses in south Italy and in Sicily under Constantinople. Complications in the East prevented him from enforcing this policy in the West. But it caused another breach between East and West, which was only closed with the Council of Nicaea in 787. The iconoclast council in Constantinople of 815 opened it once more, however, during the second period of power of the iconoclasts. The course of events had an indirect effect on the formation of the Frankish Empire in the West.

It may be noted that at a council in the West at Frankfurt in 794 Charlemagne refused to accept the decisions of that of Nicaea in 787 because of a mistranslation of its decrees. His information was that the council had recommended the payment to icons of *servitium* and *adoratio* as to the Godhead. But the Pope was better informed and refused to act against the decisions.

## Organisation of the Western Churches

Justinian's reconquest of the West and restoration of the dominions of the Empire did not last. Belisarius had conquered Ravenna for him in 540, and it became the centre from which Justinian and his successors tried to rule their western territories. It remained the seat of the Exarchate until it was captured by the Lombards in 751.[6] But although the Lombards did not succeed in taking Ravenna for another two hundred years, in the sixth century they swept down the centre of Italy and cut the peninsula into several disconnected parts. By the year 590 they had extended their control further south than Naples. Only the areas round Naples, Rome, Perugia and Ravenna, as isolated pockets, remained under the control of the local imperial authorities.

For the life of the Church this had important and far-reaching consequences, for it meant that in the area round Rome there was no further effective central imperial control. The Pope therefore became the leader of the area in a political as well as in an ecclesiastical sense. This situation coincided with the reign of one of the greatest of the Popes, Gregory the Great, who succeeded to the bishopric of Rome in 590 and ruled until 604. Because of the impracticability of sending to Constantinople for consent, he followed his predecessor Pelagius without imperial permission, though his election was later recognised by the Emperor Maurice. He was a man of immense determination and self-confidence; and he imposed his will in all matters of church and government in Rome. By his energy he organised defence against the Lombards and held them at bay, while using the resources of the Church to sustain the defenders: and it was he who negotiated agreements with the attackers.

The last years of the sixth century were particularly important for future developments in the relations of the churches. A number of turning-points occurred, which, though products of previous developments, in their subsequent histories indicate new developments.

In 589 in Spain a council was held at Toledo: it was the third church council to be arranged in that city. This particular council seems to have accepted for use in the West the Nicene Creed with the addition of a new clause, known from its Latin as the *Filioque*. (There is some difference of opinion among historians as to which of the Councils of Toledo did this.) This clause appears in the English version of the creed as follows: 'I believe in the Holy Ghost, the Lord, the giver of life, who proceedeth from the Father *and the Son* . . .' The words 'and the Son' had no place in the creed as it was originally approved by the councils of Niceaea (325), Constantinople (381) and Ephesus (431), and it therefore did not have the authority of the Christian Church as a whole. Moreover, these Ecumenical Councils, besides deciding on the wording of the creed, had pronounced anathemas against anyone who dared to change or add to it. The introduction of the *Filioque* into the creed in the West was the biggest single subject of controversy throughout the succeeding centuries.

The *Filioque* did not gain general use immediately. Several Popes resisted its use, and Leo III, Pope from 795 to 816, had the text of the creed without the *Filioque* engraved on silver tablets in St. Peter's. It was the Franks who were the chief supporters of its use. They campaigned to have it more widely adopted, and after the year 1000 it was adopted for use at Rome. From the time when it first came to the attention of the East by its use in the Frankish monastery in Jerusalem in 847 it caused trouble with the Christians of the eastern tradition. The dispute about its meaning and its use will be found to recur again and again: in the second half of the twentieth century it is still being discussed.

## The British Isles

Christianity at the end of the sixth century had already been established in the British Isles, though by then it was mainly to be found among the Celts. In Ireland it had taken firm root, and seems to have been chiefly spread through the influence of the monasteries, some of which are reported to have had as many as 3,000 monks. From Ireland, Scotland and the north of England were evangelised, though St. Patrick himself seems to have been originally sent from England for the purpose of bringing better religion and culture to the Irish, an operation which has been unsuccessfully tried on a number of occasions since then. The form of Christian organisation which the Celts favoured had several features of its own. Not only were the monasteries large but they seem to have exhibited many of the characteristics of tribes or clans. The head of the monastery was to all intents and purposes the chieftain of a clan to whom all owed unquestioning obedience. Bishops, instead of being the rulers of the Church in the countryside, were often members of the monastic community, just as much subject to the abbot as any other members. Their activities in ordaining and in exercising other episcopal functions were therefore subject to the directions of the abbot, who used them as he thought fit. It is interesting to note that this way of using bishops was thought to consist perfectly well with their episcopal powers, and it suggests that in any discussion about unity between different Christian churches there is a good deal of room for manoeuvre in the way in which bishops may exercise their functions. The pattern with which we are familiar in the twentieth century includes a good many accidental features which have little or nothing to do with the essential spiritual work of a bishop.

This matter of episcopacy is of importance in Christian unity, and some words of Dr. G. L. Prestige may be quoted to make the point clearer. 'Episcopacy has clothed itself in very different shapes at various times and places. Sometimes, for instance, churches have been organized in small and numerous city dioceses; sometimes in regional dioceses few in number and vast in extent; sometimes again in tribal areas with monastic bishops who had no diocese to rule at all. At one moment a bishop has been virtually an independent potentate, at another he has enjoyed scarcely any independence whatever. The specialized uses to which different parts of the Church have put this gift within the general Church pattern have varied enormously.'[7] We see the truth of these words in practice when we compare the position of the bishops within the Celtic monasteries with that of Gregory the Great in Rome.

In 597 one of the greatest of the Celtic missionaries died, St. Columba. In the same year Augustine, sent by Gregory the Great, landing in Kent to convert the English, reached Canterbury. By this event the form of Christianity closely allied to Rome was brought into potential contact with the Celtic form, which was marked by its own traditions and customs, different from those of Rome itself. Celtic missionary energy was not confined to the British Isles: it had been extended widely through France and what is now Western Germany, where its monastic foundations had a great influence. But in England, with the arrival of St. Augustine and his success in converting Kent to Christianity, it was inevitable that sooner or later there would be a struggle for power between the two forms of church organisation.

The most obvious ways in which the Celts differed from the Romans were in the form of tonsure which they adopted and in the date on which they celebrated Easter. The controversy which these differences caused was eventually settled by the Synod of Whitby in 664, when the Roman system was adopted and the Celtic date dropped. Yet, although this synod formally decided the issue, one is not surprised to learn that for some time the Celtic customs continued in parts of the country which were not easily amenable to central discipline.

For early English history the historian Bede is far the most important source. Known as 'The Venerable Bede', he lived from about 673 until 735 and wrote *The Ecclesiastical History of the English Nation*. He showed himself a true historian, being careful to state the source of his information and to gather it from the best authorities available to him. Writing on the controversy about Easter (generally known as the Paschal Controversy), Bede explained (Cap. xxv) that 'those that came from Kent or France affirmed, that the Scots kept Easter Sunday contrary to the custom of the universal church'. In the account of the Synod of Whitby King Oswy listens to both sides, represented by Bishop Colman for the Celtic customs and Wilfrid (then a priest, but soon to be Bishop of York) for the Roman. According to Bede, the King decided, not on the merits of the practice itself, but on that of the respective authority of St. Columba, on the one hand, and the Bishop of Rome, on the other. On the grounds that Peter had the keys of heaven and that the Pope was his successor and obviously could claim Peter on his side, he thought it more expedient, so as to make sure that he got into heaven when he reached the gates, to come down on the side of Rome.

In 668 a new Archbishop of Canterbury, Theodore, educated at Tarsus and Athens, was appointed. To him was due the general organisation of the English Church. He engaged in extensive visitations and was responsible for calling the first important synod of the whole English Church at Hertford in 673. His efforts, however, brought him into direct conflict with Wilfrid at York, who not surprisingly objected to having his diocese divided into four without his consent. He appealed to Rome and won his case, but it did him no good, as he was imprisoned on his return. There was irony in the fact that Wilfrid was the great instrument in establishing Roman practices in the north of England and that at the same time he was at loggerheads with Archbishops of Canterbury, themselves appointed by Rome and engaged in setting up a country-wide organisation very much in accord with Roman principles. Wilfrid himself, by his appeals to Rome against Canterbury, undoubtedly contributed to the general recognition of Rome as the final court of authority in disputed cases.

In the seventh and eighth centuries England and Ireland originated important missions to the continent of Europe. Columbanus from Ireland (died 615) went via England to Gaul, where he set up a number of monasteries, and from there went to Lake Constance. He aroused opposition by the Celtic practices which he followed. He died in Italy. His monasteries spread all over Gaul, where they were a strong missionary influence. Willibrord (658–739) was the apostle of the Low Countries and Boniface (c. 680–754) the apostle of north Germany. Both these outstanding missionaries were brought up in English monasteries. Willibrord was educated in Northumbria and went to Frisia via Ireland, and Boniface from Crediton in Devon.

These facts indicate a considerable traffic between the British Isles and the Continent, in which the variation of customs which we have already noted was bound sooner or later to disappear, if and when the Church became more centrally organised.

*Growth of Papal Power*

Meanwhile political details in western Europe need not take our attention, where they do not bear directly upon the details of church relationships. The Pope played a more and more important part in the development of political events, both through his own action and through the Christianisation of the non-Christian peoples who penetrated into Italy and France. Eventually the Franks consolidated their power and established their own dynasty. Pippin the Short in the middle of the eighth century 'occupied a central place in the affairs of Europe such as no prince had held since the days of Theodoric the Great'.[8] His assistance was sought by the Islamic leaders as well as by the Roman Emperor in Constantinople. He died in 768 and was succeeded by Charles the Great (known as Charlemagne), who soon ruled his dominions alone, since his brother Carloman died at an early date (771). Charles, who supported Pope Leo III in a number of important ways, was rewarded on Christmas Day 800 in St. Peter's in Rome by being crowned by the Pope and named 'Augustus' and 'great and pacific Emperor of the Romans'. Under his son, Louis the Pious, Ebo and Anskar took Christianity to Denmark and Sweden, and in doing so contributed significantly to the unity of each.

The increase of the power of the Pope is often seen by those who dislike it as a deliberate plan of gaining power on the part of the papacy and nothing more. There is little doubt that papal ambition for power did play an important part in the development, but it could hardly have been successful unless the political and ecclesiastical needs of western Europe had provided favourable conditions. The fact that the Church was organised under the Pope, and that in the Church was concentrated all the learning of western Europe, almost exclusively confined to the clergy (to which the phrase 'clerk in holy orders' as a description of a priest still bears witness), powerfully reinforced the influence which the organisational head of the Church exercised. Moreover, it is difficult to see how order could have been brought out of the chaos of the dark ages if the papacy had not filled the rôle which it adopted for itself. There were therefore very powerful, perhaps irresistible, forces encouraging the papacy to develop its authority and control.

These non-religious forces were strongly supported by the appearance of documents now known as the Forged or False Decretals. They seem to have originated from a Frankish source in the eighth or ninth century, and to have been put together with considerable skill. They purported to be letters of Constantine to Pope Sylvester I giving him supreme authority, not only in his ecclesiastical position in the Church, but also over the lands of western Europe. They were used by Pope Nicholas I in 865, probably with the knowledge that they were spurious. But throughout the Middle Ages until the fifteenth century these documents were universally accepted as genuine. For our purpose the most important of them is the so-called 'Donation of Constantine' dealing with the position of the Pope. It contained the following passages. 'We attribute to him (sc. the Pope) the power and glorious dignity and strength and honour of the Empire, and we ordain and decree that he shall have rule as well over the four principal sees, Antioch, Alexandria, Constantinople and Jerusalem, as also over all the churches of God in all the world. And the pontiff who for the time being presides over that most holy Roman Church shall be the highest and chief of all the priests in the whole world, and according to his decision shall all matters be settled which shall be taken in hand for the service of God or the confirmation of the faith of Christians.'

The document went on to award the Pope the right to occupy the Lateran Palace and to wear crown, mitre, imperial stole and imperial robes. It continued: 'We convey to the oft-mentioned and most blessed Silvester, universal pope, both our palace, as preferment, and likewise all provinces, palaces and districts of the city of Rome and Italy and of the regions of the West; and, bequeathing them to the power and sway of him and the pontiffs, his successors, we do (by means of fixed imperial decision through this our divine, sacred and authoritative sanction) determine and decree that the same be placed at his disposal, and do lawfully grant it as a permanent possession to the holy Roman Church.'[9]

By its historical influence, this document must be adjudged the most successful and influential forgery ever perpetrated, since it held undisputed authority for more than 500 years. But it could not have done so, had it not fitted in with the tendency of men's minds at the time. Two aspects strike the observer. First the unquestioned acceptance that the Emperor had the power to give to the Pope the position and privileges which the forged 'Donation' purported to bestow. Second, the extra approval gained by the Pope for his claims was something added to his position, not something new. As we have seen, it supported in an effective way the inevitable developments of the authority of the papacy, and gave it a spurious but impressive appearance of justification in principle. Just as in the West the eighth to the tenth centuries were periods of important evangelisation in the north of Europe, so in the East the Christian faith was spreading. The history of these centuries, little known to the general reader, shows a remarkable power of expansion in the Christian Church on all its borders, except where it was losing ground to the advance of Islam in the area of the eastern Mediterranean. A significant period began in the East during the ninth century as the result of the lives of 'the apostles of the Slavs' Cyril (originally named Constantine) and Methodius. They were Greeks who began a work of evangelisation in Moravia, having been sent there in 862 by the Emperor. This work they conducted in the language of the people, and before long they found it desirable to introduce a new script, now known as the Cyrillic alphabet, which was adopted by most of the Slav countries of eastern Europe.

In the western world Latin was the common medium of communication, since it had become the only civilised language available. The course of events strengthened its position. In the East Greek remained predominant, but the introduction of another language for ecclesiastical purposes began. Later, when the Slav languages became the media of national feeling, it was to affect the political situation as well as the ecclesiastical.

## Tension between East and West

After the death of Methodius Moravia was forcibly Latinised, thus losing the benefit of its new language and being secured for the western Church. In the ninth century Bulgaria accepted Christianity, its king, Boris, being baptised in the year 865. His conversion was due more to an act of statesmanship than to personal conviction, for he judged that his own future lay in alliance with the Christian nations.[10] Boris, however, wished to secure for himself an independent church which would not lay him open to interference from authorities outside the country. He began by inviting a mission from the Franks, which had the immediate effect of provoking an invasion from Constantinople, which was not prepared to see western control over an area so vital to its own security. The Pope did his best to persuade the Bulgarians to remain under his wing, but in the end he could not be successful in the political situation of the time.

The tensions aroused between Rome and Constantinople over Bulgaria coincided with a serious quarrel between Pope and Patriarch, which has become known as the Photian schism. Photius was Patriarch of Constantinople, and it would appear that Pope Nicholas I dealt rather more tactfully with the Bulgarian king than did his rival. He also hinted in his letter that the Greeks were of doubtful reliability, as they were in the habit of having contact with Armenians and others. Rome was the only place from which Orthodox teaching could certainly be secured.

The Pope sent a mission to Bulgaria, at the head of which was a certain Bishop Formosus. He seems to have been a man who did not know the meaning of the word compromise and who nursed a steady dislike of the Greeks, against whom he was ready to lay any complaints which would seem acceptable to their enemies. He was eventually recalled from Bulgaria, but his activities there caused Photius to write a letter of complaint setting out those actions to which he took exception; this protest in the form of an encyclical letter was sent to the Patriarchs of Alexandria and Jerusalem and the Church of Antioch and was based on four main grounds. The Latin missionaries 'draw the faithful away to their uncanonical customs, Saturday fasting, and drinking milk and eating cheese in the first weeks of Lent. They deny the validity of priests' confirmations. They call married priests adulterers, and their children bastards. What is worst of all, they teach a new and strange version of the Nicene creed.'[11] The new version of the creed was, of course, the addition of the *Filioque* clause. Photius also wrote to Boris complaining about western customs.

What is significant about this dispute is that it gives clear evidence of the way in which the two areas of the Christian Church had drifted apart from one another. The systems of church discipline and fasting have now become different. Though small in themselves, it is often the variation in popular observances of religion which causes the hardest feelings, since it is through these varying practices that the consciousness of division reaches ordinary people. The question of priests confirming arose from the fact that eastern Christians were in the habit of administering the rite of Confirmation by the anointing of oil. The oil had been previously blessed by a bishop, but was actually administered by the priest, immediately after baptism. This is still the Eastern Orthodox custom, though it no longer arouses any difficulty.

Eastern Christians have always maintained a married priesthood among those priests who were not monks. Priests have to be married before ordination or else to remain in the celibate state as monks. The objection which Formosus had expressed seems to be somewhat strange in the light of the fact that Hadrian II, who became Pope in 867, seems to have been himself married, since his wife and daughter were abducted and murdered in the following year. But the most important difference was the introduction of the *Filioque* into the dispute between Pope and Patriarch, where it was to crop up again and again until the present day. (A note on the subject is appended to this chapter.)

*Photian Schism*

Photius, one of the most cultured men of his age, first became Patriarch in 858 and continued in office until 867. In the summer of that year a large council was held in Constantinople which included the eastern Patriarchs and which took the step of excommunicating and deposing the Pope for exceeding his powers. The Pope had already earlier declared that he did not recognise Photius but continued to regard his predecessor Ignatius as the rightful Patriarch. There was therefore a condition of mutual recrimination and anathema. But in the same year, 867, the Pope died, the Emperor at Constantinople was assassinated, and Photius was dethroned and replaced by Ignatius.

Ignatius ruled until his death ten years later, and during this period the Church of Bulgaria was more firmly linked with Constantinople. Photius returned too during these years and became tutor to the princes at the palace; and on the death of Ignatius to whom he had been reconciled he resumed his position as Patriarch. The question of the Bulgarian Church remained a matter of dispute, but eventually Photius, in order to re-establish good relations with Rome, agreed to cede the Bulgarians to the Pope's jurisdiction. Pope John VIII sent legates to restore relations, and at a council held in 879–80 in Constantinople, known as the 'Photian' Council, agreement was reached between the two sides. All additions to the creed were condemned, though there was no particular mention of the *Filioque*. The Pope removed the ban which he had placed on the Bulgarian Church forbidding them to use the Slavonic liturgy; and, although in theory the church came under his jurisdiction, it did not in the long run change the situation whereby the Church of Bulgaria became one of the churches associated with the Patriarch of Constantinople. Pope John VIII died in 882, and Photius was once more removed from the Patriarchate in 886 by the new Emperor Leo VI.

For many years it was held that the final schism between East and West began with the Photian schism and continued until the final break nearly 200 years later in 1054. The first part of this theory is now seen to be false, since the breach was healed before the death of Pope John VIII. But the difficulties were evidence that the two sections of Christendom were growing apart, the effect of which was eventually to cause a final division between them. It must be remembered that technical communion between the eastern and western parts of the Church often obscured the fact that they went their own ways without much regard to one another. It was not a case of full unity which was later broken. The various sections of the Christian world were constantly seeking for a unity which was never achieved, and from which they were diverted to a lesser or greater extent by the political, economic or dynastic events of the historical conditions in which they lived.

There are in history many examples of bodies of Christians splitting away from a unified section of the Church to which they belonged. Such divisions will appear later. But the idea that Christendom was once one great united Church is a figment of the imagination. Much more the history of Christendom is a travailing in pain to bring forth the unity which its own gospel requires, an effort which has never reached its end and in which Christians are as much engaged today as they were in the past.

## The *Filioque* Clause

Since the clause has been such a subject of contention between eastern and western Christians throughout the centuries, it is desirable to examine what the debate in fact covers. The creed approved by the first three General Councils expressed belief in the Holy Spirit in these words—'I believe in the Holy Spirit, the Lord, the Giver of Life, who proceeds from the Father; who with the Father and the Son together is worshipped . . .'; the *Filioque* adds the words 'and the Son' in the clause dealing with the procession of the Holy Spirit—'who proceeds from the Father and the Son'.

To many it appears that the doctrine of the Trinity is a speculative affair in the best circumstances, and that it is not possible to speak of the nature of the Godhead with any certainty. Disputes, therefore, about the relation of the 'Persons' of the Trinity seem to them to be largely meaningless. But this did not appear to be so to the Christians of an earlier age. It is, however, important to realise that Christian thought and language about the nature of the Godhead and the relations of the 'Persons' of the Trinity are not concerned with the matter mainly from a speculative or philosophical point of view. Christian interest and concern in the doctrine arises from a sense of the vital need to safeguard certain aspects of Christian experience, without which Christian teaching and the Christian gospel would lose their power.

The aspects of experience mainly concerned are those of the reality of God's work in Jesus Christ and the validity of God's work experienced by Christians in their own life through the power of the Holy Spirit. Both these are truths which Christians have always thought it essential to preserve. They have therefore felt it necessary to maintain that in Jesus the fullness of the action of God is found, and that it is equally to be found in the action of the Holy Spirit in the Church.

The formulations accepted to express these truths in the doctrine of the Trinity had to be safeguarded from the kind of attack mounted by those who wished to turn the Gospel into something different from what had been generally received. The defence therefore concentrated on the points under attack. It is of some importance to realise that the doctrine of the Trinity is not meant to be a description of God: it merely states certain truths which must be part of the truth about God if the Christian message is to be received.

There are some eastern theologians, notable among them the late Vladimir Lossky, who hold that the difference made to the doctrine of God by the *Filioque* is one of great importance, and that it represents a serious divergence between East and West in their understanding of the Christian Gospel. On the other hand, there are theologians in both parts of the Church who think that it is largely a matter of wording, and that no serious principle is at stake. All are agreed that the phrase 'who proceeds from the Father and the Son' must not be taken as indicating that there are two sources (*aitia*) in the God-head: there is only one, namely the Father, and no western theologian holds that there are two. The *Filioque* is defended by the West on the grounds that it is a way of making sure that the position of the Son is equal to that of the Father. In various discussions which have taken place, a phrase of St. John Damscene, an eastern theologian, has been accepted by both sides as satisfactory, namely 'who proceeds from the Father through the Son'.

A Roman Catholic theologian of authority has written: 'What, then, it may be asked is the real point and importance of the dispute about the *Filioque*? In the course of the dispute the real reason for both the Greek and the Latin formulas tended to be obscured. The Greeks added the formula that the Holy Spirit proceeds from the Father in order to repel the Arian and Macedonian heresy that the Holy Ghost is a creature made by the Son; the Latins added the *Filioque* in order to oppose the Adoptionists, who maintained the inferiority of the Son to the Father because he does not share with the Father the procession of the Holy Spirit. Thus both formulas were adopted in order to maintain the perfect equality of Father, Son and Holy Ghost, and both formulas were and are most orthodox in intent.'[12]

But whatever may be said about the inner meaning of the phrase, there can be no doubt that its addition to the creed in the West in the teeth of an absolute prohibition to add anything to the creed cannot be justified except as a local aberration or need. If there is in fact no essential difference between East and West in what is taught, then it would seem that there can be no serious objection on the side of the West to dropping a phrase which is no longer needed as a safeguard against adoptionism, and which on its own showing does not make any difference to the essential meaning of the creed. If it is thought that western Christians would find it too difficult to abandon their habits of saying it, its use could at least be made optional, since it has never had ecumenical authority.

[1] Alexander Schmemann, *The Historical Road of Eastern Orthodoxy*, New York, 1963, p. 167.

[2] Schmemann, *op. cit.*, p. 146.

[3] Henry Bettenson, *Documents of the Christian Church*, Oxford, 1946, p. 128.

[4] Every, *op. cit.*, p. 80.

[5] Gervase Matthew, *Byzantine Aesthetics*, London, John Murray, 1963.

[6] The title 'Exarch' originally an imperial term, is now used in the Orthodox churches to denote the representative of a Patriarch in a country abroad.

[7] Sermon before the University of Cambridge, 10 May 1953.

[8] Oman, *The Dark Ages*, London, Rivington, 1901, p. 333.

[9] Henry Bettenson, *op. cit.*, pp. 138 *ff.*

[10] Every, *ibid.*, p. 125 *passim.*

[11] Every, *ibid.*, p. 127.

[12] Bernard Leeming, *Rediscovering Eastern Christendom. Orthodox–Catholic Relations*, London, Darton, Longman and Todd, 1963, pp. 29–30.

# 6

## Hostility Replaces Ignorance

### The Crusades

ON Christmas Day in the year 800 Charlemagne was crowned by the Pope in St. Peter's Rome and hailed by the crowd as Emperor. 'Long life and victory to Charles Augustus, crowned by God, great and pacific Emperor.'[1] The significance of this act in the light of subsequent history was very great, since it was a symbol of the rejection of the Roman Empire in the form in which it had continued to exist in the East. It had repercussions which were both political and ecclesiastical, though many of them could not have been understood at the time. Later the re-establishment of the Holy Roman Empire in the West gathered around itself a theory of Christian government and unity which was to have results of far-reaching importance.

The coronation of Charles the Great was the outcome of a number of factors which happened to coincide at that moment. His personal power was one of the most significant. It was combined with an intense interest in the spread of Christian influence under his own leadership. At the moment of his greatest power Italian and German interests happened to coincide, and an alliance between the two led to the same wish to restore the authority of Roman rule in the West. Charlemagne saw himself raised to the highest position to which his mind could aspire, while the Romans saw in him the chance to restore the glory of their own tradition which had been in eclipse for so long. At the same moment the Pope, Leo III, had been restored by the power of Charles to control over Rome, and, uniting in his own person the chief magistracy of the city and the head of the western Church, found himself in a position to exercise both aspects of his rule in combining the recognition of the Church with the rights of the head of the Roman Senate.

At that moment, although in the East the Empire was in a condition of weakness, it naturally refused to recognise the setting up of a rival emperor in the West. Ironically it was not many years before the western Frankish kingdom fell into a state of confusion, whereas under the Macedonian dynasty 867–1025 the eastern Empire attained its greatest power and prosperity. The Dynasty's founder, Basil, was probably an Armenian by descent, and during the period of this dynasty the control of the Empire was re-established over its former territories of the East. The emperors profited by the disruption of the Muslim powers on the borders of the Empire, where a new power in the shape of the Seldjuk Turks was making its appearance.

The effect of these developments on church relations was to encourage the tendency towards separate growth, since there was no motive for eastern Christians to seek closer contacts with those of the West. The prosperity of the Empire encouraged its members to be content with their own flourishing culture and to look down on that of the West, where newly converted warring tribes had lately been brought into the Christian fold. For the most part, therefore, no efforts were made to concert any Christian action, and the popular customs of East and West continued to grow apart.

The differences were made worse by psychological tensions arising from different outlooks. The Byzantine Empire was an old cultured society, sophisticated and erudite: the new western power was young and crude, revelling in the force of arms, adventurous in seeking excitement and new fields to conquer. Each side despised the other, the West considering the Byzantines to be decadent and ageing, and the East looking upon the westerners as uncivilised upstarts. Modern parallels can be found in relations between the old civilisations of Europe and what the Europeans regard as the crudities of modern Russia and the United States.

Official relationships between the two sees of Rome and Constantinople were also distant. If we judge by the official mention of the Pope on the diptychs at Constantinople it must be concluded that relations continued to be correct until the year 1009, when the Pope's name ceased to appear. But there is no other reason for taking this as a decisive year, apart from the fact that it was then that the last Pope named on the diptychs died—John XVIII. When the 'systatic' letter, announcing his succession, was sent by the next Pope the

Patriarch refused to put his name on the lists because his profession of faith included the *filioque*.[2]

As the eastern Empire recaptured its territories, travel for the West became safe again, and there was a renewal of contact through travellers. But this, instead of causing closer relations, was often the origin of further tension, because the differences in custom became an irritant to Christians, especially to those who were engaged in religious pilgrimages. At the end of the tenth century pilgrims were numerous and could travel easily across Europe and Asia Minor to the holy places. As Runciman[3] points out, the increase of pilgrim traffic coincided with the reforms of monastic life in the West, which stemmed from the centre at Cluny. These reformers were particularly interested in the promotion of the pilgrim traffic, but part of their reforming zeal was to emphasise the claims of the papacy and its jurisdiction and supremacy. In 1024 there was an effort to try to reach a compromise which would give recognition to the primacy of Rome while at the same time retaining the supremacy of the Patriarch of Constantinople in his own sphere. The latter wrote to Pope John XIX with the approval of the Emperor suggesting that they should agree on a formula that 'with the consent of the Roman bishop the Church of Constantinople shall be called universal in her own sphere, as that of Rome is in the world'. His motive in making this proposal may have been to come to a general agreement, but it is more likely that he was primarily moved by a desire to re-establish his authority over the Byzantine churches in South Italy where there were signs of difficulty.[4] The Pope's apparent readiness to agree aroused the determined opposition of the Cluniacs, and he withdrew in consequence, an action which ensured that his name was not placed on the Constantinopolitan diptychs.

But in spite of these differences between the two chief sees, other ancient sees in the East at Antioch and Jerusalem seem to have continued to recognise the Pope and to regard themselves as being in communion with him in spite of the *filioque*.

In 1020 the Normans appeared in southern Italy supporting a revolt against Byzantine power. The attitude of the Pope to this effort was one of acquiescence at first, since, although the Normans were not allies of his, at least they belonged to the western Church, and the consequence of their conquest of Byzantine areas was to bring the churches in them under papal jurisdiction. But when they began to threaten districts closer to him, he thought it advisable to seek an alliance against them with the eastern Emperor. Yet he did not wish to see the churches revert to eastern customs, partly for reasons of power and partly through a desire to encourage a uniformity of use as a means of reform.

When therefore the Pope found himself ecclesiastically supported by the Normans, although opposed to them politically, he had no desire, even if he had had the power, to prevent them from trying to change the customs of the Byzantine churches in South Italy to those of the West. As is to be seen throughout the ages, nothing irritates ordinary people more than having their religious observances interfered with and changed without their consent. The fury aroused by such changes has no relation to the importance of the matters under dispute. There are many examples in our own day of bad feeling engendered by the innocent actions of a rector of a parish, full of good intentions but lacking in tact. The attempt to change centuries' old habits of worship among the Byzantines in South Italy may be assumed to have resulted in protests by them to the Patriarch of Constantinople.

## Michael Cerularius

From 1043 the patriarchal throne of Constantinople was occupied by an able and ambitious prelate, Michael Cerularius. His aim was to establish the independence of his church from Rome and, so far as might be, from the Emperor. Indeed, it was his exaggerated claims to control the Emperor which eventually led to his downfall and death. He shared many of the ideals of the reforming parties in the western Church, and in the interests of his own control desired to establish greater uniformity of practice among those subject to the eastern Emperor. It is a sad, but not uncommon thing, to see that it is often the proper ideals of good men rather than the evils of bad ones which cause division. In the case of the dispute between Cerularius and the Pope an added irony was the fact that both of them wished to see greater unity in their own churches through a closer uniformity of custom. Tension arose not out of a direct clash in the first place, not merely from a competition between customs as such, but out of a desire to have church customs so arranged that they stressed the unity of Christians rather than their differences. Laudable though this may have been, it has showed itself both then and since to be gravely mistaken, and the events of the mid-eleventh century can still speak to our own times.

In the East an element which affected the view of Cerularius seems to have been a desire to persuade the Armenians to follow the customs of the Greek Church rather than their own. Armenia had within recent years been once more brought under the control of the Emperor, and there was a natural tendency to regard ecclesiastical unity as a buttress of the unity of the State. Just as in earlier years the big divisions of the East had been deeply affected by the fact that the dissidents identified their national aspirations with their church organisation and doctrine, so now when Armenia once more came within the control of the eastern Emperor (1046) the Patriarch as a matter of course tried to tie its church to that of Constantinople by overcoming or abolishing those things which were the outward expression of a different outlook. In 1049 the Armenian Patriarch visited Constantinople, where no doubt the customs, and perhaps the doctrinal teachings, of his church were discussed.

Among Armenian church practices there were a number of peculiarities which seem to have been continued from early times and to have derived from Jewish origins. Two of these practices corresponded with those of the Latins, namely the use of unleavened bread in the Eucharist (called *azymes*) and the beginning of Lent at Septuagesima, with the dropping of the use of *Alleluia* from that point until Easter. The Patriarch of Constantinople, therefore, trying to get the Armenians to change their habits, could hardly avoid objecting to the same customs among the westerns when the matter became a live issue—and of course there had been objections made on earlier occasions.

The combination of these factors, not unmixed with personal ambition, led Michael Cerularius to take action in Constantinople itself in 1053 by persuading Leo, Archbishop of Ochrida, to write a letter to John, Bishop of Trani, warning him against the errors of the Latins. Four objectionable practices were mentioned in the letter— the use of unleavened bread, the practice of fasting on Saturdays in Lent, the eating of things strangled and of blood, and the singing of *Alleluia* at Easter only.[5] Michael asked that the letter should be circulated among the bishops of the West. By chance the letter arrived shortly before Cardinal Humbert of Silva Candida, a close associate of Pope Leo IX, came on a visit to the Bishop of Trani, and he took the letter, which was in Greek, and translated it into Latin, sending it to the Pope, Leo IX.

The problem of language again proved to be a fruitful source of misunderstanding, for, although the original text of the correspondence is lost, there seems little doubt that the translation of Greek terms into Latin was misleading, to say the least, and in some cases probably completely false. The word *oekumene* seems to have been a special stone of stumbling. It was used by the Patriarch of Constantinople to mean the Empire, that is to say, that area over which the writ of the Emperor ran. But literally it meant the whole inhabited world, and it was this sense which was given it in Latin. It seemed, therefore, to the Pope that the Patriarch was claiming authority over the whole world; and his inevitable reaction to such a claim was to reiterate those of the papacy. He wrote a protest to Michael Cerularius entitled *In terra pax hominibus* which contained the following passages: '. . . You are said to have publicly condemned the Apostolic and Latin Church, without either a hearing or a conviction. . . . In prejudging the case of the highest See, the see on which no judgement may be passed by any man, you have received the anathema from all the Fathers of all the venerable Councils. . . . As a hinge, remaining unmoved, opens and shuts a door, so Peter and his successors have an unfettered jurisdiction over the whole Church, since no one ought to interfere with their position, because the highest See is judged by none . . .'[6] He went on to add that if the Scriptures did not provide enough authority for this claim, at least the Donation of Constantine was clear enough, and he quoted this forgery at great length, quite ignorant of its false character. He protested at the action of shutting down the Latin churches and monasteries in Constantinople, although in Rome the Byzantine customs had been allowed to continue without interference.

As the Emperor and the Pope were at this time in alliance against the inroads of the Normans in Italy, the sharpening of difficulties was not welcome and the Emperor Constantine X intervened to make Cerularius show a more friendly attitude. Both he and the Patriarch therefore wrote to the Pope to conciliate him. Another interpretation of this gesture is that the Patriarch did not act in this way because of imperial pressure, but that his concern was solely with the practices of Latins within Constantinople and that he had no serious objection to their practices within their own domain,[7] so long too as they did not interfere with the Byzantine areas of jurisdiction. Runciman thinks that the peace-maker was probably John of Trani. But whatever the origin of the gesture of conciliation, it came to nothing. If Cerularius must bear some of the blame, Humbert must carry even more. He was a man of aggressive character, whose knowledge of Greek was not great: his translations of the communications from Constantinople probably exaggerated anything in them which was offensive to papal ears, and the signature of Cerularius as 'Ecumenical Patriarch', interpreted to mean Patriarch of the Universe, was, as we have seen, a cause of irritation and a challenge.

In 1054 Humbert and two other legates were sent to Constantinople with letters from the Pope, who at the time was a captive of the Normans. It is possible that Cerularius sincerely doubted the genuineness of the letters and the messengers who claimed to be the Pope's spokesmen. He declined to recognise them, but the legates determined to bring things to a head, and in July 1054 the legates placed a bull of excommunication of Michael Cerularius on the altar of his cathedral St. Sophia. It may be noted that the condemnation was personal, and that the members of the Church of Constantinople were specifically excluded from it. It cited ten heresies of which the easterns were supposed to be guilty, and the bull was never actually confirmed by Rome, although in historical accounts it has generally and misleadingly been accepted as the act which finally separated the two sections of Christendom. It remained in force until it was formally withdrawn by action of Pope and Ecumenical Patriarch in the year 1965. A joint declaration was issued by Pope Paul VI and Patriarch Athenagoras I on 7 December 1965 regretting 'the offensive words, the reproaches without foundation and the reprehensible gestures which, on both sides, have marked or accompanied the sad events of this period'. They regretted and removed the sentences of excommunication which followed, for the excommunication by Rome had soon been followed by similar action on the part of Constantinople.

But at the time the situation was not changed much by these particular excommunications, for while the general differences remained, the other patriarchal sees do not seem to have been affected in their attitudes by these particular events. Much later it is observed that there was no inhibition of communion between members of the Latin Church who found themselves in the East during the crusades. Nevertheless, it was a further cause of exacerbation between the two chief authorities of the churches. Cerularius tried to persuade the Patriarch of Antioch to support him and with this aim wrote a tendentious letter about the events, but he was unable to pursue the matter because of his own personal problems at home, and the reply which he received was not altogether sympathetic. Michael Cerularius eventually brought about his own ruin by his unbridled ambition, posing as equal or superior to the Emperor, and he was removed in 1058, dying soon afterwards.

During the rest of the eleventh century there were convincing signs that neither Rome nor Constantinople regarded the churches as being out of communion with one another, and writings of men of good sense showed how easy it would have been for them to continue to live in peace and concord if only aggressive prelates could be restrained. The Greek Archbishop Theophylact of Bulgaria, in reply to questions about western use from a deacon in Constantinople, expounded an attitude of tolerance and understanding which allowed for differences of practice without attaching to them undue importance, and even the *filioque* he thought should not be overemphasised, though he disapproved of adding to the universal creed without universal authority. On the western side Pope Urban showed a peace-loving outlook and Anselm, one of the greatest of the Archbishops of Canterbury, while defending the use of the *filioque* as a proper expression of western theological understanding, clearly did not wish to impose it on the eastern churches and regarded the original form of the creed which they used as perfectly legitimate.[8]

But in spite of his peaceful intentions, Pope Urban in his zeal to promote the interest of the Church was to be the instrument of events which were finally to sever the ecclesiastical unity of East and West.

## The Holy Places

The see of Jerusalem occupied a special place in Christendom, since it was the focus of the immense pilgrim traffic which was at its height in the eleventh century. An acceptable *modus vivendi* had been achieved with the Muslim authorities, and the patriarchate was able to organise its affairs as it found most suitable to its spiritual and economic purposes. The Patriarch kept on good terms with both East and West, and it is probable that the Pope was commemorated in the diptychs there throughout the century. The Patriarch was Greek, and the main services at the centre were Byzantine in character. In the village churches, however, the services were in Arabic, the language of the people, and one can see even at this early date the basis of tension between Greek and Arab Christians, which has not yet been satisfactorily resolved within the Jerusalem Patriarchate. The Patriarch exercised a territorial jurisdiction which included a number of churches of the Latin rite, and he does not seem to have made any serious difficulties about such churches following their own customs.

In 1071 the eastern Emperor Romanus set out to try to recover control of Armenia. In the process he suffered a calamitous defeat at the hands of the Seldjuk Turks at the battle of Manzikert. This battle has been described as 'the most decisive disaster in Byzantine history'.[9] The Byzantine Army was destroyed, the Emperor taken prisoner, and in one stroke Asia Minor was laid open to the power of the Turks. They did not seriously invade the area until two years later, but meanwhile they were establishing their mastery over the Muslim Fatimids. In the same year Jerusalem was captured by one of Alp Arslan's (the Seldjuk leader) subjects, and although it was re-taken by the Fatimids, it again fell to the Turks. The Christians were not molested, though the Patriarch thought it expedient to retire to Constantinople for much of the time. Meanwhile the struggle for power went on in Anatolia, and by the end of the century the emperor Alexius had done much to strengthen his position by establishing his power in Europe. At the same time it seemed that the Seldjuk power was on the wane, so that conditions seemed favourable for further action.

In the West the idea of holy war had already been widespread and accepted against the infidel in Spain. The great reforming Pope Gregory VII not only encouraged action to drive out the Muslims from Spain by force but he also promised that those who gained control of lands in the process could keep them. It was therefore not difficult to transfer the idea of the defeat of Muslim powers in Spain to their defeat elsewhere as a Christian duty. Moreover, because of the thousands of pilgrims who were familiar with the holy places, and because of the particular renown which those places held in Christian thought and devotion, there was a much greater direct appeal to religious motives for a crusade to rescue them from the hands of the enemy of Christendom.

Everything therefore conspired to favour the launching of a crusade for the holy places. The Emperor had stabilised his position but lacked man-power. The great devotional pilgrimages had been made very difficult, though not altogether impossible. A holy war in Spain had already conditioned men's minds to the idea of such action, and it had been accompanied by promises of spiritual benefits as well as material loot.

In March 1095 a council was held at Piacenza at which Pope Urban tried to put down a rival of his own, an anti-Pope supported by Henry IV of Germany. At that council two representatives from the emperor Alexius were present and were permitted to speak to the council. They had been sent to try to recruit men for the imperial forces, and they were so successful in appealing for help in the East that they convinced their listeners that an army should be raised for the purpose. Later in the year Urban held a council at Clermont, and on that occasion preached a sermon which was to have consequences far beyond any he could have foreseen, for he called all Christian Europe to take part in a holy war to recover the holy places for Christian control. His motives were admirable. He was responding to an appeal of the Christian Emperor of the East: he wished to restore a great devotional treasure to access for Christians. The end result of the crusades, which he initiated, was to be the final separation of eastern and western Christendom and the loss of control over the Holy Land until the twentieth century, though two hundred years were to elapse before these consequences became clear.

It is unfortunate that so many western students have been brought up to look at the crusades through a haze of sentimental old-fashioned chivalry. They associate them in their minds with noble ideals of rescuing ladies by jousting knights, and other quite unrealistic myths of early medieval romanticism. An effort of imagination is needed to see what the crusades were like for the ordinary eastern Christian who had the misfortune to live in a part of the country through which the crusaders passed. Even in the modern world, in which the licentiousness of the soldiery is restrained by strict discipline, the passing of an army through any country is something to be avoided at all costs, even if it is supposedly friendly. When the troops have to provision themselves and live off the land a plague of locusts is a small burden in comparison. Moreover, there was nothing in common between the western and eastern Christians as far as their daily habits were concerned. They spoke different languages; they had different customs of living; even their religious services were unlike one another. It was not long, therefore, before the western armies aroused the fiercest resentment among eastern Christians, and indeed threatened many of them with economic ruin in the process of rescuing them from the threat of the infidel.

The idea of a holy war was not nearly so attractive to eastern Christians as it was to the West, and many of them did not approve of the concept, quite apart from whether it was to their advantage or not. The Emperor had in the crusading armies far more than he had wanted or bargained for. He was anxious to secure his frontiers against those who threatened them, but he had no particular animosity against Muslims as such, with whom for several centuries there had been an amicable arrangement about Christians visiting the holy places. The sight of warlike bishops and clergy among the crusaders shocked many of the Byzantines, who took a far less cheerful view of war than their western coreligionists.[10]

There is no opportunity here to follow the tortuous course of the crusades, and we must be content with picking out those events which more than others typify the problems to which the crusades gave rise. The capture of Antioch by Bohemund and his crusaders immediately provoked a crisis. Bohemund felt that he had been let down by the Emperor and decided to claim Antioch as his own, although it was a key city in the Empire. He was opposed by some of the other crusaders, but supported by his own troops, and in taking control he deliberately broke a solemn oath which he had given to the Emperor. So as to make it appear less bad, he forged a document purporting to give imperial authority for his action.

## Ecclesiastical Rivalries

The Orthodox Patriarch of Antioch was John the Oxite, who had acted with devotion and courage in refusing to desert his people. He remained with them during the siege and was abominably treated by the Turks. When the crusaders captured the city he was restored to his throne, but in the course of subsequent events he was more and more ignored by the ecclesiastical authorities, who corresponded with the Pope as though there were no lawful Patriarch of the see. He was eventually driven into exile, and a rival line of Latin Patriarchs begun.

In Jerusalem there was no Patriarch, and the Latins elected one from among their own bishops. He was accepted by Christians throughout Palestine as their bishop, since there were no rival candidates from the Byzantine tradition. Christians of other customs received hard treatment from some of the Patriarchs in Jerusalem, but the see continued to be occupied by a Latin until the city was captured by Saladin in 1187.[11] What was clear was that in the Patriarchate of Jerusalem there was no schism between the Byzantines and the Latins, whatever causes of friction there may have been. It seems probable, however, that there was a rival line of Byzantine Patriarchs of Jerusalem kept going elsewhere after the death of Symeon in Cyprus during the first crusade.

The brute facts of the matter were that there was a constant struggle for power, both ecclesiastical and military, wherever the western crusaders went. The ecclesiastics were often difficult to distinguish from secular lords: they behaved very like them, had their own soldiers and were often hand in glove with their military colleagues, many of whom were their near relatives. Whenever they could, they expelled or overruled their Byzantine colleagues, and when western crusaders were in command there was little the Byzantines could do except protest and leave. Many Byzantines came to think that it was better to be under the rule of a Muslim power than to be governed by the Latins. Michael Anchialus, Patriarch of Constantinople from 1169 to 1177, actually stated this point of view unequivocally: 'Let the Saracen be my lord in outward things, and let not the Italian run with me in the things of the soul, for I do not become of one mind with the first, if I do obey him, but if I accept harmony in faith with the second, I shall have deserted my God, Whom he, in embracing me, will drive away.'[12]

The Latins were expelled by Saladin after his conquest of Jerusalem in 1187. Two years later he entered into an agreement with the Emperor for the restoration of Greek and Syrian rites there, as a consequence of which a Greek Patriarch once more occupied the see.

## Constantinople Sacked

But these difficulties, which made relations between East and West so strained, paled into insignificance compared with the effect of the fourth crusade of 1204. The great Innocent III was Pope at Rome, and encouraged the formation of another crusade supported by the Venetians, who had agreed to provide transport for the crusaders if they would first capture the city of Zara, a Christian city under the rule of the King of Hungary, but a trade rival of Venice. This act

E

brought the condemnation of the Pope in 1202, and it was while they were celebrating success there that Alexius, son of the deposed eastern Emperor Isaac Angelus, came with a request that they would restore him to the throne. The Venetians, whose greedy eyes were attracted by the riches of Constantinople, agreed to take the crusaders there, and the western forces arrived outside the city in 1203. After a series of political manoeuvres the vital decision was taken in 1204 that the crusaders should break into the city.

They succeeded in doing so on Good Friday 1204, and Constantinople was subjected to a ghastly sack, worse than any other in its long history. The soldiers, who were vowed to a campaign against the enemies of the Christian Church, turned their arms against the centre of Christian civilisation. In three days they destroyed the Christian Empire, the unity of the Church, and made the success of the Muslim powers inevitable by removing the only effective bastion against them.

Constantinople contained immense treasures of Christian and ancient art. It was the repository of all the greatest achievements of art and learning of many previous centuries. 'For three days, a wild crowd of drunken and blood-thirsty soldiers killed and raped; palaces, churches, libraries and art collections were wantonly destroyed; monasteries and convents were profaned, hospitals and orphanages sacked. A drunken prostitute was placed on the Patriarch's throne in the Cathedral of St. Sophia and sang indecent songs to the applause of the crusaders, whilst the Knights were busy hacking the high altar to pieces; it was made of gold and adorned with precious stones.'[13]

Pope Innocent III played a double game. He deplored the events, but showed himself ready to take advantage of them. The victory of the crusaders over their supposed allies was followed by the establishment of a Latin kingdom at Constantinople and the election of a Latin Patriarch to replace the eastern tenant of the post. Thomas Morosini, a young Venetian, was made Patriarch, and although Innocent began by annulling his election, he afterwards accepted him and made every advantage he could out of the situation. From the instructions which he issued it appears that he hoped that it would signify the permanent rule of the Latins over the Greek churches there and elsewhere. For many years there were rival emperors, sometimes as many as five in all, and rival Patriarchs laying claim to the same titles.

The fearful havoc executed at Constantinople in 1204 could never be forgiven. It continued to live in the minds and consciousness of Eastern Orthodox Christians for centuries afterwards, and its effects are still traceable in attitudes held today. It was the final proof of the enmity and deceit of the West, and confirmed eastern Christians in the view that life under the Muslims was to be preferred to the hegemony of the so-called Christian West. A legacy of hatred of Christians for other Christians had been implanted deep in the hearts of the Christian East.

## The Rise of Russian Christianity: Efforts at Reunion

During the period when relations between Christian East and West were deteriorating a new church was growing in the East, the Church of Russia, destined to be the largest and most influential of all the churches of the Eastern Orthodox tradition. Its name derives from that of a Scandinavian tribe, the Rus, who were settled in the area round Kiev in the tenth century. The earlier conversion of the Bulgars had spread the influence of Byzantine Christianity north and east of Constantinople, and, like the Bulgars, the Russian Christians had to decide whether they would adopt Christianity in its Byzantine or in its Latin form. But there was not to be the same struggle for power between Pope and Patriarch as in the case of the Bulgarian Church, for geographical and political factors told heavily in favour of close relations with Byzantium.

The critical date for the 'conversion' of Russia is usually given as 988, the year when the Prince Vladimir was baptised and adopted the baptism of his subjects as his ruling policy. But for several decades there had been Greek bishops at Kiev, where a number of highly placed persons had accepted the Christian faith. Like Rome in the West, the civilisation of Byzantium was a powerful attraction and influence on peoples which were coming into living contact with an old and cultured civilisation. Vladimir seems to have toyed with the idea of some other faith and to have decided on Byzantine Christianity as a result of the enthusiastic reports brought back by his emissaries of the services in St. Sophia. His grandmother Olga was a Christian. Perhaps this foreshadowed the vital part Russian grandmothers were to play in educating the Russians in Christianity during succeeding centuries.

The Russian Church thus became part of Byzantine Christianity and derived from Byzantium its religion, its laws and its culture. The Cyrillic alphabet was adopted, and through and in it Russian religion and learning was formed. During its first period the Russian Church formed an ecclesiastical province dependent upon Constantinople: and, with two exceptions, the Metropolitans who were heads of the Church were Greek. Other bishops were, however, chosen from among the Russians. In the second period from 1238 to 1448, in spite of pressure for more Russian influence, out of ten Metropolitans five were Greek and only three Russian, the remaining two being Bulgars or Serbs.[14] This last period was one of Tartar domination, from which Russia emerged at a critical ecclesiastical moment, for it was in the middle of the fifteenth century (1453) that Constantinople fell finally to the Turks and ceased to be the centre of eastern Christian civilisation.

Christianity had already been spread in Serbia and Rumania. In Serbia it followed the script and language of the other Slav churches, Bulgaria and Russia. But Rumania contained a people primarily Latin in race, and with a language much influenced by Latin. Because of its position, it was also affected by its Slavonic neighbours, and adopted many of their terms and concepts. It was the only one of the group of Orthodox churches in eastern Europe neither Slav nor Greek in origin and language.

A feature of Russian Christianity, which can also be observed in post-Christian communism, was a consciousness of a special task laid upon the Russian Church to mediate true Christianity to the world. It is impossible to trace the origin of this special Russian emphasis found in its history, and no doubt it owed something to the national character which was formed over centuries of development. But it proved of great importance, especially when allied to political or racial outlooks and policies. From earliest times Christian churches had tried to claim apostolic foundation, since there was often a direct link between the status of the founder and that of the church he founded. The most obvious and persistent case was that of Rome, where the link between the Pope and St. Peter was so much emphasised as sometimes to seem to identify the two. On this link have hung many of the papal claims, based on the supposed authority given to Peter by Jesus himself, especially the recorded words of Jesus that it was 'on this rock' that he would build his church.

At first the apostolic founders were connected with sees and only later cast their mantle over a wider area. Thus Alexandria claimed St. Mark; Cyprus, St. Barnabas; Malabar, St. Thomas; The Church of the East, SS. Simon and Thaddeus; and Constantinople, St. Andrew. There was a tendency, if not a settled practice, to invent a legend of an apostolic founder where no historical evidence was available. So Russia in the eleventh century quoted a supposed visit of St. Andrew. But quite apart from this tendency, there was in many minds a clear conviction of the special calling of each church. The additional glamour of an apostolic founder highlighted the desire for a sense of self-identity. The Jews originated the belief that every nation had its 'celestial patron in the person of an angel', an idea which was familiar to the Russians.[15] Hilarion of Kiev expressed the Russian attitude in words which have been frequently quoted in Russian literature: 'The Roman country praises with laudatory words Peter and Paul by whom she was led to believe in Jesus Christ, son of God; Asia— Ephesus and Patmos, John the Theologian (Evangelist); India, Thomas; Egypt, Mark. All countries, cities, and nations venerate and glorify each their own teacher who had taught them the orthodox faith.'[16]

The Russians were, it seems, possessed of an earnestness which made them specially open to the suggestion that they had a unique mission. Perhaps in origin it was little more than the normal national consciousness which is always liable to exaggeration. But, whatever its exact cause, the events of Russian history joined with national feeling in Russia to produce a conviction of religious vocation, which has often been observed, and is generally given the title 'messianism'. The most important incident in the development of this consciousness was the fall of Constantinople (1453) at the moment when the Church of Russia was beginning to feel its strength. From the middle of the fifteenth century Russian Christianity was no longer concentrated on Kiev, and from 1461 onwards there were two Metropolitans of the Church, one in Kiev and the other in Moscow. With the establishment of Moscow as a patriarchate in 1589, the centre of the Church was to be found there.

The collapse of the eastern Empire with the capture of Constantinople by the Turks in 1453 seemed to be the collapse of the eastern form of Christianity except in Russia, which alone of the ancient churches of the East found itself free from Muslim rule. Russian Christians became convinced that upon them had fallen the rôle of preserving the pure form of Christianity for the future, in distinction from the sullied form believed and practised in the West. At that time there was little or no friendly contact with the West, as the Russians throughout their history had constantly to defend themselves against attack from the West, their attackers being not only national enemies but also representatives of the western church intent on imposing their religious allegiance on those whom they conquered. They faced Teutonic Knights whose attitude towards them was more that of crusaders against the enemies of Christianity than of fellow Christians. Their experiences strengthened the hostility to the West which had been brought to such a high pitch by the crusades.

Constantinople fell in 1453. In 1472 the Tsar Ivan III married the niece of the last of the Byzantine emperors of the house of Palaeologus, and was thus dynastically identified with the continuation of the old Empire. The first Rome had become unorthodox; the second Rome in the shape of Constantinople had been vanquished by the infidel; the third Rome now began in Russia. In this way the idea of Moscow as the third Rome began to have currency and was readily accepted everywhere. The first appearance of this idea in literature is in a letter of Philotheus, a monk of Pskov, who wrote to the Grand Duke Basil III: the Orthodox Church found no peace in the second Rome 'because of the union with the Latins at the Eighth Council. Then the Church of Constantinople fell, and the empire fled again to a third Rome, which is in New Great Russia. . . . All Christian empires bow down to you alone: for two Romes are fallen, but the third stands fast; a fourth there cannot be; your Christian kingdom shall not be given to another. . . . You alone are Emperor over all Christians under the sun.'[17]

The following centuries saw the Russian Church playing a more and more important rôle in eastern Christianity, and, closely identified with the State, it helped to produce an identification of nationality and religion found in many other parts of the world in some degree, but particularly marked in the case of the Eastern Orthodox. We shall have occasion to return to this aspect of developments at a later stage.

### Last Years of Byzantium

After the Christian sack of Constantinople in 1204 the Latin kingdom survived until 1261. The city was regained by Michael VIII (Palaeologus). Having made himself master of the eastern Empire with its centre at Nicaea and defeated a combination of various powers to the north and east, he entered Constantinople on 15 August 1261. The eastern Empire was therefore once more established there and was to survive for almost another two hundred years, but the weakening of its strength through the fourth crusade had spelled its eventual doom. For in its restored form the new Empire was merely one among a number of contending states, surrounded by powerful rivals. The defeat of the Latin kingdom was a blow to papal prestige, and the war which accomplished it hardened yet more the deep hostility of Greek and Latin towards each other, in which religious, ecclesiastical, linguistic and national elements were fused into a single enmity and hatred.

Between 1261 and the fall of Constantinople to the Turks in 1453 two important efforts at reconciliation between the two parts of Christendom were made. The overruling motive in each was political rather than religious. Evidently political alliance was made more difficult by the fact that the differences between the sides had a deep-seated religious aspect, and some kind of *modus vivendi* on the religious question was a necessary prerequisite for an effective political détente. In the East, there was still a distinction between the political and ecclesiastical authorities which no longer obtained in the West. The Pope found himself simultaneously head of a political institution with powers which had to be defended and promoted by the normal methods of political alliances and military conquest, and at the same time the supreme religious authority of the western Church. His religious interest in reunion often waxed or waned according as it seemed to the occupant of the papal see to be to his political advantage or disadvantage. In the East when the Emperor wished to promote political alliances he brought pressure on the Patriarchs to support his policies by suitable ecclesiastical action, when necessary.

It was the threats of Charles of Anjou which in the 1270s threatened the political interests of both Pope and Emperor. Gregory X became Pope in 1271, and had two main ambitions, to regain control of the Holy Land and to achieve reunion with the Greeks. The former could not be done without the latter. The pressure and threats of Charles of Anjou, who had secured for himself the theoretical rights over the Latin kingdom of Constantinople, and was King of Naples and Sicily, induced the Pope to make advances to Michael VIII in favour of reunion. A General Council was convoked by the Pope at Lyons in 1274 to deal with reform, reunion and the recovery of the holy places.

The Emperor thereupon began to try to persuade the Orthodox (as we may now call them) to support the effort towards closer unity with the Latins. He was not unsuccessful, though the Patriarch of Constantinople, Joseph, steadily refused to give any approval to the project. Nevertheless, numbers of the clergy were prepared to go forward on the basis of the primacy of the Pope, the replacement of his name on the diptychs at Constantinople and the recognition of a right of appeal to the papacy in disputed matters.

## Council of Lyons

The legates of the Emperor attended the Council of Lyons and agreed to the demands which the western Church made. The *filioque* was accepted and repeated three times at the High Mass which was held in celebration of the agreement. The papal claims were also largely accepted. But when this had been done it still remained for the union to be accepted in the East, and the Emperor, in spite of many efforts, never succeeded in bringing this about. Because of his own part in the submission, he was refused the burial of the Church and died excommunicate. The Popes again and again tried to get the agreement enforced, but without success. They in turn over-reached themselves, by making demands which could not possibly have been met even by the most cooperative ruler of the East. An ultimatum to the Emperor from Pope Nicholas III in 1278 made these demands: '(1) to send a fresh statement of his adherence to the confession of Lyons, (2) to compel the Patriarch and the clergy to swear to it, (3) to introduce the *filioque* into the creed, (4) to renounce all usages which the Pope might deem contrary to the faith, (5) to receive papal envoys and assist them to visit the churches of the Empire and see that all is done there as agreed, (6) to accept a permanent nuncio at Constantinople, (7) to require his subjects to seek absolution from the envoys for their adherence to the schism, (8) the envoys, on their part, to confess and absolve all returning from the schism, and (9) to excommunicate the enemies of the union; finally (10) the creed or confession of Lyons once accepted, the Patriarch and clergy to seek confirmation in their office from Rome.'[18]

These terms, though not of great importance historically, provide an interesting indication of the difficulties which had now become fixed in improving relations between the two parts of Christendom. The psychological outlook of each side was far apart from the other, and the papal demands bring the fact out starkly. It is easy to interpret the difficulty by making moral judgments about the unreasonableness of one side or the other, and there is no doubt that this element is one of those which can be discerned. But if we give way to the temptation of saying, for example, that the papal demands show the power-hungry nature of the western papacy over the proper independence of the East; or if, on the other hand, we say that the confusion and lack of organisation of the East made it impossible for them to reach agreement we only blind ourselves to other aspects of the situation which also need to be understood. The Popes were not merely concerned with their own power. Their attitudes had been formed by the historical situation in which they had to live and to survive. They were genuinely concerned to try to achieve Christian unity with the East, and many of their motives were right. But they were unable to conceive of such unity except in the terms of their own experience.

No doubt in reaching their conclusions as to what was needed there were many hidden and perhaps even disreputable elements, but these were only the mixed motives of every man in trying to reach a decision which affected him deeply. As we saw earlier, the Popes were more or less forced into becoming political and military powers, as well as religious leaders, by the requirements of the world in which they found themselves. In the west of Europe the spread of Christian influence had been mainly achieved through kings and other rulers who had accepted it, and it had only been maintained and organised through an ever widening and ever more centralised policy of authority centred on Rome. For several hundred years, therefore, Christian civilisation had seemed to depend on a union between the ecclesiastical and secular power, in which the Pope combined elements of both in his own person.

The demands made by Pope Nicholas III show this clearly. For they tried to establish a thoroughly centralised control over ecclesiastical affairs under the Pope, enforced by the secular power. Had it been possible to put such a programme into effect, it might have begun to make effective over the whole Christian world the kind of unity which the Pope succeeded in establishing in western Christendom in the Middle Ages. From one point of view it was a high ideal, and represented what appeared to its promoters as the only kind of unity which could have reality. But it was in the thirteenth century quite impossible to expect eastern Christians to accept a form of church unity which denied their deepest convictions and way of thinking.

The desire for unity did not die. It was always to be found beneath the surface, even when there were few signs of it above. The fact that church unity was considered important for political purposes is not merely a testimony to the political undesirability of church division but a silent witness to the fact that church unity had an important positive part to play in human relations, if it could be achieved. Sadly enough, the attempts to reach it only too often resulted in other divisions, one split being healed at the expense of creating another.

Political events in the East became more and more uncertain as the power of the Turks spread, and eventually their authority controlled so much of the surrounding territory that the capture of Constantinople could only be a matter of time.

## Council of Florence

John VIII became Emperor of the East in 1425 and, as the Turks closed around him, he again, like some of his predecessors, sought help from the West. He offered to unite the eastern church with the West if the Pope would organise the powers of Europe in his defence. Such a proposal had attractions for a Pope who, besides desiring to extend his own supremacy, wished to appear as the leader of Christian Europe. In consequence, the two sides met in the longest of the abortive councils aimed at unity, the Council of Florence. In fact, the council first met at Ferrara in 1438, moved to Florence in the following year and continued at Rome from 1442 to 1445. It was attended both by the Emperor and by the Patriarch Joseph of Constantinople, and also by representatives of other eastern patriarchates. The main questions under discussion were the *filioque*, the use of unleavened bread at the Eucharist, the primacy of the Pope and the teaching on purgatory. The two vital questions were, as usual, the position of the Pope and the *filioque*. The main opponent of agreement on the eastern side was Bishop Mark of Ephesus, who refused to sign the documents to which the other easterns agreed. The actual formula about the Pope's position which was accepted was by no means clear as to the power of the Pope, the text being: 'We recognise the Pope as Sovereign Pontiff, Viceregent and Vicar of Christ, Shepherd of all Christians, Ruler of the Church of God: saving the privileges and rights of the Patriarchs of the East.'[19] Such a formula was open to varying interpretations. But the need for military help was pressing, and it could not be obtained without paying for it. A decree of union including the *filioque* was signed by all except Mark of Ephesus on 5 July 1439.

However, when the Emperor returned home he found it impossible to persuade the people to accept the decree. In 1443 the Patriarchs of Alexandria, Antioch and Jerusalem formally dissociated themselves from it and declared the Patriarch of Constantinople a heretic.

Later in the council Jacobites, Syrians, Chaldaeans and Maronites were all said to have been reconciled, but the achievement was not one which had any marked permanent effects. It is also worth recording that when the Greek Isidore, Metropolitan of Moscow, returned to Russia from Florence he met with no support for the union. He was imprisoned by the Grand Duke and eventually left the country. His successor was for the first time elected by the Russians themselves in 1448 without reference to Constantinople, and thus effective Russian independence of the Greeks was established.

The union of Florence did not really exist and was never established. It perished totally with the fall of Constantinople. Some forces from the West reached the city before the Turks began the siege on the night of 28/29 May 1453. There was a moving demonstration of Christian unity as events moved to their climax, perhaps the best example of what the Council of Florence might have achieved, if Christian aims had been unmixed with those of baser metal. The imminence of defeat and possible death brought all Christians together in the presence of their common Lord as they faced that mortal danger together. The final act may be recalled in the words of Sir Steven Runciman. 'The day was nearly over. Already crowds were moving towards the great Church of the Holy Wisdom. For the past five months no pious Greek had stepped through its portals to hear the Sacred Liturgy defiled by Latins and by renegades. But on that evening the bitterness was ended. Barely a citizen, except for the soldiers on the walls, stayed away from this desperate service of intercession. Priests who had held union with Rome to be a mortal sin now came to the altar to serve with their Unionist brothers. The Cardinal was there, and beside him bishops who would never acknowledge his authority; and all the people came to make confession and take communion, not caring whether Orthodox or Catholic administered it. There were Italians and Catalans along with the Greeks. The golden mosaics, studded with the images of Christ and His Saints and the Emperors and Empresses of Byzantium, glimmered in the light of a thousand lamps and candles; and beneath them for the last time the priests in their splendid vestments moved in the solemn rhythm of the Liturgy. At this moment there was union in the Church of Constantinople.'[20]

## Western Middle Ages

It was Pope Nicholas I (858–867) who first used the forged decretals to justify papal claims of supremacy in many fields, but it was Gregory VII (1073–1185) (Hildebrand) who formulated them in a way which laid the basis for future expanding claims: many of them could not be realised in his time, but they set the foundations for the policy of his successors for the next 250 years. During the tenth century western Europe was in a condition of political chaos, and the position of the Popes reflected this fact. In the middle of the following century a new order had emerged in which the chief power had moved from the West Franks to Germany. At the same time there had been a revival of spiritual ideals through the monastic centre of Cluny, aiming at reforming the lax discipline of the Church, especially in the lives of the clergy.

But reform of the Church also meant reform of the papacy itself. In 1033 Benedict IX became Pope 'despite his extreme youth' and proceeded to lead a wild and licentious life which scandalised the Romans to such an extent that they were eventually driven to set up a rival in 1044 or 1045—Sylvester III. But Benedict still had supporters, and, being pressed, he sold the papacy in the following year to a successor who called himself Gregory VI. Benedict, however, tried once more to come back into power, and the result was the unedifying sight of three claimants to the papal throne, no one having the power to decide between them. A synod at Rome invited the German Emperor Henry III to end the scandal. At another synod called by Henry at Sutri in 1046 two of the claimants were removed, and the third was later thrown out by yet another synod held in Rome. A new Pope was elected through Henry's influence and was accepted as Clement II.

These events were of great significance for the subsequent history of relations between the Empire and the papacy. The struggle between the two was the most important aspect of European history for more than two centuries. The book dealing with the period 918–1273 (in a well-known series on the history of Europe) was entitled *The Empire and the Papacy*.[21] In acting as he did, Henry III behaved as the eastern emperors had done from earliest times, and it seemed natural to him and his contemporaries that he should take upon himself the task of putting an end to a disgraceful ecclesiastical situation. No doubt political motives were not entirely absent, but Henry was a genuine supporter of reform in the Church, and his main objects seem to have been religious. Indeed, it would have been difficult at that time to have distinguished clearly between the two.

His action in this case heralded a bitter struggle between the temporal and ecclesiastical power. The reform of the papacy, if successful, must inevitably carry with it an increase of influence and efficiency. This in turn meant that the more able and disinterested the Popes were, the more they wished to restore the position of the papacy as it was reflected in the forged decretals and in the practice of earlier centuries, when the emperors received their throne and their crown from the hands of the Pope himself.

## Pope Gregory VII

With the accession of Hildebrand to the papal throne as Gregory VII the claims of the papacy were put forward in their full form. He began by a vigorous reform. The celibacy of the clergy was to be enforced, and married priests were to be rejected by the laity. Simony, that is the payment of money for ecclesiastical or spiritual privilege or position, was to be abolished, and in order to strengthen this reform, no one was to be invested into any spiritual office by a layman. Gregory claimed for the Church complete independence of the secular power, and went on to make it clear that this independence could only be considered complete with the supremacy of the Church over the Empire. In all Church matters he exercised absolute power of all causes and appointments.

In the dramatic confrontation of Gregory VII and the Emperor Henry IV at Canossa in 1077 the Emperor was humiliated before the Pope by having to wait three days in mid-winter for absolution. But it was a victory which did not prove permanent, and aroused a resentment more deep-seated than the previous rivalry. Moreover, by his absolution Henry regained his spiritual status. He refused to give up his power of investiture, and in Henry's struggle with his rival Rudolf, the Pope took the side of his enemy and pronounced Henry's excommunication, purporting to deprive him of his territories. But Henry, supported by the German bishops, deposed the Pope, electing instead the Archbishop of Ravenna, who assumed the title Clement III. The matter could only be settled by war. Henry captured Rome, but was driven out by the Normans, to whom Gregory had appealed for help. Before them Henry retired and the Normans took the city against the desperate defence of its inhabitants. They sacked the city with horrible outrages and massacres, and made thousands of Romans into slaves. Gregory retired from the city and died at Salerno not long afterwards with the famous words on his lips: 'I have always loved the law of God and hated iniquity. Therefore I die in exile.' His rival remained in Rome for only a short time and then went back to his old home at Ravenna.

Gregory, by his ability and by his extravagant claims, had created a state of affairs which was to do the utmost harm to Christian Europe. Some might hold that more harm was done when the papal claims were successful than when they were defeated, for their success blinded men's eyes to the true nature of the gospel and the Church, which was formed to proclaim it. The long-drawn-out quarrel, known as the investiture contest, sprang directly out of these claims, though it must be recognised that the right of independence in appointments to spiritual office was an essential part of the freedom of the Church. On the other hand, if the Pope had not claimed unjustified rights over the secular power the problem of investitures would not have arisen in the extremely fierce form which it assumed. The setting up of an anti-pope came directly from the papal claim to depose and rule the Emperor. And it is a tragic fact that the better the Popes were, the more they were inclined to press the secular claims of their office, for these claims belonged to a frame of thought which they could not reject. They are not to be blamed for thinking in the terms of their time, but they must perhaps be convicted of too little application to themselves of the principles which the Christian religion ought to embody.

The struggle between the ecclesiastical and the secular power also laid the foundations for the later division which was to split Christian Europe into fragments at the Reformation. The simple and obvious fact was that the Pope regarded temporal power as something he should do everything possible to acquire. His attempt to use religious sanctions for the gaining of temporal power became deeply embedded in the outlook of the papacy, and it was not shed until the twentieth century, though it took a number of different shapes during the course of history. When the nation states came to power the hidden influence of past history was a strong factor in the rejection of papal authority.

Nevertheless, the concept of spiritual freedom and the ideal of a united Christendom were powerful factors in men's minds and corresponded to their own inner convictions of truth. There would have been no possibility of the Pope's successful influence in temporal affairs had he not exercised a deep sway over the loyalty of those who in the light of their own times and thought found in the Christian faith the answer to their basic needs. Moreover, the alternative to papal power might well have been the complete subjugation of spiritual principles to the requirements of secular rulers, and the consequent humiliation and dependency of Christian leaders. It was unthinkable in the terms of that age for such a possibility to be accepted without resistance.

The investiture controversy was the focus for the struggle between the two interests. From the time of Gregory VII constant attempts were made to enforce the rulings against lay investiture of bishops with the ring and staff and the requirement of homage before consecration. Eventually a compromise was reached in which the lay authority bestowed the temporalities only, homage being paid six months later, except in Germany, where homage was still permitted beforehand by the settlement reached in 1122 at the Concordat of Worms. In England St. Anselm was in conflict with Henry I on the subject, and there, too, a compromise like that in Germany was agreed in 1107. On balance, it is probable that the papacy gained more than the secular power in the result.

It is not relevant to follow the developments of this and other controversies which did not directly affect relations between Christians as such, except in so far as they throw light on attitudes of mind which were later to issue in divisive action. Because in its main features it was a struggle for political power, the tension between popes and secular kings and emperors had the result of hopelessly confusing the question of spiritual principles with temporal questions.

It encouraged the leaders of the Church to see their problems in terms of secular power; it encouraged lay leaders to use political methods in dealing with the Church and also to use ecclesiastics and their spiritual sanctions for the pursuance of their own temporal interests.

A frank examination of events, however, must force the admission that the most notable attempt to identify the Pope with sanctity ended in ignominious failure. In reaction against the strife and factious intrigue accompanying the struggle for a papal election, the electors in 1294 elected as Pope, with the name Celestine V, a holy hermit. His nomination called forth immense enthusiasm and whenever he went out he was thronged by crowds seeking his saintly blessing. But he was totally ignorant of how to conduct any business, still more of the complications of the papacy, and he became the tool of the King of Naples. While his personal life was the cause of inspiration to many, 'the Cardinals groaned in secret dismay over the perils with which his incompetence threatened the Papacy'.[22] Such a man could not fulfil the requirements of supporting and discharging the duties of the institution as it actually was, and he proved useless for the task for which he had been named.

*Thomas Becket*

The struggle between Empire and papacy was seen in miniature and in highly dramatic form in England in the quarrel between Henry II and Thomas Becket. Becket's change of front after he had become archbishop exactly reproduces the psychology of the age as observed in events on the Continent. His thought moved in the same forms, and he saw his duty to the Church as being its victory over the king through freedom of action and the establishment of its privileges. The agreement called the Constitutions of Clarendon in 1164 showed the subjects at issue, and although Becket agreed to them at the time, he bitterly reproved himself afterwards for doing so. The debates concerned such matters as presentation to benefices, whether the trials of those in orders should take place in the king's courts or in ecclesiastical courts, and other matters, almost all of which dealt with the borders of authority between king and church. It must be remembered too that the 'clerks' in question covered large numbers of ordained men in minor orders, and included most of those in the kingdom who could read and write.

The conflict between a hot-tempered king and an obstinate and infuriating archbishop was bound to lead to a clash, and it ended in the archbishop's dramatic murder in Canterbury cathedral. There was a terrible inevitability about the course of these quarrels, because, given the conditions and outlook of the time, they were bound to occur and had to be fought fiercely to the end. And they helped to condition men's minds for future action, which left no room for compromise.

But within their limitations it is also necessary to recognise the deep hold which high ideals had upon men in the Middle Ages. It was a time of renewal, and although the Church suffered from the shortcomings of its own time, yet it contained far-seeing and powerful positive forces. The reform of the monks, first from Cluny and then from Citeaux and elsewhere, is evidence of the deep desire of men to be true to the call of the Christian gospel. The appearance of the friars—Dominicans and Franciscans—in the thirteenth century was further evidence of the seriousness with which men took their religion. The crusades, too, whatever their failures and scandals, sprang from a genuine religious wish of men to give themselves to the cause of the Christian faith.

Moreover, a remarkable intellectual renaissance took place during these centuries, reaching its high point in Thomas Aquinas (1225–74), the famous Dominican whose intellectual grasp and amazing power of thought established a method of philosophy and theology which continued to be paramount in his own church until the twentieth century, and which very deeply influenced the thought of western Europe for hundreds of years. Religious ideas were powerful factors in influencing men's actions in many aspects of their lives.

The thirteenth and fourteenth centuries also witnessed a great movement of mystical life in Germany and elsewhere. England was the home of some remarkable mystical writers whose works bore witness to the popular desire to strengthen and deepen the spiritual life for ordinary churchmen as well as for those who had embraced the monastic life (technically known as the 'religious' life). But there was an unfortunate tendency also to admit two standards, one for those who were professionally religious and the other for those who lived in the world and pursued secular occupations.

Nevertheless, in this period there was an immense flowering of Christian life, in practical, intellectual and spiritual activities which bore witness to the power of religious ideas and beliefs in western Europe and which were to play an important part, when combined with other elements, at the time of the Reformation.

### Rival Popes

At the end of the thirteenth century Boniface VIII (1294–1303) made claims for the papacy greater than ever before. They brought him to ruin, not because he was conquered by the Empire, but because he underestimated or failed to notice a new kind of power, that of the nation-state, which in the shape of France struck him down, and inaugurated a period of deplorable scandal and weakness for the papacy. First the Popes were established at Avignon, which remained their residence from 1309 to 1377. In 1378, with the forced election of a new Pope at Rome, Urban VI, further strife broke out in the Church, and the same body of Cardinals, who had elected him, four months later elected a rival, Clement VII, who settled in Avignon. There was no means by which the scandalous schism could be settled, since both could claim the authority of the same body, and the secular powers supported one or the other as it suited their policy. It was a scandal to the whole of Christendom, and it also considerably increased the total revenues which had to be raised for their support.

By the beginning of the fifteenth century there were actually three Popes. In 1409 the Council of Pisa had met with the aim of ending the outrageous situation of the Great Schism: it had purported to depose the two existing Popes and had appointed a third, Alexander V, succeeded by John XXIII. The fact that the most famous Pope of the twentieth century took the title John XXIII indicates that the position of his predecessor is not officially recognised. The three rivals were still opposing one another when a General Council was called for the purpose of resolving the matter—the Council of Constance in 1414. The other two claimants were Gregory XII and Benedict XIII. John and Gregory were forced to resign, but Benedict refused to do so, and he was deposed by the Council in 1417.

The position of the papacy was inevitably brought into disrepute by the Great Schism, and in its circumstances the claims of the great earlier Popes would have seemed ludicrous. The series of events had an important influence in making Christians ask themselves questions as to where the ultimate authority of the Church was to be found.

It gave great impetus to the conciliar movement, whose adherents claimed that the only final authority was to be found in a General Council of the Church. In the action which it took the Council of Constance certainly acted in a way which implied ultimate authority, and in its decrees it attempted to perpetuate this authority for the future. With the election by the Council of Martin V in 1417 the Great Schism was brought to an end, but it had left a dangerous scar and weakness in the authority of the Church.

## Heretical Strains

Throughout the history of the Church heretical tendencies have appeared again and again in different forms and in different places, and caused the authorities of the Church considerable trouble both in East and West. One such tendency was a strain of doctrine which is usually called 'dualist', the essence of which was the belief that matter was evil, and that there were two powers, opposed to one another, who created the world, whose struggle was manifested in the world itself. This teaching was an attempt to meet the problem of evil which has baffled all the best thinkers of the world, and it is not surprising to find that the heretics, too, failed to answer the problem.

From the earliest times of the Gnostics dualism under different names was found. In an appendix to his study on the subject entitled *The Medieval Manichee*, Sir Steven Runciman lists no less than fifteen different names applied to these heretics in Europe, and many of these names had varying forms. In Bulgaria they were called Bogomils after the name of their leader. In the West the most common names for them were Cathars or Albigenses. The first of these names derives from the Greek word meaning 'pure', and the second from the district of Albi where some lived. They were found at one time or another in most of the countries of the Balkans and of the West, though the names were sometimes loosely used.

The Albigenses were strongly opposed to the Church, and rejected most of its practices. Their belief that all matter was evil had the effect of making them extremely rigorist in their practices: they fasted from all forms of meat and animal produce, and condemned the institution of marriage. In the twelfth and thirteenth centuries they were condemned by a number of church councils. Some of their hold on the popular imagination seems to have derived from their extreme asceticism when contrasted with the laxity of the lives of many clergy. The Dominican order was founded as a means of counteracting them. In 1208 a crusade was mounted against them which was notorious for its cruelty and massacres. After this their extirpation was confided to the Inquisition, which did its work to such effect that the Albigenses had entirely disappeared by the end of the fourteenth century.

Although they rejected the sacraments of the Church, they had their own religious meal, and seem to have retained some elements of early Christian rites. These dualist heretics were always rejected by the Church, but in their practice there was a use of Scripture which was later to be more and more widespread, not in following dualist interpretation, but in the conviction that men should feel themselves free to interpret the Scriptures in senses which did not have the approval of the Church.

## Waldenses

Another Christian division arose from the Waldenses. The origin of the Waldenses was reminiscent of Francis of Assisi. Peter Waldo of Lyons took literally the text telling the young man to sell his goods and give the money to the poor. He was a rich man and became a wandering preacher and mendicant, attracting followers by his life towards the end of the twelfth century. They formed settlements in the French Alps, and might perhaps have escaped trouble had they not attacked the worldliness of the Church and its clergy. They tried to secure recognition from the Church, but a Council of Verona in 1184 rejected them and condemned their activities. In consequence, they found themselves deprived of the ordinary ministrations of the Church, and so they formed their own ministry and celebrated their own sacraments.

The Waldenses were quite different from the dualist heretics in that they were basically Orthodox Christians and were not associated with any fundamental denials of Christian doctrine. On the contrary, they tried to purify the Christian life. They based their attitudes on a strict adherence to the New Testament, and lived a simple life. In their use of the sacraments they continued the practice of confession and celebrated the Lord's Supper, but rejected prayers for the dead and purgatory as being unscriptural. They were the first organised church to embrace many of the beliefs and practices later widespread through the Reformation. The Waldensians suffered severe persecution in the thirteenth and fourteenth centuries, and they had their own internal differences which caused divisions. But they persisted in their church life, and when the Reformation began they immediately made contact with the Reformers. They have continued to exist ever since that date, and in the twentieth century are confined to Italy, where they have a well-ordered Protestant church. Their sufferings during history have been immense, and they did not receive freedom until 1848, their survival after the Reformation being assisted by the help and friendship of other Protestants.

## Wycliffe and Huss

There were significant movements of thought in the fourteenth and fifteenth centuries before the beginning of the Reformation which were heralds of changes to come. The dominance of scholastic thought begun by Thomas Aquinas and carried on by the Dominicans was not unchallenged. The systematic totality of scholastic thought, based on Aristotelian concepts, was criticised by adherents of the Platonic tradition, and a notable feature of some critics was an appeal to Augustine and to his categories and frame of reference. Foremost among such thinkers was John Wycliffe (c. 1329–84), the most eminent English theologian of his day. He has often been described as a forerunner of the Reformation, and the ascription is justified so long as its sense is understood. He did not escape the limitations of his own time, but his rejection of the ruling nominalist philosophy in favour of realism was an important feature of his outlook.[23] More important still from a religious point of view was Wycliffe's appeal to the Bible and to St. Augustine, for it was this double appeal which was later to form the basis of the new teaching about the Christian religion which the Reformers spread.

Wycliffe was an Oxford don, and for a time Master of Balliol. In some ways his career seems to have been disappointing, first in failure as warden of Canterbury College in Oxford and later in the wider influence of the outside world when he was the protégé of John of Gaunt. It was not difficult to attack or criticise the Church for the behaviour of the clergy, and in doing this Wycliffe did no more than many of his age. But from this he proceeded to make far more radical criticisms of the doctrine and discipline of the Church, which led inevitably to hostility against him, but secured his place in the history of religious thought. Coupled with his growing deviation from received doctrine, his fame rests on his English translation of the Bible from the Vulgate, undertaken between 1382 and 1384. How much translation he did himself is uncertain, but there is no doubt that the translation was widely circulated and that its influence was important both from a religious and from a linguistic point of view.

Wycliffe exercised a strong influence on the Bohemian theologian John Huss. Huss derived many of his doctrines from Wycliffe, and in the conditions of his country at the time became an influential figure. He was induced to go to the Council of Constance under a safe conduct from the Emperor Sigismund, but when he reached Constance the promise was ignored and he was put into prison. The Council began by condemning Wycliffe and ordering his body to be exhumed and burnt. Huss was ordered to admit the Council's authority in everything, but he would not betray his conscience, and was condemned and burned to death in 1415.

The points at which the teaching of Wycliffe and Huss diverged from that of the Church may be gauged from some of Wycliffe's propositions which were condemned by the Council of Constance.

'1. That the material substance of bread and the material substance of wine remain in the Sacrament of the altar.

'3. That Christ is not in the Sacrament essentially and really, in his own corporeal presence.

'4. That if a bishop or priest be in mortal sin he does not ordain, consecrate or baptize.

'10. That it is contrary to Holy Scriptures that ecclesiastics should have possessions.

'14. That any deacon or priest may preach the word of God apart from the authority of the Apostolic See or a Catholic Bishop.

'16. That temporal lords can at their will take away temporal goods from the church, when those who hold them are sinful (habitually sinful, not sinning in one act only).

'18. That tithes are mere alms, and that parishioners can withdraw them at their will because of the misdeeds of their curates.

'30. That the excommunication of the Pope or of any prelate is not to be feared, because it is the censure of antichrist.

'42. That it is fatuous to believe in the indulgences of the Pope and the bishops.

'43. That all oaths made to corroborate human contracts and civil business are unlawful.'

These few extracts[24] from the council show clearly enough why Wycliffe earned the determined enmity of the powerful office-holders in the Church, and from them may also be seen the mixed nature of Wycliffe's opinions. Some of them dealt with fundamental truths, whereas others were merely expressions of opinion or wild generalisations. One of the opinions condemned was that 'all of the order of mendicants are heretics'. If this were Wycliffe's view it would bear witness to some confusion of thought in spite of his theological reputation.

But whatever judgment we may reach about the truth of Wycliffe's opinions, his activity was bound to undermine the authority of the Church and to cut at the root of a number of doctrines which were thought to be of high importance. The influence which he had on Huss and Bohemia shows how closely the thought of England and that of the Continent were bound together: they belonged to one intellectual world. It also showed that rebellion against the condition of the Church and some of its teaching easily aroused sympathy in widely different places. While Huss was detained at Constance, his followers in Bohemia first began to use the cup for the laity at the Eucharist—from which they were called Utraquists (both kinds)—another small sign of new opinions.

In England Wycliffe's followers were called 'Lollards', though the title was often applied loosely to anyone who was critical of the Church. The teachings of the Lollards were disseminated by poor preachers who claimed that the Scriptures were the only authority in religion and that every man had a right to interpret them, attacking various practices of the Church then current. They were fiercely persecuted, and in 1401 the bill *De Haeretico Comburendo* was passed and a number of the Lollards were burnt as heretics. Lollardy gradually changed its character, but continued underground into the second half of the sixteenth century.

By the end of the thirteenth century most of the youthful energy of the new movements in religious life and thought was beginning to wane. The new forms of monastic life and those of the friars had lost their first enthusiasm and become established, property-owning and power-exercising bodies, differing little from the condition of affairs which their orders had first been set up to rectify. The Church itself, besides the obvious failures of which mention has been made, was efficiently organised, but its unity was based on a canonical and legalistic structure rather than on a freely accepted loyalty and co-operation. Its rigidity, and the diminishing quality of the life of the Church, made it susceptible to criticism and at the same time unable to adapt itself to the expanding needs of the civilisation in which it lived.

Into this state of affairs came that complex of exciting new thought and experiment known as the Renaissance. It is impossible accurately to date the Renaissance, as its roots were in the past and its expression in the different aspects of life did not occur at the same time. It is a title which covers a turbulence and revolution in men's thinking and attitudes, and corresponds to the break-up of the Middle Ages in every part of its life. Politically it covers the rise of the nation states of France, England and Spain; economically it includes the rise of the importance of industry and the fading away of feudalism; artistically it refers to an entirely new way of painting and of revival in the other arts; it means the rising power of the people against those who had hitherto ruled them; it brought national literatures and new national consciousness; and, with all seeming to need renewal, it rejected many of the ideas which had been predominant in religious life and doctrine. No doubt it seemed newer to those who lived in it than it does to later historians, who can see how many of the former ideas still governed men's outlooks, but the Renaissance was the greatest outbreak of new ideas the world had ever seen. Its influence on the Reformation was immense: the Reformation itself was part of the totality of the Renaissance.

[1] M. Creighton, *A History of the Papacy*, I, 11, London, 1897.
[2] Runciman, *The Eastern Schism*, p. 32.
[3] *Op. cit.*
[4] Runciman, *op. cit.*, p. 36.
[5] B. J. Kidd, *The Churches of Eastern Christendom*, p. 210.
[6] Henry Bettenson, *Documents of the Christian Church*, Oxford, 1946, p. 134.
[7] Every, *The Byzantine Patriarchate*, p. 167.
[8] Runciman. *op. cit.*, cap. iii *passim*.
[9] Runciman, *A History of the Crusades*, I, Cambridge, 1951, p. 64.
[10] Runciman, *Crusades*, I, 83.
[11] Runciman, *Crusades*, I, 88.
[12] Every, *op. cit.*, pp. 184–5.
[13] Nicolas Zernov, *Eastern Christendom*, London, 1961, p. 107.
[14] B. H. Sumner, *Survey of Russian History*, London, 1947, pp. 176–7.
[15] G. P. Fedotov, *The Russian Religious Mind*, New York, 1960, p. 406.
[16] Quoted, *ibid.*
[17] Quoted Schmemann, *op. cit.*, pp. 312–13.

[18] B. J. Kidd, *op. cit.*, pp. 270–1.

[19] Kidd, *op. cit.*, p. 289.

[20] *The Fall of Constantinople*, Cambridge, 1965, p. 131.

[21] London, *Rivingtons*, 1898.

[22] Creighton, *op. cit.*, p. 28.

[23] Nominalism is the theory of knowledge which denies reality to universal concepts. Its opposite—realism—held that universal concepts, such as species, had an independent existence apart from the individual components which make them. Both are technical philosophical terms.

[24] Bettenson, *op. cit.*, pp. 243–5.

# 7

---

# The Reformation and After

## Reform

POLITICAL conditions at the beginning of the sixteenth century were such as to break up the unity of western Europe into competitive national states. The rise in their power and the national consciousness which accompanied it produced a situation which had never before existed. It is important to realise that the tendency to create separate states was not in any sense a falling away from a better condition which had hitherto existed, but an expansion of strength, prosperity and learning which could have no other result. The growth of these states was an inevitable expression of the growth of civilisation. The increase of industrial wealth meant that it was in more hands, and the interests of more people were therefore engaged in its promotion and defence. For this a new structure of society was needed with smaller and more manageable units, and the new national states provided it.

The unity which existed had been gradually weakened over the previous two centuries by the growth of these new powers, and it proved to be a form of unity which was suitable only for the particular stage of human development which it served. The tendencies which were promoting new national consciousness and the divisions which came with them directly affected the Church too. In spite of the struggle between Empire and papacy which distinguished between the interests of the two groups, men felt that their religion and their national sense ought to correspond. It had always done so, and there seemed no reason why it should now cease. Moreover, there was a tendency to adopt concepts which had applied to the Empire as a whole and to transfer them to the new political units which had now come on the scene. Thus the medieval theory of the two swords—the spiritual sword in the hands of the Pope and the temporal sword in the hands of the Emperor—had behind it an implicit assumption that the head of the Church and the head of the State were but two facets of the same social, religious and political body. When this idea was transferred to the nation state, or to smaller units, it became the principle of *cujus regio, ejus religio*—the religion of a state is that of its ruler. This has often been described as a Protestant doctrine aimed at justifying changes of religious allegiance in Protestant states. But when examined it is found to be no more than the medieval principle translated into different political terms.

Conditions had been ripening for changes in religious outlook. The invention and rapid spread of printing had made new thought widely available, and copies of the writings of such eminent men as Erasmus were circulating all over Europe. For the first time new ideas could be spread without the personal contact which teaching by word of mouth required.

It is also important to allow sufficient importance to the purely religious motivation of the Reformation. While it would be misleading to suppose that events were governed only by religious motives, there is no doubt that they played a vital part. The Reformation was a religious movement, even when full allowance has been made for the many other factors which contributed towards it. One of the most telling influences was the undoubted fact that a certain sterility had overcome the presentation of the Christian faith. Forms which had been inherited from the Middle Ages no longer met the religious needs of sincere Christians. The problem was not merely one of remedying abuses, though this was certainly one aspect: it went deeper, for men were seeking for greater depth in their own religious lives.

For some time there had been widespread criticism of the abuses in the Church. People complained about the ignorance and immorality of the lives of clergy, of the weight of church taxes, of absenteeism of those who were charged with spiritual responsibility, of laxity in monasteries and nunneries, of the awarding of lucrative church posts to foreigners. These were all things which ordinary people saw every day, and which impinged on their lives in practical fashion. In addition, there was the scandalous behaviour of Popes, which included their entry into battle fully armed at the head of their military forces, as well as the deplorable character of some of their lives in private. Savanarola protested about these scandals in Florence and succeeded in persuading many people to support his puritan reforming programme: he was burnt for his pains in the Signoria, the main square of his own city, in 1498.

Another tension which had made itself clear was that between the superstitious devotion of the uneducated people and the attitude of the growing educated and intellectual class. It had the effect of tempting the authorities to exploit superstitious beliefs by action which disgusted those with sincerity and intelligence. This was seen in the controversy about indulgences which occasioned Luther's best known public action.

## Luther

Luther himself illustrated most of these sides of the reforming movement. He was a religious figure of immense power and a certain crudity. There is no doubt that his message sprang in the first place from his own religious needs. He himself had found that his religious experience did not bear out the claims made by the authorities of the Church, nor did it give him what he needed for his own spiritual growth. He suffered from a feeling of guilt, and he found that the sacraments of the Church, as he knew them, did not succeed in giving him the assurance of forgiveness which he craved. He himself was a monk of the Augustinian order, and there he had deeply studied both Augustine and St. Paul. Through the Augustinian emphasis on free forgiveness and love, based on St. Paul, he found the assurance which the formal structure of the Church's ministrations had failed to provide.

The immediate occasion of Luther's movement was the sale of indulgences. This was being promoted all over Europe in order to pay for the rebuilding of St. Peter's in Rome. An indulgence was a supposed guarantee that the temporal penalties due for sin were remitted, and it was thought that this guarantee could be applied to souls in purgatory as well as those at present living. At the time when these indulgences were being peddled Luther was on the teaching faculty of the university of Wittenberg, and on 31 October 1517 he nailed on the door of the Schloss Kirche in that city a statement of ninty-five theses against the use and sale of indulgences. It is not to be supposed that Luther had the slightest intention of starting a wide movement, or that he had any idea of what the results of his action were going to be. The posting of notices on the door of the church was the usual way in which disputations were announced, and there was no reason to suppose that this particular occasion was thought to be out of the ordinary. But it was a significant moment, as it was the first time Luther came out publicly in opposition to the Church authorities.

In a letter written to Albrecht, Archbishop of Magdeburg and Mayence and Markgrave of Brandenburg, Luther explained his attitude in the matter, and probably thought that reasonable and sincere men would all agree with him. His letter contained these remarks:

'With your Electoral Highness's consent the Papal Indulgence for the rebuilding of St. Peter's in Rome is being carried through the land. I do not complain so much of the loud cry of the preacher of Indulgences, which I have not heard, but regret the false meaning, which the simple folk attach to it, the poor souls believing that when they have purchased such letters they have secured their salvation, also, that the moment the money tinkles in the box souls are delivered from purgatory, and that all sins will be forgiven through a letter of Indulgence, even that of reviling the blessed Mother of God, were anyone blasphemous enough to do so. . . .

'In addition, reverend father, it has gone abroad under your name, but doubtless without your knowledge, that this Indulgence is the priceless gift of God, whereby the man may be reconciled to God, and escape the fires of purgatory, and that those who purchase the Indulgences have no need of repentance.'[1]

These few words of Luther revealed the essence of the matter quite clearly, for, although it is possible for a subtle theologian to make some defence of indulgences, there can be no doubt that the picture which Luther painted of the common beliefs was accurate. Yet his protest would probably have been no more regarded than those of many others but for the particular combination of circumstances at that moment. Luther found himself with a growing volume of support for his attitude of criticism and, probably unwillingly at first, he became a symbolic figure of resistance against the Pope's authority and of the expression of popular discontent. Together with this popular support, Luther was backed by the Elector Frederick of Saxony. Although in theory the Empire still existed, in fact its power had been divided among the separate kingdoms of Germany, whose rulers were sufficiently independent to take a line of their own if they wished. Frederick wanted to support his own university, and was perhaps not unwilling to embarrass the scheme to raise more money for church dignitaries out of the pockets of his own people. In religious matters he was influenced by his chaplain Spalatin, who was a close friend of Luther.

The Church authorities determined to silence Luther and to see that he was condemned, and set the machinery in train for this purpose. In 1518 he appeared at Augsburg before the Dominican Cardinal Cajetan, who based his complaints on Luther's defiance of the Pope's authority rather than on any criticism of indulgences. Luther did not retract as he was ordered and, finding himself in direct opposition to the Pope, he appealed from him to a General Council of the future. In the following year, 1519, he took part in a public disputation with John Eck at Leipzig on behalf of his fellow professor at Wittenberg, Carlstadt. This event was an academic disputation in the familiar style of the time, but it led Luther, in opposing Eck, not only to question the decisions of the Pope but also to admit the fallibility of General Councils of the Church. Leipzig was near enough to Bohemia to remind him of John Huss and his scandalous condemnation and death by the authority of the Council of Constance.

By his criticism of the external authorities of the Church, both Pope and General Council, Luther found himself forced to rethink his own attitude. It brought forcefully to his mind the antagonism between the authorities of the Church as he knew it and that of the Bible. In the following year, 1520, Luther wrote three of his most influential treatises which launched the Reformation on its course throughout Europe—'To the Christian Nobility of the German Nation', 'On the Babylonian Captivity of the Church', and 'The Freedom of a Christian Man'.

## Appeal to the State

In the first of these he frankly appealed to the secular powers against the Pope . . . 'Poor Germans that we are—we have been deceived! We were born to be masters, and we have been compelled to bow the head beneath the yoke of our tyrants, and to become slaves. Name, title, outward signs of royalty, we possess all these; force, power, right, liberty, all these have gone over to the Popes, who have robbed us of them. They get the kernel, we get the husk . . .'[2] His doctrinal point of view was expressed in the second of the treatises. It was meant for theologians and was written in Latin. Together with the first, it formed a two-pronged attack, appealing to men of intelligence and independent spirit in State and Church. Several of his friends tried to get Luther to suppress his first treatise to the nobility, but the effort came too late to stop publication. Luther had written, as he was often to do later, in a style which was more powerful and unrestrained than he himself realised.

His second treatise on the Babylonian captivity was a criticism of the sacramental system of the Church as it was then presented. Luther himself was not in any way negative in his attitude to the sacraments. Indeed, his turn of mind was rather conservative, as can be seen when he is compared with other continental Reformers. But he rejected the way in which the sacraments were presented, and wished to retain only three as the basis for normal Christian life. He dedicated this work to Professor Hermann Tulich of Wittenberg, to whom he wrote on 6 October 1520: 'Eck and Emser opened my eyes as to the Pope's sovereignty; for although at first I maintained his right to the human title, I now see that the Papacy is the kingdom of Babylon, and the tyranny of Nimrod, the mighty hunter. I must now go and lecture on giving the sacramental cup to the laity, and deny the seven sacraments, retaining only three—Baptism, Repentance, and the Lord's Supper, in all which the Roman Court has imposed a miserable captivity upon the Church.'[3]

Luther was extraordinarily gifted. He was not moderate in speech, however, and some of his expressions are not only lacking in taste, but quite disgusting. Had he been a moderate man, either in thought or word, he would not have exercised such an influence. It is of interest to note that Henry VIII of England wrote a refutation of Luther's work on the Babylonian captivity and earned from the Pope the title *Defensor Fidei*, which, like the pallium still appearing on the arms of the Archbishops of Canterbury, is still used as a title by the sovereigns of England, although it has no possible connection with the meaning which it originally bore. Besides Luther's religious power and mastery of strong language, he was a brilliant hymn writer and musician within his limits. The hymns which he wrote had an enormous strength of language, and his tunes exhibit a parallel strength of musical line. For his own protection he was hidden in the castle at Wartburg for eight months. He was taken there after appearing at the Diet of Worms in 1521, called by the Emperor, where he again refused to recant. It was a pregnant time, for out of those months came Luther's translation of the Bible into German, an event of vast influence on the development of the German language. He used popular speech, and for the first time the Bible came alive in a language which spoke directly to the minds and hearts of the German people.

1524 to 1526 were the years of the peasants' revolt. In this Luther had begun by trying to mediate, but had ended by an ill-judged and over-stated condemnation of the peasants, whose rising had been provoked by miseries and grievances which were all too real. Luther's pamphlet on the subject encouraged the Protestant princes to put down the revolt ruthlessly. Its tone and contents lost him much sympathy. In consequence of these political developments, taken in conjunction with his open defiance of and condemnation by the Pope, many who shared his critical views drew back from open identification with his cause. His party was becoming more clearly organised. It was now a definite Protestant movement supported by certain political authorities which for one reason or another wished to see it succeed. Luther's followers were first called Lutherans by their opponents; but they adopted the name for themselves after 1530, when the confessional document known as the Confession of Augsburg or *Confessio Augustana* was framed. This document has been accepted by all the Lutheran churches as their basic statement of doctrinal belief.

Lutheranism established itself as a church organisation in Germany and conquered Scandinavia. It spread also to a limited extent in south-eastern Europe, especially among the Slovaks; and it was later taken by the German barons into the Baltic states of Estonia and Latvia, where it remained the dominant form of the Christian religion. The main reformer in Sweden, Olaus Petri, was studying in Wittenberg at the time when Luther first placed his theses on the church door, and he was therefore in close touch with events from the start. There had already been a Catholic reform movement in Denmark and Sweden, and among the Reformation strands Lutheranism had almost a monopoly of influence in Scandinavia. At that time Norway was ruled from Denmark and Finland from Sweden, and the Reformation penetrated through the two key countries. In Sweden the powerful personality of King Gustavus Vasa (1523–60) was decisive, for it was his decision to use the Reformation to break the power of the episcopate in Sweden and to establish a national church. He succeeded in keeping a continuance of episcopal ordinations in Sweden, for the new Lutheran bishops were consecrated by those who had been themselves consecrated under the papal régime. In Denmark and Norway, however, there was a break of consecration, although the structure and office of episcopal government was preserved in their churches. All the bishops in Denmark and Norway were deposed in 1537 and their successors were consecrated by Johannes Bugenhagen, a priest who was a close collaborator of Luther's.

The word 'protestant' derives from the protest which a group of German princes put forward at the Diet of Speyer in 1529. At the time they were linked in a political league, called the Schmalkaldic league, which was ready to fight against the Emperor and the Catholic powers. It was within this framework that the Protestants found freedom to order their religious life and to set up new church organisation. It is not to be supposed that religious motives were those which chiefly influenced the action of the Protestant princes, and one must recognise that there were Catholics on the other side who did not wish to see the complete defeat of the Protestants or their total disappearance.[4]

## Zwingli and Calvin

In Switzerland the Reformation began in Zürich under the leadership of Zwingli. He was an admirer of Erasmus and, like many others of his time, highly critical of the Church. But it was partly the effect which Luther was having in Germany which helped to launch the reforming movement in Zürich. Zwingli was by no means a follower of Luther in the doctrinal sense, but the influence of a successful revolt in Germany showed men that action could be effectively taken to put their ideas into practice. Zürich was a free city, and Zwingli's reforming activities were given the full support of the city council, who rejected the attempts of the Bishop of Constance to restrain them. In all the reforming actions economics played some part of more or less importance, and in the case of the cities which revolted against Rome there is no doubt that the acquisition of church property and revenues was a strong encouragement, though many saw in their removal from church use a form of public duty.

F

Zwingli's form of teaching was at variance with Luther's, and it was not long before the differences became obvious. In his teaching on the Lord's Supper, for example, Zwingli upheld a view that it could be interpreted in an exclusively symbolic fashion, whereas Luther upheld the less radical doctrine of consubstantiation. In 1529 at Marburg attempts were made to reach an agreement between the two views, but it proved impossible, and Zwingli's views spread to other centres in his own country.

Calvin, the greatest of the Swiss reformers, was French in origin. He was prevailed upon to stay and become a minister in Geneva when passing through in 1536, but his first stay lasted only until 1538, when he was temporarily expelled from the city. Geneva had accepted reform under the guidance of Farel, who was a preacher but no organiser. Calvin, who had been trained as a lawyer, had an extremely orderly mind which expressed itself not only in lucid exposition but also in organisation. He saw his task in Geneva as being to apply in church and civic affairs the principles of Christian living which he derived from his theology. He had a remarkable power in the city from 1541, when he returned to Geneva after exile, until his death in 1564. Geneva was a city of refuge for many Protestants, primarily from France but also from places as far away as Scotland. In 1554 John Knox was at Geneva in flight from the rule of Queen Mary in England. Two years later he came to Geneva again, and he was English chaplain until his return to Scotland in 1559. He was influenced deeply by Calvin's theology and outlook.

The zeal of the Reformers did not include any attempt at tolerance. Both in Zürich and Geneva heretics were executed for their heresies. In the former an Anabaptist was put to death by drowning, and in Calvin's Geneva Michael Servetus was burnt as a heretic in 1553 because of his views on the Trinity. Men were convinced of the truth of their views and were determined to enforce them if they could. So in Geneva there was a Protestant version of the claims which the papacy had earlier made. Calvin did not rule Geneva, though his influence was immense. But the principles on which Geneva was governed were that the civil power ought to enforce on the population the standards of life which were derived from the doctrine of the Reformers: and to a large extent this was done.

Calvin's *magnum opus* was his 'Institutes of the Christian Religion'. This work originally appeared in Latin, and was succeeded by enlarged editions at various later stages of his life. His original views were influenced by another reformer, Martin Bucer of Strasburg, though the logical and systematic way in which they were expressed and developed was his own. His opinions about the sacrament of the Eucharist were neither Zwingli's nor Luther's but somewhere between the two. But Calvin and Calvinism are best known for their great emphasis on the power and omnipotence of God, which led adherents to the conviction that, as God knows all, he knows who will and who will not be saved. This led further to the teaching that not all, but only the elect, were destined or created for salvation. This led to the view that some men are predestined to salvation and others to condemnation, a doctrine which not unnaturally roused great opposition, as it is difficult to fit it in with any convincing doctrine of the love of God.

The doctrine of predestination is expressed in Calvin's *Institutes* in the edition of 1559 quite clearly: 'By predestination we mean the eternal decree of God, by which he has decided in his own mind what he wishes to happen in the case of each individual. For all men are not created on an equal footing, but for some eternal life is pre-ordained, for others eternal damnation. . . .' Not all Calvinists were later content to accept such teaching, and it was denied by Calvin's more moderate successors in various parts of Europe, such as the Arminians in Holland some years later.

All the reforming movements appealed to the New Testament to justify their attitudes and actions. Printing and vernacular translators had made the Bible more and more available to ordinary people as well as to scholars. All could now refer to the Scriptures to judge for themselves what was said there. This appeal accounted for many of the differences of view among the Reformers, since there was no one agreed method of interpreting the documents, and no authority recognised as binding in such interpretation. Some observers have considered this confusion to be nothing but a calamity, whereas others have taken the view that it was a happy result of a proper freedom. The truth certainly lay somewhere between these two opinions.

The movement of Christian man and woman out of a condition of ignorance into one of new knowledge can only be regarded as welcome, in spite of the difficulties which accompanied it. The same process has been repeated in different circumstances throughout

history. Every advance in human thought, knowledge and poten-
tialities has brought with it new openings for fuller living, but at the
same time intense difficulties of adjustment. It has taken decades, and
in some cases centuries, for men to adapt themselves to new conditions of life. It could be said that the confusion which sprang out of
the Reformation in the West inaugurated a period of adjustment
which has not yet finished in the twentieth century, and may well
continue beyond it. The differences of opinion therefore should not
be regarded as tragic failures, but as an inevitable stage of developing
understanding and insight.

The dispute at the Reformation between Catholic and Protestant
has often been represented as that of private judgment versus the
authority of the Church. This is a superficial way of regarding it,
and to adopt such an interpretation can only falsify the real questions
at issue. It may be shown as a difference between those who were
prepared to submit to the Church and those who were not. But,
whichever decision was taken, it was equally a matter of the private
judgment of the person in question. It is impossible to take away the
right or power of private judgment without destroying the essential
humanity of man. In every case private judgment was exercised, but
it reached different conclusions.

In appealing to the New Testament it is not surprising that there
was a great variety of opinions, for the documents comprising the
New Testament are themselves representative of many uncoordinated
elements. By a process of selection it was possible to derive from the
Scriptures almost any doctrine which appealed to the person who was
examining them. In this way there came into being different convictions about the ministry of the Church, which have continued ever
since. Some rejected the Pope as unnecessary or anti-Christian, and
retained the bishops; some retained bishops without thinking the
apostolic succession of ordination to be important; some retained
merely the name, and made them into general superintendents,
sometimes changing the title; some thought bishops altogether
undesirable and abolished the system in favour of a congregational
method of ordination; some thought there should not be any separate
order of ministers at all. There were adherents of views which covered
the whole spectrum of opinion. These differences became particularly important when men's minds turned to trying to achieve
greater unity among Christian bodies.

But variations did not merely concern the ministry of the Church. They also affected questions of infant baptism and rebaptism. The Reformation produced a number of different groups who fixed upon the question of baptism as the main issue. Some disapproved of infant baptism and maintained that only believers' baptism was countenanced in the New Testament, a view for which there is a good deal of evidence. They refused to recognise children's baptism and insisted on believers' baptism for all their adherents. For this reason they were known as Anabaptists (rebaptisers), and such groups were found in Germany, Switzerland, Bohemia and the Low Countries. They were fiercely denounced by Luther, Zwingli and Calvin, and persecuted on all sides, Protestant and Catholic. Among them were groups known as the Swiss Brethren, Hutterites, Mennonites and Socinians. Anabaptists were one of the earliest proponents of toleration,[5] a natural reaction of a small group which was undergoing severe persecution. In later times the name Anabaptist became a term of reproach, and for this reason was repudiated by the Baptists, who, however, maintained many of the original doctrines.

The Anabaptists and Baptists did not succeed in gaining strength sufficiently to 'take over' any one country, but remained a minority in many countries of Europe. The Calvinists became particularly strong in France, Holland and Hungary, as well as Switzerland, with strong minorities elsewhere, especially in western Germany. The name 'Calvinist' when applied to churches is synonymous with 'Presbyterian' and with the word 'Reformed' when used as a title of a church.

### English Reformation

If it is true that in some countries the Reformation was a political revolution with religious consequences and in others a religious revolution with political consequences,[6] events in England certainly place it among the former class. The development of the Reformation in England followed a different course from that in any other country, reflecting the peculiar traditions of an insular State, and in particular the position and attitudes of the crown. Nevertheless, the same basic elements were present in England, and its close connections with the Continent, especially in religious matters, meant that it was open to influences of thought which had their centre abroad. Professor Chadwick even affirms that until the end of the sixteenth century there was not a single English theologian 'whom we should naturally regard as an original and constructive thinker'.[7] Yet this did not mean that English churchmen were unable to think clearly about the issues being debated throughout Christendom. They viewed them with a certain detachment, and, as has been seen in other eras, they did not commit themselves wholeheartedly to any of the great figures. Certainly English religion was deeply influenced by Calvin and Luther and others, but it did not, like Scotland, ally itself with one against the rest. The influence of Huguenot and other Protestant refugees from the Continent had important effects on English economic life as well as on religious attitudes.

The power of the king in England was undisputed and unchallenged. He ruled Church and State without any objections either from his subjects or from the Pope. Henry VIII, who occupied the throne from 1509, was popular, and the power of the nobility had been greatly weakened by the Wars of the Roses, leaving the King without serious rivals. In his religious outlook Henry was conservative, and interested in theology. We have already noticed that he wrote a tract against Luther and was rewarded by the Pope for his effort. While Cardinal Wolsey was in power in his reign a policy of conservative reform was initiated in church affairs which had included the dissolution of some smaller religious houses. As papal legate, Wolsey had dealt with most church cases which might otherwise have gone to Rome, and had thus to some extent encouraged a feeling of self-sufficiency in the ordering of church affairs at home.

Crisis arose when Henry wished to get rid of his wife, Katharine, who had been unable to provide him with a son and heir. She had been his brother's widow, and for this reason it had been necessary to obtain a dispensation from the Pope for the marriage, since it was within the forbidden degrees. Use of the word 'divorce' in this connection is misleading, since it was not a divorce but an annulment which Henry was seeking. He was in fact wanting a ruling that the marriage had not been permissible in the first place, and that therefore it never had been a true marriage and should be regarded as being non-existent. He asked the Pope to annul the marriage for which he had originally given permission, but the Pope at the time was more or less a prisoner in the hands of the Emperor Charles V, Katharine's uncle. Henry, because of the Pope's refusal to do as he asked, accepted the suggestion of Thomas Cranmer, to appeal to the universities for an opinion; but this was not of much use. The death of Archbishop Warham of Canterbury enabled Henry to appoint Cranmer as his successor, who at once 'heard' the case and gave judgment as the King wished. Katharine was supplanted by Anne Boleyn, whose love affair with the King doubtless induced him to press the matter to a conclusion whatever the consequences.

This event began the Reformation in England, and it continued as a rather unpleasant mixture of political expediency, royal tyranny and greed, *force majeure* exercised on the clergy, the robbing of the Church and its institutions of their riches, and an appeal to nationalist sentiment. But in spite of this unholy mixture, there were real and powerful religious elements at work too, such as were growing on the Continent. It is not to be supposed that most Englishmen thought that they were starting a new church: they certainly were of the opinion that they were engaged in a work of reform, and the continuity of offices and structure which was a mark of the English Reformation undoubtedly expressed in most men's minds the reality of what they were doing. The Church was being reformed of abuses in its life and practice, and was being freed from foreign interference and usurpation.

Henry would not have been able to pursue his independent course had it not been for influential support in the nation. An important element was the Pope's claim to interfere with freedom of trade in which many Englishmen were directly or indirectly engaged. In 1493 Pope Alexander VI had purported to award to the Spanish monarchy large parts of the world, not yet conquered or annexed. England, in an expansionist frame of mind with its growing power at sea, was in no mood to acquiesce in the alliance of the Pope with its chief rival.

One of the means by which ideas were spread from one country to another was through refugees. England during the sixteenth century was the home of successive waves of refugees, who changed their character according to who was in power. And the changes which took place under Edward VI, Mary and Elizabeth in their turn sent Englishmen scurrying to the Continent for safety until the present dangers had passed. The Italian Peter Martyr and the German Martin Bucer were only two of the continental theologians who held influential positions in English universities.

In 1529 a parliament was elected which earned the name the Reformation Parliament. It would be an error to suppose that it was representative in the sense that we attribute to a modern parliament. More than half its members were royal officials, and many of the rest were appointed by the direct influence or favour of the King. It was therefore a body of men likely to be pliant to the royal wishes. From the start the King's financial interest in changes became apparent by the transference to him of payments in connection with wills and with pluralities. This was followed by a monstrous tax upon the clergy for accepting Wolsey, the former favourite, as papal legate. These steps preceded the annulment of the King's marriage.

### The Pope Rejected

In 1534 the King took steps to break entirely with the authority of the Pope and to set himself up in an undisputed position in Church as well as in State. Three years earlier Henry had forced the submission of the clergy upon them, and it was now embodied in an act of supremacy. In their submission the clergy had been forced to recognise Henry as 'especial Protector, only and supreme Lord, and, as far as the law of Christ allows, even supreme Head'. The limiting phrase was significant, and evidently left loopholes wide enough for almost any conscience. Henry never explicitly claimed, indeed he repudiated, spiritual powers, but when the Act of Supremacy was passed all qualifications were omitted. 'Be it enacted by authority of this present parliament, that the king our sovereign lord, his heirs and successors, kings of this realm, shall be taken, accepted, and reputed the only supreme head in earth of the Church of England, called *Anglicana Ecclesia* . . .' and it went on to spell out the powers which he would exercise in this capacity. The phrase *Anglicana Ecclesia* is not new, having been used to describe the Church of England in *Magna Carta* of 1215. It witnessed to the belief that no new church was being set up, but the old one reformed.

The members of the Church included people who reacted in many different ways. It is fair to guess that most of them had mixed feelings; they were glad to have their national independence proclaimed in Church as well as in State, but they were uneasy at the direction in which things seemed to be going. There were good men who were able to accept the Act with clear consciences, but there were others who were not. Among those who resisted were the finest spirits of their time, notably Bishop John Fisher of Rochester and the former Lord

Chancellor of the land, Thomas More. Both were executed for treason in 1535, and many others suffered a similar fate.

But when all is considered one has to admit that the change took place with remarkably little disturbance, even allowing for the pressure and threats which accompanied it. This bears a silent witness to the fact that many Englishmen were not sorry to see the power of the Pope transferred to English hands and the revenues of the Church prevented from going abroad. Henry promoted as his agent Thomas Cromwell, an unscrupulous character, who could be relied upon to carry out his orders even beyond the letter. He was given the office of Vicar-General with wide powers in Church matters. By a second Act of Annates in 1534 these papal revenues were taken by the crown and a method of appointing bishops was instituted, which has continued in the Church of England ever since. By this method the sovereign sends to the cathedral body a *congé d'élire* or permission to elect, but at the same time directs them to elect his nominee under penalty of severe punishment.

In 1536 the lesser monasteries were confiscated by the crown after a series of damaging charges, many of which were patently exaggerated and some of them untrue. It was, however, true that the condition of the religious houses left much to be desired. Their wealth and the character of some monastic lives did not accord with the principles on which they were founded and the purposes for which they existed. They were certainly open to damaging criticism. Had this not been the case, Henry's plans might have met with less success. In 1537 the greater monasteries met the same fate, and vast wealth became free for the disposal of the King. In this latter year Henry's actions against the monasteries provoked a revolt in the north of England, which became known as the Pilgrimage of Grace. It met with some initial success, but subsequently its leaders were arrested and executed. With the suppression of this opposition there was nothing which could stand in the way of Henry's depredations.

The march of events was not hindered by the action of the Pope. In 1535 he issued a bull which perhaps was never promulgated because there was no means of putting it into practice. But it made a break which was to be fateful in the coming years, and it exhibited just that use of spiritual means to attain secular ends which caused men to turn away from the papacy, and which confused the issues in an already confusing situation. The bull, issued by Pope Paul III, was called *Ejus qui immobilis* and was dated 1535. It declared Henry to be excommunicate and anathema, and the children of Henry and Anne to be deprived of all dignities and honours. And the bull continued: 'And all the subjects of the same king Henry we do absolve and utterly release from their oath of fidelity, from their allegiance and from all kind of subjection to the king and the other persons aforementioned. Commanding them nevertheless, on pain of excommunication, that they utterly and entirely withdraw themselves from obedience to the said king Henry, his officials, judges and magistrates, and do not regard them as superiors, nor obey their commands.' The same thing was to be repeated in 1570 against Queen Elizabeth. It was this sort of action which identified the Pope in people's minds as a national enemy and made Roman Catholicism seem in itself a treasonable attitude which could not be tolerated. Subsequent events were to harden this attitude of hostility still further.

It is not the purpose of this study to follow the details of the English Reformation, but to observe those facts which militated against or towards unity among Christians. The basic assumptions which were accepted by all at that time were that nationality and religion went together, and that whatever religion was adopted by the State would as a matter of course be enforced through the powers of the State. Henry VIII was succeeded by the young Edward VI, under whom the Church went further towards a Calvinistic form of religion than at any subsequent time, but his reign lasted only six years, and in 1553 the whole process of Reformation was violently reversed by the accession of Mary, who was personally an ardent supporter of the papacy and who was bitter about the maltreatment of her mother Katharine, which had been closely bound up with the rejection of the old religion. The bishops who had been deprived were restored, but Parliament, when it met, refused to sanction the return to the Church of the property which had been forcibly taken from it. There was much hostility to the proposed marriage of Mary with Philip of Spain. Mary spoiled her own case by the hardness and obstinacy of her character. She was unable to do things in a way which would retain support, and her policy provoked rebellion. She adopted a severe policy of persecution against the Reformers: heretics were burnt again and included such names as Hooper, Ridley and Latimer. Cranmer himself met his end bravely after being frightened into recantations which did him no credit, but which he withdrew before the end.

## Elizabethan Settlement

Elizabeth succeeded in 1558 to a condition of great complexity and danger. It was her skilful management which welded the nation together, and her policy gradually established the Church of England in a settlement which proved permanent. She changed the title 'supreme head' to the less odious form of 'supreme governor' and pursued a policy which would appeal to men of moderate opinion and common sense, thus encouraging an arrangement which would be conservative in its outlook and church order, while accepting the main teachings of the Reformation. The ancient order of ministry—bishops, priests and deacons—was retained; the more extreme expressions of Protestantism were removed from the Communion Service, eucharistic vestments were permitted and the forty-two articles of Edward VI were reduced to thirty-nine. Another switch of bishops took place, and those who would not comply were replaced by others whom Mary had removed.

Matthew Parker was chosen to be Archbishop of Canterbury and was consecrated in due form by four other bishops. Later, a tale known as the 'Nag's Head Fable' was put about, namely that his consecration had been an irregular sham which had taken place at a tavern in Cheapside. No reputable historian now accepts this tale, and its importance consists only in the fact that for a long period it was a weapon in the armoury of Roman Catholics who wished to prove that the Church of England had no right to claim a valid ministry depending on the apostolic succession. Disputes about the status of the ordained ministry have been an important part of inter-church strife, particularly important to Roman Catholics, whose teaching about the sacraments made them depend for their content and reality on the correctness of their celebration and on the status and validity of the minister who celebrated them. The question of apostolic succession was only one of the essential elements of a valid ministry, but without it all the sacraments dependent on the minister were doubtful or worse.

The ecclesiastical settlement was supported by the Act of Uniformity, which ordered the general use of the Prayer Book in 1559. It should, however, be noted that though the Act was passed by

Parliament, the Convocations, the only church authority in spiritual matters, were not consulted, and that in the House of Lords all the spiritual peers voted against the Act. It could hardly claim, therefore, to have any authority but that of the State. All clergy were required to use the book on pain of losing their positions and being imprisoned for six months. For a third offence imprisonment for life was laid down. Penalties were also provided for speaking against the book, and the laity were ordered to attend the services or to be fined if they had no proper excuse for absence.

This Act expressed in legal form the assumption which everyone took for granted, namely that within one nation everyone was expected to belong to the same church and to share in the same religious observances. This idea was to cause immense trouble in the coming years, and it combined elements of national and religious character, such as have been observed in other connections. After the events of the preceding reigns there was under Elizabeth a considerable group on both wings of the Church which objected to the Act of Uniformity on grounds of conscience. On one side were the Roman Catholics, and on the other the Puritans, the former rejecting the Protestant character of the Church of England and the latter resisting its Catholic elements. A number of the clergy belonged to the Puritan section and conformed as little as possible with the hope of getting things changed or 'purified' in the direction of Calvinism. As yet there was no specifically Anglican theology. Nor did such come into existence until the end of the sixteenth century with Hooker.

For some years those who disobeyed were allowed to continue without repressive measures. But in 1566 Archbishop Parker issued his 'Advertisements', which attempted to lay down a minimum observance of ceremonial, including vestments. The controversy on the subject of dress in church, known as the Vestiarian Controversy, had begun in the reign of Edward VI and became acute again with Parker's action. The dispute led to a definite schism from the Church when a group of Independents met in London and formed the first congregational organisation, so called because they held that each congregation had the power to decide all religious questions and to ordain its ministers. Thus began an important strain in English religion which was to grow to considerable strength and to exercise great influence, especially later in North America.

For a hundred years and more until the Toleration Act of 1689 the struggle to enforce religious uniformity continued, and introduced into English religious life a spirit of hatred and enmity. The seventeenth century was to see this spirit bring disaster to the whole of the country when mixed with civil and political tensions. Roman Catholics were regarded for the most part as traitors, or at least potential traitors, an attitude which was greatly strengthened by the ill-fated expedition of the Spanish Armada. English Roman Catholics played a full part in the defence of their country, but in the average English mind foreign invasion and plots against the established order became unbreakably associated with the profession of obedience to the Pope. Papists suffered severe persecution, which forced them to hide or fly the country, and this in turn confirmed their identification with foreigners in the minds of their fellow countrymen. The Pope had called upon France and Spain to drive Elizabeth from the throne, and he must bear considerable responsibility for the unhappy results for his followers and for deepening division among Christian people.

## Counter-reform

The cause of truth and historical perspective has suffered much in debates between the churches: *odium theologicum* spiced with misrepresentation is not a good recipe for a sense of perspective. From some pamphleteers one would suppose that the dissolution of monasteries was a peculiar crime of Protestant princes led on by personal greed; but there was dissolution elsewhere too. In Spain some religious houses were dissolved as a form of internal Catholic reformation, and their wealth devoted to other purposes such as hospitals. In England some of the monastic wealth benefited education as well as the private pockets of political promoters.

Some kind of reform would have come, within the papal obedience, whether the Reformation had arisen or not. The activities and successes of the Reformers brought matters to a head and caused that reform to come in a way which had disadvantages as well as good points. For when reform did come within the papal church, it was inextricably mingled with the need to resist the Reformers outside the Church and to meet the requirements of propaganda and ecclesiastical power politics.

The power politics which involved the Church were inevitably closely affected by the manoeuvres of the political powers of the day. If Protestantism was being promoted by Protestant princes in alliance against their enemies the best way to resist it seemed to be an alliance of Catholic rulers to extend their own sway, and, in doing so, to enforce observance of papal authority. This development, of necessity, strengthened the hands of secular rulers within their own countries vis-à-vis the Church, since it was to them that church leaders looked for the furtherance of their cause.

## Council of Trent

Pressure mounted in favour of the calling of a General Council of the Church. Eventually such a council met at Trent in 1545. It had three main phases and continued intermittently for nearly twenty years, concluding only in 1563. It was of vital importance to relations between the Roman Catholic Church and other churches, since it fixed the main lines of Roman Catholic thought for four centuries and shaped the Roman Catholic attack on the status of other Christian churches. It succeeded in many of its aims at internal reform, though it did not go as far as most Protestants would have wished. But in any case it came too late to affect the formation of separate churches by the Reformers who had broken away from the Pope. Protestants were present at the middle session of the council 1551/2, but their demands could not be, and were not, met.

Trent repudiated the Protestant principle of appeal to the Scriptures as the sole source of authority in the Church. Scripture and tradition were set side by side as authorities to which obedience should be paid. '. . . this Synod receives and venerates, with equal pious affection and reverence, all the books both of the New and the Old Testaments, since one God is the author of both, together with the said Traditions, as well those pertaining to faith as those pertaining to morals, as having been given either from the lips of Christ or by the dictation of the Holy Spirit and preserved by unbroken succession in the Catholic Church. . . .'[8] It rejected doctrines of the Eucharist emanating from Luther, Zwingli or Calvin, and restated the doctrine of transubstantiation. In its decisions about justification and merit it was totally opposed to the truths which Protestants were trying to express, and it affirmed the need of all seven sacraments for salvation.

Had the council been held earlier, it is not impossible that it might have reached an agreement with the Protestants who wanted reform but who did not wish to found new church organisations. But it was too late. Trent did much to make the papal church into a better and more efficient body and introduced a new spirit of earnestness. The rise of new orders, in particular the Society of Jesus, betokened fresh vigour and determination. But, for better relations among Christians, it was not only a failure, it was a disaster. Nevertheless, the root of the trouble did not lie primarily with the council but with the principle on which it rested, namely that there was only one true Church and that this was the Church which was under the authority of the Pope. Consequently, all those who called themselves Christians outside that obedience were no more than dangerous heretics.

The activities of the Jesuits were militant and chiefly devoted in Europe to the extirpation of heresy, one of the main objects for which they had been founded by Ignatius Loyola. They earned for themselves a name of abhorrence, not only among their opponents, but among others too, by their doctrines and their actions. Equally obnoxious to Christian sentiment was the Inquisition, which used torture to force men to forswear their beliefs and to embrace the authority of the Church. Torture had been first authorised by the bull *Ad extirpenda* of 1252, though it had been used long before that date. In the sixteenth century the infamous work of the Spanish Inquisition was to become a byword of cruelty. It was not finally suppressed until 1820.

The numbers of persons who suffered from the Spanish Inquisition was large but restricted. Torquemada is calculated to have burnt about 2,000. But the moral and psychological effects made a breach between Roman Catholics and other Christians which has not yet been healed. This was made worse by the horrors of forceful conversion in countries where princes of the Counter-Reformation were in power. In some countries, like Poland, Protestantism made considerable progress, but then was rooted out by the accession of a Catholic prince and the work of the Jesuits. In France serious attempts were made to find a means of agreement between the two groups, but they were smashed by Catherine de Medici through the murder of the Protestant leader, G. Coligny, and the massacre of St. Bartholomew on 23 August 1572. Fierce wars of religion continued in France until they were ended by the Edict of Nantes in 1598, which brought reasonable toleration until its revocation in 1685.

The consequences of the European struggles for power, which were complicated by rivalry between Spain and France, between Spain and the Netherlands, and by such political aims as the preservation of the power of the papal states, were that western Europe was divided in bitter rivalry between Catholic and Protestant, which penetrated deep into political and national as well as religious consciousness. The attitudes of the two parties to one another were governed for the next several centuries by the burning memories of the evils which they had respectively suffered—the massacres, the tortures, the injustices and the martyrdoms—these were the memories which formed the picture which each had of the other side.

## Uniatism in Europe

At the end of the sixteenth century a significant event occurred in the policy of the Roman Catholic Church, which was to introduce a new concept into church relations. In the development of Polish religion away from Protestantism back to Catholicism there was an attempt to end the eastern schism, represented in Poland by substantial numbers of Eastern Orthodox Christians, especially in the south-east of the country. In the manoeuvres of the struggle for power the question as to which side the Orthodox would take was of some importance. In the end most of the Orthodox bishops were persuaded to abandon the obedience of the Patriarch of Constantinople and to submit to Rome. They did so under an agreement that they would keep their own Byzantine rite and religious practices while submitting to the Pope. These included a married clergy and communion in both species.

This step had negative results of some importance in making a serious obstacle to understanding between Rome and the Orthodox. Although the participating bishops certainly knew what the Union of Brest–Litovsk of 1596 meant, it is highly unlikely that the ordinary people shared such understanding. For them the services remained much the same, the same clergy continued to minister in the same churches, and there were very few signs that there had been any change. The only outward evidence was that instead of the name of the Patriarch of Constantinople, that of the Pope was mentioned in the liturgy. But, as both these hierarchs were quite unknown to them and did not in any way impinge upon their religious lives, they had little interest in such a change. To other Orthodox churches the Union seemed to be the worst kind of religious seduction and deceit, for it appeared that their faithful Orthodox people had been persuaded unknowingly to sell their souls to the Pope while thinking that they were still carrying on the traditions of their forefathers.

On the other hand, the Union represented an implicit claim by the Pope that the only true Christians of the Byzantine rite were those who accepted his authority. Unless this were the case, there could be no point in the Union. Moreover, it also implied that there was only one way of ending the eastern schism, namely submission to papal authority. These implicit, and sometimes explicit, claims inevitably made a wider breach between East and West.

Yet there was another more positive aspect. The introduction of a uniate church into the papal fold carried with it the principle of unity without uniformity. This was not altogether new, for local rites had for long been recognised by Rome, and there had been Byzantine churches under papal jurisdiction for centuries in southern Italy. But the creation of a new church in this way meant that Latin could not logically be thought essential to the Catholic liturgy, nor could the habits of western religious life and the discipline exerted there be claimed to be more than a temporary and local phenomenon. In later years—much later—this was to be a means of breaking down the narrowness of Roman Catholicism when it tended to identify true Catholicism with the Latin rite and with western Catholic customs.

Although this union was formed in Poland, it never succeeded in practice in uniting in Poland itself Catholics of the western and eastern rites, who continued to be hostile to one another, although both were under the Pope.

## Scottish Developments

Events in Scotland followed a course quite different from that of England. In the sixteenth century the country had suffered severely in wars with England, and in its reaction against its more powerful neighbour Scotland had allied itself with France, a conjunction which was highly objectionable to the English. Scotland was a poor and remote country, but its inhabitants had the virtues associated with those who find life difficult: they were brave, persistent and independent. In Church affairs the leading lay figures of Scotland had great influence, and many of the chief families had members who were prominent in ecclesiastical offices.

The story of Scotland's conversion to the Reformation is closely associated with the personality of John Knox, who, as has already been noted, spent some years in Geneva and came much under the influence of John Calvin. The divisions between the strict Calvinists and the Church of England had not yet hardened, as may be seen from the offer of the bishopric of Rochester which was made to Knox. He declined the proposal.

The course of events was intermingled with political and dynastic questions. Many of the Scots disliked dependence on France as much as dependence on England. Mary, Queen of Scots, the half-sister of Elizabeth, married the heir to the French throne in 1558. That year Elizabeth came to the throne in England, and in opposition Mary proclaimed herself the rightful Queen of England.

There were therefore elements making up a complicated mixture in which religion played an important part. First there was the personal rivalry between Elizabeth and Mary. Within Scotland itself was to be found resentment both against England and against France, and a party which wanted to promote the Reformation had already been formed. The alliance of Mary with the ruler of France meant a political and military combination of great danger to England, made worse by the fact that France represented the Catholic and England the Protestant cause. In this situation those supporting the independence of Scotland saw as one of its forms the establishment of a Protestant church, different from that of the Church of England, and independent of it.

In Geneva Calvin had already abandoned the traditional form of Christian ministry, and had no bishops. John Knox took the same attitude, and this fitted in well with the nationalist trends in Scotland. It is impossible to measure how far its difference from the polity of the church in England swayed the Scots to regard Presbyterian polity with favour, but it is unlikely that it played no part at all. John Knox returned finally to Scotland in 1559, and just over a week later preached the reformed faith in Perth, with the result that the monastic establishments in the town were destroyed by the crowd. This was a declaration of war against Catholics and French. In the following year, in alliance with the English, the French forces and those fighting with them were defeated and a treaty agreed which debarred French forces from Scotland. Knox had been the leader in resisting those on the side of Rome, and he had been the rallying point for the forces which overthrew them. The Scottish Parliament adopted the doctrines of Calvin as the official creed of the country, repudiated the Pope and made the saying of Mass a capital offence.

In church matters Knox applied to the whole of Scotland the principles which he had learnt in Geneva, attempting to adapt them over a wide and disjointed area. Each parish was to have a minister with elders responsible for discipline, in agreement with the congregation. It has been pointed out that although this is called presbyterianism, it had in some respects a resemblance to primitive episcopacy, in that each minister was a kind of bishop and exercised the powers which bishops had in the early Church. This system was set up by 'The First Book of Discipline', which was compiled by Knox and five collaborators. It covered much more than ecclesiastical organisation. It was followed in 1578 by a 'Second Book of Discipline' composed by Andrew Melville. Both of these books depended for their implementation on support from the civil power, which was by no means forthcoming, so that neither was ever completely enforced. Nevertheless, the first book set up the framework of Scottish religion, which was to endure as the main expression of Christianity in Scotland for succeeding centuries. A 'Book of Common Order' was approved by the General Assembly for public worship in 1564.

Knox himself died in 1572, 'having influenced not merely the religion but the character of the nation more than any other man in Scottish history'.[9]

[1] M. Currie, *The Letters of Martin Luther*, London, Macmillan, 1908, pp. 18–19.
[2] Bettenson, *op. cit.*, pp. 275–6.
[3] Currie, *op. cit.*, p. 57.
[4] Owen Chadwick, *The Reformation*, Pelican Books, 1964, p. 63.
[5] Rouse and Neill, *A History of the Ecumenical Movement*, S.P.C.K., 1954, p. 29.
[6] Chadwick, *op. cit.*, p. 97.
[7] *The English Church and the Continent*, London, 1959, p. 61.
[8] Bettenson, *op. cit.*, p. 365.
[9] Williston Walker, *A History of the Christian Church*, Edinburgh, Clark, 1959, p. 373.

# 8

## Growth of Protestant Life

### Theological Debate and Reorganisation

THE Church in England at the beginning of the seventeenth century
illustrated a religious situation which had not yet hardened, as it
had on the continent of Europe, into the identification of certain
religious views with clear political attitudes. Calvinism, as it had
developed in Geneva and elsewhere, had become associated with a
form of political organisation which supported government without
monarchy. It had become closely tied with the new class of bourge-
oisie, arising through the increasing importance of trade, and it was
undoubtedly an expression of the new-felt power of which this class
was beginning to be conscious. Elizabeth in the second half of the
sixteenth century no doubt sensed this, and was therefore anxious
that it should not become the prevailing outlook in England and thus
undermine her own sway. The Church of England had been set up
and encouraged under the direct control of the monarch, an arrangement which not only suited the sovereign's political book but also
brought the crown great economic gains. The keeping of sees vacant
and the appropriation of their revenues to the crown was a useful
source of income, and was practised on a considerable scale, as was
shown in the cases of Ely, Bristol and Oxford, which between them
provided Elizabeth in sum with a total of ninety years of episcopal
revenues.

When Elizabeth died in 1603 there were only two groups which had
not been successfully kept within the national Church, the Roman
Catholics and the Independents, the latter as yet a very small group.
The Church itself was an amalgam of varying opinions, by no means
clearly delineated. But the policy of the first two Stuart reigns
achieved just what Elizabeth had avoided, dividing the national

Church into warring factions, and splitting it into churchmen and Puritans. At the beginning of the century groups were still forming of those within the Church who by tradition or personal temperament supported tendencies, either High Church or Puritan. The split was the outcome of the ecclesiastical policies of James I and Charles I. Certainly before this Puritans promoted their own ideas and tried to persuade others to support them, but differences were not permitted to come to a break, and the personal influence of the Queen doubtless weighed heavily in favour of religious peace.

*Puritan Pressure*

The dissatisfaction of the Puritans with the Prayer Book became at once apparent when James I ascended the throne. Even before he reached London on the way from Scotland he was presented with a Puritan petition, the Millenary Petition, asking for changes in the customs required by the Prayer Book. But, when in 1604 the Hampton Court Conference met to discuss the matter, James discovered that the real aim of the Puritans was to change the Church of England completely and to substitute a Presbyterian form of government for episcopacy. James, who had come from Scotland, had not found Presbyterianism there to his liking, and his reaction to it showed how it was in his mind associated with the absence of monarchy. His phrase 'No bishop, no king' put the point succinctly, and his action in disbanding the conference put the principle into practice. The only lasting contribution of the 1604 conference was the production of the so-called 'authorised' version of the Bible of 1611, generally known outside England as the 'King James' version.

The Puritans continued their campaign by bringing pressure on the King in parliament. James was not skilled in dealing with practical affairs, although he was cultured and learned. It was his incapacity in practical matters which caused Henry IV of France to describe him as 'the wisest fool in Christendom'. Moreover, he did not rightly understand the English, having himself been brought up in Scotland: England had not at that time become accustomed to being controlled by Scotsmen. He did not carry the personal authority of the Tudor monarchs, and the pattern of the country's wealth and power was shifting from the hands of the aristocracy into those of the middle classes.

Meanwhile the position of the Roman Catholics deteriorated

through the participation of some of them in plots to influence or to overthrow the Government. These activities culminated in the 1605 Gunpowder Plot to blow up Parliament. Up to this point James had been leaning towards greater tolerance for Roman Catholics, but any chances of moves in that direction were indefinitely put off. The plot made a permanent impression on English minds far beyond its importance, as can be seen from its continued yearly celebration three and a half centuries afterwards. Those events set back the position of Roman Catholics and identified them even more plainly as enemies of their country in the minds of the people. Legislation of a penal character was soon afterwards enacted: and a new oath of allegiance was enforced, including the statement that the doctrine of the Pope's power of deposing princes was 'impious, heretical and damnable'.[1] The situation has been summed up as follows: 'In the country at large the division between the Catholics and the rest of their fellow-countrymen was widening. A proportion of the squires' families of the old religious tradition returned to a strict practice, but the children of the Elizabethan "Church Papists" who did not take this course were gradually assimilated to the full Anglican position. And the Puritan feeling against Rome was growing strongly with all the vitality of that doctrine which has always possessed a curious detached integrity and an unrivalled power of focusing animus. This horror of Rome, perhaps concentrated on the Jesuits, was also characteristic of wide Anglican circles and it seems indisputable that this sentiment was growing during the first forty years of the century.'[2] The increasing success of Roman Catholics in regaining lost territories on the continent of Europe did nothing to assuage the fears of those who had known attempts from the Continent to conquer England and Scotland not many years earlier.

The differences of view between the Puritans and the middle-of-the-road members of the Church of England reproduced in some ways the disputes which were being conducted on the Continent between the extreme and moderate Calvinists. Jacob Arminius (Hermann), a Dutchman, opposed the pitiless logic of Calvinist teaching about predestination, and upheld the reality of free will in men. Because Arminians were in opposition to the main Calvinist body in Holland, they were suspected of being in league with Spain, the traditional enemy of Holland, another example of why and how religious opinions aroused fierce enthusiasms: men were not capable of believing that a religious opinion was not expressive of some definite political outlook. Arminian doctrines were discussed at the Synod of Dort in 1618–19, at which a number of English theologians were present, and the teaching was there condemned. The Arminians or Remonstrants were thus compelled to leave the national church of Holland. Their opinions were moderate and liberal, and in spite of their condemnation they continued to have considerable influence on later Protestant thought. So far as England was concerned, the decisions of the Synod of Dort were formally accepted and supported by James I, but they did not prove to have the power to halt views which were more and more coming to the fore among Anglican divines.

## Anglican Britain

During the seventeenth century an Anglican position was developed in relation to Romanism, on the one side, and Puritanism, on the other, and as time went on Anglican attitudes came more and more to be identified with the interests of the monarchy against those of parliamentary government. In broad terms the Church of England was for the king, so far as that church could be identified with the new Anglican thought and the conservative traditions of episcopal government and the Prayer Book, while those who wished to overthrow these elements were gradually developing not only into a coherent religious opposition but into a political opposition which eventually became an armed revolt against the crown. At first the struggle was concentrated on trying to gain the governing influence within the Church of England itself, and was thus an internal strife for power. But with the clear alliance of the parliamentary forces with Scotland, and with the Presbyterian system there established, a new situation developed.

The position of Anglicans gradually formed itself into an attitude which was to mark the Church of England in succeeding centuries, differing from that of any other church which had separated from Rome. Leading Anglican thinkers claimed that their church was no new church: it was the Catholic Church of the land, continuous with that which had been founded by the earliest missionaries: it had never abandoned the Catholic faith, but merely reformed and purified it: it appealed to the early fathers of the 'undivided' Church for its doctrinal standards; and it maintained the Catholic order of the Church in the form of bishops, priests and deacons.

This approach was not merely theoretical and theological: it went deep into the outlook and devotion of the Church's members. In Bishop Lancelot Andrewes, Nicholas Ferrar, George Herbert and others it produced fine flowers of devotion, piety and poetry. It valued the liturgical traditions of the Prayer Book and those outward ceremonies which caused most irritation to the Puritans. The leaders of this new Anglicanism were immensely learned, and their works breathed a spirit of reason and scholarship, besides making notable contributions to English literature by their style and content.

Charles I, who succeeded his father in 1625, was thoroughly in sympathy with these Anglican religious outlooks, and did all he could to support them. But at the same time he acted in a way which more and more alienated the sympathy of his subjects, especially the elements which were becoming more powerful as time brought increasing possibilities of trade. His method of raising revenue caused resentment and opposition.

## Archbishop Laud

But the worst calamity was Archbishop Laud, appointed to the see of Canterbury in 1633. He was a man of clear ideas, many of which would commend themselves to men of sense, but he had no notion how to put them into effect or to commend them to others. If he had been less clear, intelligent and efficient he would have been far more wise and have avoided untold harm. He was determined to enforce the requirements of the Prayer Book in outward forms of worship throughout the country, and he thought he could do this by sheer force. He was not himself narrow-minded, but he gave the impression of being so, and he tried to force men to conform to religious practices which they did not want and to which some of them were conscientiously opposed. By doing this he brought ruin to his church and king, and created a running sore of hostility between Church and Presbyterians which has by no means disappeared, even in the second half of the twentieth century.

The first serious trouble came with the Scots, and here again we may see how religious differences and enmities, when combined with ancient national rivalries, intensified hostility. Laud issued a new prayer book for the Scots in 1637. Up to that time the Scots had admitted a mild form of episcopacy, but against this new measure they rebelled, uniting themselves in a Covenant, and provoked what is known as the 'First Bishops' War' in 1639. Nothing very warlike happened in it, and in the next year it was followed by the 'Second Bishops' War', in which the few inadequate troops which Charles had managed to send were thoroughly defeated at Newburn.

All this trouble involved Charles in expense, the funds for which he could only secure from Parliament, which was extremely hostile to him. The same policy which had caused revolt in Scotland was making Laud and the King enemies in England among the many members of the church who objected to Laud's policy, and especially to the use of the Star Chamber to punish those who opposed it. The stage was being set for the final tragedy. In Ireland in 1641 a Roman Catholic rising took place, followed by ghastly massacres which did nothing to reassure the king's opponents in England, who thought they themselves might be subjected to the same medicine.

Civil war ensued, ending with the defeat and the beheading of Charles. Laud himself had been executed in 1645, Charles followed in 1649. Both died thinking that their cause was that of church and country, and both were regarded by many as martyrs. Both of them believed in the divine right of kings, as did many of their followers. This was the belief that a king in the hereditary line of succession had an absolute right to the loyalty of his subjects, whether he were a good or a bad ruler. If he were a bad one this was a punishment for past sins. To rebel against the king was to rebel against God. Almost all leading Anglican writers upheld this notion during the seventeenth century, and though it seems extraordinary to a modern man, there is no reason to suppose that it was not held sincerely. As has been amply demonstrated, in earlier centuries men found it impossible to distinguish between what they believed as Christians and what they believed politically and nationally, the two aspects being inextricably part of one another.

### Differing Opinions

The development of Anglican doctrine was one result of church life in the seventeenth century, but it also produced in England a Puritan statement of great import for subsequent generations. In 1643 there met at Westminster an assembly of divines for the purpose of organising the Church of England on the basis of Presbyterian principles. It produced the 'Westminster Confession of Faith' which laid down the basis for such organisation. Later in the century, when in 1689 the

Episcopal Church in Scotland was disestablished by the parliament of that country, this confession became the official formulary of the Presbyterian Church of Scotland, and remained so for subsequent centuries. It followed the Calvinist doctrine of election to salvation or damnation, and it maintained the distinction between the visible and invisible church, which held that the true church was invisible and known only to God. Moreover, it put great stress on the identi-fication of Sunday with the Jewish Sabbath and applied to it the restrictions which were to be found in the Old Testament. The charac-ter of the Scottish Sunday was to be much affected by this peculiar theory. It also adopted the theory of the total depravity of man, in its article IX of Free Will—'Man, by his fall into a state of sin, hath wholly lost all ability of will to any spiritual good . . .'[3]

The first part of this century also saw the organisation of the Baptist churches, the first of them appearing in London in 1612. They and those who joined them were known as 'General Baptists', and their theology was somewhat Arminian. But later, in 1633, some strict Calvinists adopted the practice of believers' baptism and be-came known as 'Particular Baptists'. Like others who formed small minorities and who had no chance of acquiring control of political power, they had no temptation to try to persecute their opponents, and became advocates of a policy of toleration and freedom of con-science. Seven London congregations in 1646 drew up a confession of faith following the Calvinistic teaching about predestination.

An important though little noticed event early in the century was the departure of a small group of independent Christians from England to North America. In 1620 a group of rather more than 100 persons sailed from Plymouth in the ship *Mayflower*, landing in Massachusetts in December of that year. They had originated in two separatist churches in Lincolnshire in the early years of the century, some of whose members had fled to Holland in 1608. On reaching America they established the colony of Plymouth and set up their own form of religious practice. They had fled in order to gain freedom to worship in the way they wished, and it is an interesting sidelight on the psychology of their day that they saw nothing strange in imposing by law their form of worship on others in the territories which they controlled in the new world. This group is known as the 'Pilgrim Fathers'.

*Efforts for Unity*

The spread of reform, and with it the increase in division among Christians, were not the only tendencies to be seen in the century after the Reformation. When separations occurred it was not long before men of far-seeing Christian view began to try to bridge the gulfs which religion exhibited, and to work for better understanding and cooperation. After the Reformation there were attempts to make new contacts with eastern Christendom and to forge links between Protestants in the West and Orthodox in the East. Even before the Reformation there had been efforts to make contact between the Utraquist followers of Huss (sc. those who advocated communion in both kinds for the laity) and the eastern church authorities. It came to nothing, but the Greek Church leaders showed themselves willing to enter into discussion with western Christians after the breakdown of the temporary agreements reached at the Council of Florence.

Lutherans also made attempts to enter into negotiations with the Orthodox during the second half of the sixteenth century, both from Sweden and from Germany. Tübingen theologians had correspondence with the Patriarch Jeremiah II of Constantinople, but this was prematurely published by a Polish priest as a weapon in the struggle of his own country against Protestant ideas and came to nothing. The most interesting character of this period from the point of view of Orthodox relations with the West was the Patriarch Cyril Lukaris. He had been in Poland during his early years, and in 1602 at the age of thirty was made Patriarch of Alexandria, a post which he held for eighteen years before becoming Patriarch of Constantinople for another eighteen. In Poland he had engaged in vigorous opposition to the Roman Catholic Church, and when he returned to his own church he wished to promote many reforms of which it stood in need. Lukaris entered into correspondence with the Dutch Minister, and also through the British Ambassador at Constantinople with Archbishop Abbott of Canterbury, sending his chaplain Metrophanes Kritopoulos to Oxford, where he studied for five years. Later he presented to Charles I the famous *Codex Alexandrinus* (an early fifth-century manuscript of the Bible in Greek) which now reposes in the British Museum. In 1629 Lukaris published a confession of faith over his own name which caused a sensation, for its Protestant tendencies caused much opposition among some of the Orthodox.

The career of Lukaris was interrupted by exile or deposition on four occasions as a result of his enemies' intrigues. He was finally brought to a tragic end by the action of Roman Catholic agents, by whom he was trapped, strangled and buried ignominiously in a pauper's grave. In a judgment on his life Archbishop Germanos of Thyateira wrote, 'Perhaps he may have failed to reconcile his duty as the Primate of the Orthodox Church with the exigencies of high politics and with his aims as spiritual leader of his nation.'[4] Lukaris remained for centuries a Greek national hero, regarded as a martyr for the faith.

Lukaris began a process which brought the East once more into touch with the theological climate of the West, and his ideas formed the subject of constant discussion and controversy during the following century. Peter Mogila, Metropolitan of Kiev, strongly opposed Lukaris's standpoint, whose views were finally repudiated by the Synod of Jerusalem in 1672, findings which are considered basic documents for the understanding of the Orthodox faith, ranking as one of its five 'Symbolic Books'. Two of the other Symbolic Books also come from the same period—'The Confession of Metrophanes Kritopoulos' of 1625 and 'The Orthodox Confession of Mogila'. The Acts of the Synod of Jerusalem were accompanied by 'The Confession of Dositheus', Patriarch of Jerusalem, written to correct the views of Cyril Lukaris. Some of these Orthodox documents show certain Latin influences which many later Orthodox would repudiate.

Generally speaking, the seventeenth century was a period during which Christian divisions hardened, both those between Protestants and Catholics, and those between different Protestant confessions. But this negative tendency was relieved by efforts made by individuals from time to time, and in the first half of the century two personalities are of special interest, one a Roman Catholic and the other a Scottish Protestant.

### Christopher Davenport, Friar

Christopher Davenport was brought up in an Anglican middle-class family, and educated at Oxford, where he was admitted to Merton College in 1613 at the age of seventeen or eighteen. His brother John was also at Oxford at the same time. Whereas John became a Puritan, Christopher at some stage became a Roman Catholic. It is not known exactly at what point his change of allegiance took place, but in 1616 he was admitted to the English College at Douai, remaining there for only one year. He then joined the Franciscan order at Ypres in 1617. He adopted the name Franciscus a Sancta Clara and showed himself extremely able both in practical affairs and in academic work. It is not necessary to follow his career except to note that he went to England, reportedly as one of the chaplains to Queen Henrietta Maria, the wife of Charles I. Here he made himself well liked and had numerous and friendly connections with people in high station, both in Church and State. He moved easily in court circles and had contact with Laud and other leading churchmen.

At the time the Roman Catholics in England were divided among themselves between those who regarded everything Anglican and official with complete hostility and a more moderate group, who were anxious to show their loyalty to their own authorities in the State and to come to a *modus vivendi* so far as relations with the established Church were concerned. Davenport identified himself with the moderates and worked hard to try to create a better understanding with Anglicans. But he did more than this; he tried to initiate discussions which would lead towards reunion between the churches, and with this aim in mind he wrote a study of the Thirty-Nine Articles in order to show that they were not incompatible with the faith of the Catholic Church.

This remarkable effort appeared as an appendix to a larger work with the title *Deus, natura, gratia*, in which he spoke in favour of peaceful reconciliation. In his own words: 'I have laboured as you see, pious reader, to reconcile the articles of the Anglican Confession with the decrees of the Roman Catholic Church. I thought that men ought to be brought back to the Church in which (by the aid of the grace of God) they must be saved, not the church whence they have fallen off. . . . But in these newfangled expressions, I beheld Christ divided . . . who would not mourn such a sight? Who would not advise reunion? Who would not persuade it by every means he could?'[5] The book appeared in 1634 and was dedicated to Charles I. Davenport made attempts to have the book licensed for printing in England, but was not successful because of the opposition of the Archbishop of Canterbury.

His attitude to the Articles is the first evidence of the great liberty of interpretation which was possible in accepting them with Catholic presuppositions. A great number of them were simply stated to be Catholic doctrine—fifteen—without qualification. The others were in some cases considered to be inadequate, or needing to be understood in one particular sense, but there was almost nothing which was a final obstacle to their acceptance when rightly understood. Indeed, his interpretation of them anticipated by some centuries a point of view which was to be adopted by Anglicans of the Catholic tradition when justifying their own formal acceptance of them before ordination in the Church of England. For example, in Article XXVIII Davenport held that 'the authors of the Article are condemning, as does the Catholic Church, the old heresy of the Capharnaites which claimed the carnal presence of Christ in the Sacrament'.[6] And in Article XXXI he maintained 'that this Article says nothing against the Sacrifice of the Mass but only the false opinion—false to both sides—that the Mass is a sacrifice independent of the Cross'.[7]

Davenport lived until 1680, and both during the Commonwealth period and after the Restoration remained in England to try to keep relations reasonably good. But his efforts towards reunion failed to advance matters at that time. Protestant interpretations won the day. The reawakening of a Catholic interpretation had to await the nineteenth century, when the insight of Christopher Davenport was to be justified, not by an outsider seeking reunion but by Anglicans themselves seeking a fuller and richer understanding than a Protestant interpretation alone could provide.

### John Dury, Presbyter

The other enthusiast was a Scot named John Dury. He was born in 1596, and he died at Cassel in the same year as Davenport, 1680. Much of his early life was spent on the Continent, where he acquired a knowledge of languages studying at Leyden University. From there he went to a French Huguenot academy, and probably returned again to Leyden after several years there. In 1624 he spent some months at least at Oxford, where he learnt about the Church of England. He became a Presbyterian minister at Dort in Holland, to qualify to minister to an English and Scottish congregation at Elbing in West Prussia. The Swedish conquest of Elbing under Gustavus Adolphus involved it in the attempt, encouraged by the Swedish king, to further a union of Protestants, and Dury's contact with Dr. Caspar Godemann, a Swedish Privy Councillor, turned his mind to the whole subject of Christian unity.

Sir Thomas Roe, the English diplomat, visited Elbing in 1629, the same ambassador who, when in Constantinople, had had close contacts with Cyril Lukaris, and who had tried to promote better relations between the Orthodox and Anglican churches. Roe took Dury up and encouraged him in his reunion interests, seeing the Church of England as a possible middle man in the reconciliation of the churches.

Encouraged by Roe, Dury went to England in 1630, where he had a rather cold reception and found the atmosphere in Church and State not particularly favourable to a union of Lutheran and Reformed churches on the Continent, though the Church leaders offered some modified encouragement. From 1631 to 1633 he was travelling continuously on the Continent from one conference to another trying to bring the Protestant churches closer together, though his efforts were weakened by the death of Gustavus Adolphus in 1632. He then returned to England and had further discussion with Archbishop Laud, who told him that if he wanted to speak on behalf of the Church of England he would have to receive episcopal ordination. Urged by Roe to comply, Dury agreed and was ordained in Exeter Cathedral on 24 February 1634. In justifying his action Dury wrote: 'As for the Church of England. . . . I did look upon it as a Church of Christ, true in respect of the doctrine professed therein, and eminent for all spiritual gifts bestowed upon it; that I judged the government thereof by bishops with indifference and that I took them as men commissioned by the king to be his delegates.'[8] But he did not receive from Laud the support in his plans which he had been led to expect. He returned to the Continent in 1634, but was back in England before the end of the year.

Soon after his return he visited Scotland and interviewed leaders of the Scottish church, but he was not unnaturally viewed with some suspicion by convinced Presbyterians after his re-ordination in the Church of England. He continued to work indefatigably, in spite of financial difficulties, and travelled incessantly from one country to another, going next to Holland and Sweden. He persuaded the professors of theology at Uppsala to put down the conditions on which they would be willing to unite with those of the Reformed tradition, though, when they did so, the conditions appeared to be aimed more at hindering than promoting such unity.

Dury protested at the execution of Charles I. Although this caused suspicion among the new rulers, Dury continued his work for unity, and in 1650 he supported the 'Engagement' of loyalty which the parliamentary government drew up as a pledge. This put him back on to the side of the authorities, and he was encouraged and used by them, undertaking the translation into French of Milton's *Eikonoklastes*. Much of the period of the Commonwealth was spent by Dury on the Continent continuing his unity efforts; and on the restoration of Charles II to the throne Dury sent the King a letter proposing methods for 'treating about peace and unity in matters of religion between the Episcopal and Presbyterian parties'. The new authorities responded, however, by dismissing Dury from his position as library keeper of St. James, which he had occupied since 1650, and so in 1661 Dury left for the Continent for the last time. He did not fail to continue his efforts for unity by interview and publications, and died after consecrating the whole of his life to the promotion of Christian unity.

Dury's story certainly included many misjudgments, and failures to see below the surface in certain theological disputes. Yet his life witnessed to a truth which was only too rarely seen during that period, and there is no doubt that, although he achieved very little in terms of formal agreement, he stimulated and kept alive in men's minds the importance of unity and understanding, at a time when it was at a discount in the religious world.

**Deism and the Enlightenment**

In 1648, the year before Charles I was beheaded in England, the Peace of Westphalia brought the Thirty Years War on the Continent of Europe to an end. It has been said that this marked the end of the wars of religion[9] and, although the truth of the statement may be granted in one sense, there is another sense in which religion was to continue to play a part in international strife. Men like to invest their wars with moral and religious justification, and under some guise or other they continued to introduce moral and religious justification for their warlike activities long after the seventeenth century. But specifically religious institutions had ceased to wield the political power which they had earlier possessed. By the middle of the seventeenth century the papacy was no longer able to enter the struggles of the political powers as an equal. It might fulminate, but any religious or military threats were no longer taken seriously, and this was an important change in the new national groupings.

If religion had ceased to have the same place in international rivalry, it continued within the various nations to be the ostensible cause of political and economic differences, and the expression of hidden struggles for power. A change was beginning to come in men's attitudes towards toleration, although intolerance was common enough. Yet the religious break-up stemming from the Reformation was to force toleration upon the churches and their members, whether they wanted it or not. The variety of men's religious convictions meant that there were minorities, sometimes substantial, in every nation which held beliefs contrary to the main religious body. There was still a general opinion that there ought to be one church for one state, and that each would benefit the other by its monopoly of ecclesiastical or political loyalty, but it gradually became more and more difficult to enforce such a principle against small groups which clung tenaciously to their own beliefs and practices. And so in time it became clearly the interest of the State not to antagonise groups, however small, whose members by a policy of tolerance could be turned into contented citizens.

It was the small groups who were the leaders of propaganda in favour of tolerance, for they had everything to gain and nothing to lose by it. Moreover, policies of repression were slowly beginning to show themselves ineffective, so that they had not even the merit of success to recommend them. Such developments did not mean that there was a cessation of struggle for power, either for religious or political ends. Toleration by no means carried with it the removal of all disabilities from minorities. At first it only stretched far enough to abolish actual threats to their life and liberty, though even this took time to develop.

In England the victory of Cromwell and the Parliamentarians over Charles I resulted in the establishment of a Presbyterian form of church order and the abandonment of the Book of Common Prayer. The Protector began with a lenient policy, and the 'Anglican' element (if they may now be so called) was faced with the problem of whether to acquiesce in the changes and influence them in a conservative direction from within or whether to adopt an attitude of open or concealed defiance. In the event, those who temporised with the new order gradually lost their influence as exponents of true Anglicanism, and the task of representing it fell on the active resisters in England and with the body of exiles who fled to the Continent because they

G

would not swallow Cromwell's church policy. These groups, whether in England or abroad, were the proponents of the 'high church' views which Archbishop Laud had held. Indeed, a study particularly devoted to this subject has used the term 'Laudian party' to describe them, though such a term is not an exact description.[10] Their policy was in essentials the same as that which Laud had so disastrously tried to enforce upon the nation.

### Anglican Restoration

The influence which this 'Laudian' group had upon the exiled Charles II and his ministers was decisive for the policy which his government followed when it was once more in power after the restoration of 1660. In its early manoeuvres it deceived and weakened the Puritan element in the church so that, when the critical moment of decision came at the Savoy Conference of 1661, the Puritan groups found themselves in a position of weakness, and the high-church Anglicans took complete control. They were supported by the Parliament which succeeded the 'Covenant Parliament' of the Restoration. But Parliament transferred the responsibility of enforcing conformity to the new Prayer Book from the crown and church to itself, and in doing so did away with the last vestige of the independence of the church. 'The political strength of the High Church party was bought with a price—the Church surrendered to Parliament its last shred of independence.'[11] An Act of Uniformity was passed requiring obedience to the Book of Common Prayer. St. Bartholomew's Day 1662 was the day on which conformity was required on pain of deprivation: its effect is known as 'The Great Ejectment', when more than 1,700 ministers left their parishes for other work or for other lands.

The Act of Uniformity was followed by other Acts which had the aim of enforcing conformity. By the Corporation Act of 1661 all holders of civil office had to be communicants of the Church of England; the Conventicle Act of 1664 made it an offence to attend any other religious meeting than those of the Church of England; in 1666 The Five Mile Act forbade any nonconforming minister to live within five miles of the place where he had previously worked; in 1673 the Test Act made it necessary for those holding civil or military office not only to receive communion in the Church of England but also to take oaths of supremacy and allegiance and to make a declaration against the doctrine of transubstantiation.

These ill-advised measures were taken with the aim of stamping out nonconformity. Their actual effect was to make a clear division between church and nonconformity which could never afterwards be bridged. The middle classes were on the whole the supporters of nonconformity, and the landowners and the poor stood by the church. These years saw the last serious efforts, doomed before they were taken, to force men into a pattern of religious belief and practice determined upon by the Government. Before the end of the century toleration was to take the first steps in a long onward march.

The Commonwealth period, besides establishing Presbyterianism, also saw the rise in strength of independent sects, especially the Congregationalists, descended from the Brownists and properly called 'Independents'. The Baptists had also grown in numbers, and, as is shown by the years in gaol suffered by John Bunyan, were subject to persecution after the Restoration.

In the middle of the seventeenth century the word Quaker was first used to describe the religious sect, later called the Society of Friends. George Fox organised them in England during the Commonwealth period, and they, too, suffered harsh treatment after the Restoration. They were open to oppression, since they refused to hold their meetings in secret. One of them, William Penn, in 1682 founded Pennsylvania in America as a settlement where Quakers could enjoy freedom of religious practice, and extend the same benefit to others. Their religious beliefs were founded on the basis of direct spiritual guidance without the aid of a visible church or outward observances.

The details of ecclesiastical politics should not be allowed to obscure the fact that the seventeenth century was important for its theological thought. Although religion was associated with many activities which had little connection with the pure milk of the gospel, yet it was immensely powerful in influencing men's minds. The shortcomings of their Christian views are always least obvious to those who hold them, but this should not lead us to underestimate the power of religious conviction. In their rebuttal of the Roman Catholic position Anglicans in the seventeenth century forged for the Church of England a point of view which held together traditional Catholic elements of order and outlook with reformed ideas; ministerial authority was given a place of significance combined with personal responsibility for individual judgment; reason was combined with an awareness of the limitations of theological speculation. It is easy to romanticise the balance of Anglican theology, yet there can be little doubt that it made a distinctive contribution to thought and practice, including within itself the English distaste for logical extremes together with a preference for moderation in practice.

The stress which the Church of England put upon the retention of bishops did not lead it to 'unchurch' those churches which lacked bishops, although Anglicans regarded non-episcopal Protestant churches as suffering a disability, perhaps through no fault of their own. Bishops, they held, were necessary to the perfection of a church, but not to its existence. Yet this high idea of bishops did not always produce the action which it seemed to require. Bishops in England during the Commonwealth period declined to take part in a plan for securing the continuance of episcopal consecrations, because of their political fears, and it cannot be said either then or later that bishops of the Church of England showed any particular desire to give episcopal care for the members of their own church in the Americas. The Church of England saw itself as maintaining a tradition of its own, which it did not feel called upon to extend to other churches, even if they originated as off-shoots of its own life. There was no conviction of a duty to promote episcopal systems elsewhere, and the idea that English bishops might have spiritual obligations overseas would have appeared strange to seventeenth and eighteenth century bishops in England, even though the Bishop of London had some theoretical responsibility for the spiritual welfare of members of the church abroad. The history of the Church of England somewhat weakens the force of its arguments for episcopacy in modern times.

*End of the Stuarts*

The reigns of the last two Stuart kings, Charles II and James II, brought a new crisis through their predilection for Roman Catholicism. Charles II was too fond of his own interests to act openly in a way to threaten his position: he had been in exile for long enough already. But his brother James II came to the throne with the definite intention of bringing back the old religion. The acts which had borne hardly on nonconformists of the Protestant sort also affected Papists, and indeed the Test Act of 1673 had been aimed against the latter. The Act required office holders to receive the sacrament of the Holy Communion and to take oaths of supremacy and allegiance. James II's efforts were ill-timed and unsuccessful. Their consequence was to put off until a much later date the toleration which might have been granted to Papists, and also to produce a schism within the Church of England itself.

James issued a 'Declaration of Indulgence' in 1687 which granted general religious toleration, but it was recognised for what it was, an attempt to make the country once more Roman Catholic. He had already shown his hand by his appointment of Papists to important offices in defiance of the Test Act. Because of his obvious purpose he found that the declaration was opposed not only by members of the Church of England but by other Protestants who objected even more strongly to his Roman Catholic policy, although they benefited greatly from the measure. The Indulgence was ordered to be read in all churches in 1688, and was resisted by seven bishops. These bishops were brought to trial and acquitted among scenes of public enthusiasm. A movement was organised to get rid of James, and William of Orange, the husband of Mary, James's daughter, was invited to accept the throne. When William landed in 1688 James fled, and William and Mary were declared joint sovereigns in 1689.

The Revolution was successful and the Protestantism of the throne secured. But this change in royal masters posed severe problems for those who had cherished a belief in the divine right of kings. It was difficult to square such a doctrine with change of sovereigns whenever it seemed politically desirable. Moreover, solemn oaths of fealty had been sworn to James II, and they were not compatible with the promises to William and Mary which were now required. Six bishops found themselves unable in conscience to take the new oaths. Among them were some of the best bishops in England, including William Sancroft, Archbishop of Canterbury, and Thomas Ken: they were joined by about 400 of the clergy. The Church of England thus lost some of its best elements at a time when they were much needed. The seceding ministers were known as Non-Jurors, and the non-juring schism persisted until the later years of the eighteenth century, when it gradually disappeared. Its members were unable to take any part in official church life, but nevertheless they made a notable contribution to the devotional life of the eighteenth century, among their most distinguished writers being William Law. As in many schisms, those who were turned out of their benefices regarded themselves as the true Church and looked on their supplanters as schismatics. But for most members of the clergy compromise seemed to be the lesser of two evils in the new situation.

The Toleration Act of 1689 greatly increased the freedom to worship as conscience might require, but it was still necessary for office-holders to abjure the Pope and the doctrine of transubstantiation, the mass and the invocation of saints, and to subscribe to most of the Thirty-Nine Articles. The last requirement was not a difficult hurdle, since the Articles were drawn with such latitude as to permit most Protestants to accept them, and the restrictions which continued against Roman Catholics were not surprising in view of the circumstances which had brought William and Mary to the throne.

## Jansenism

On the Continent in the seventeenth century a long-drawn-out dispute within the Roman Church had begun on the subject of Jansenism. Jansen, Bishop of Ypres, died in 1638, and five propositions from his book *Augustinus* were condemned in 1653. Jansenism was a combination of Augustinian theory with a strict form of religious life. It is best known because it caused Pascal to write his *Lettres Provinciales* in 1656, in which the moral casuistry of the Jesuits was unmercifully attacked. At this time the Church of France, referred to as the Gallican Church, was resisting demands from the Pope to control appointments to bishoprics and to enjoy their revenues during vacancies, and the Gallican Declaration of 1682 claimed independence for the Church of France in such matters. The dispute continued into the next century, when the papal Bull *Unigenitus* in 1713 once more condemned Jansenist teaching. But the movement was eventually defeated and the claims withdrawn.

The Jansenist controversy produced a permanent schism from Rome which has persisted to the present day under the name of the Old Catholic Church. There were many sympathisers with the Jansenists in Holland, and when Archbishop Codde became Archbishop of Utrecht the Jesuits launched a campaign against him which eventually persuaded the Pope to order him to be deprived of his office. But the cathedral chapters of Utrecht and Harlem refused to accept the decision, maintaining that the Pope had no right to remove an archbishop without trial. As a result of pressure from the Dutch Government, Codde was allowed to return from Rome in 1703, but he found that his people were divided between him and his opponents.

The differences between the Jesuits, who supported the absolute powers of the Pope, and the Dutch, who maintained the rights which the local chapters had always possessed, were never solved, and in 1724 the chapter of Utrecht secured the consecration of Cornelius Steenoven as their archbishop. The Pope was officially informed, but replied by censuring the action and declaring the election null and void. From that time the Old Catholic Church continued as a small group, divided from the Pope, but claiming doctrinal orthodoxy according to the Catholic faith.

At a much later date after the first Vatican Council in 1870 this church was joined by groups of former Roman Catholics in Switzerland, Germany and Czechoslovakia who refused to accept the decrees of that council on the subject of the infallibility of the Pope.

## Contacts with the Orthodox

The Jansenist controversy was the occasion for an approach to the Eastern Orthodox. The Russian Tsar, Peter the Great, visited Paris in 1717 at a time when the French Church was still engaged in disputes arising from the bull *Unigenitus*. A group at the university of the Sorbonne, known as the Appellants, opposed the Bull and looked for allies elsewhere. They approached the Tsar with a proposal for unity and embodied their proposals in a document which was despatched to Russia. But the reply was evasive and took refuge in the answer that the Russian Church could come to no conclusion on such a matter without the agreement of the other Orthodox churches.

At about the same period the Non-Jurors also made an approach to the Orthodox. There had been contacts with the Eastern Orthodox towards the end of the seventeenth century, when Gloucester Hall in Oxford was used as a college for the training of Greek theological students: it proved to be economically unsound and only lasted from 1698 to 1705. But it was evidence of a growing interest in the Christian East. The Non-Jurors wished to strengthen their position by linking themselves with a church of undeniable authority, and in 1716, as a result of contacts which had been made with him in England, the Metropolitan Arsenius of Thebais forwarded to the Eastern Orthodox Patriarchs the draft of an agreement from the Non-Jurors between 'the Orthodox and Catholic remnant of the British Churches and the Apostolic Eastern Church'. Its contents may be described in the words of a modern Russian bishop.[12] 'The principal idea of the draft was the establishment of communion in prayer and liturgy. The draft of the agreement drew attention to points where there was no divergence between Anglican and Orthodox believers as well as those on which the Anglican bishops (the authors of the draft) did not agree with the Orthodox Church. In addition the document proposed practical measures that ought to be taken if agreement were to be reached. In particular, the suggestion was made that a church called the Concordia should be built in London, subordinate to the Patriarch of Alexandria, where services would be held for British Catholics, and that a Greek bishop visiting London would have the right on certain days to conduct services in the cathedral church of London.'

The correspondence went on for some years, and the Orthodox authorities were friendly but cautious. It is difficult to know just how much they understood of the situation produced by the non-juring schism. In the end Archbishop Wake of Canterbury heard of the matter and wrote to the Orthodox authorities advising them to have nothing more to do with it. It is not difficult to see why he was not in favour of the scheme, for it would have made a number of complications which he was anxious to avoid. (The name 'Concordia', chosen for the projected church, was adopted in the twentieth century by the main Lutheran publishing house in the United States.) In his concluding message, Archbishop Wake assured the Patriarch of Jerusalem that Anglicans held the same basic faith as the Orthodox and expressed the hope that relations between them would not be diminished.

It is somewhat ironic that the settlement of 1662, which was intended to produce a national church based on episcopacy, should in the end have caused not only a schism with the Puritan element but also, because of its connection with the crown, a schism of the most high-minded Episcopalians. Archbishop Wake prevented the latter from strengthening their position by an agreement with the Eastern Orthodox, but he was himself ready to pursue closer understanding with Protestant and Roman Catholic alike.

According to Professor Norman Sykes, the 'outstanding innovation of the Anglican restoration settlement was the unvarying requirement of episcopal ordination for the ministry in whatever capacity in the church'.[13] This was the practical expression of the high-church point of view which triumphed in 1662. It did not necessarily carry with it any particular theory of the theological necessity of episcopacy, but it was commended as being in accordance with the oldest traditions of the Church and as the best form of church government. Later it was to acquire interpretations which gave it more importance, but, even as a practical measure, it made a clear division between Anglicans and Protestants, who did not value or did not possess such a ministry. One effect of the settlement was to cause churchmen to adopt different attitudes to non-episcopal churches at home and abroad. At home those who rejected the settlement and the episcopal ministry which went with it were schismatics pure and simple, and had to be treated as such. It did not necessarily carry with it any judgment about the spiritual values of their ministries: they were merely dissenters who were resisting the established order. Churches on the Continent, on the other hand, which at or after the Reformation had abandoned or lost the episcopal order were not regarded as schismatic, since they did not appear as rivals to the Church of England.

*First Signs of Toleration*

With the Toleration Act of 1689 considerable relief was gained by Nonconformists, as we have seen. It had been intended that the Act should be accompanied by a Comprehension Bill aimed at revising the Prayer Book in such a way that the majority of Nonconformists would be able to become members of the established Church *ex animo*. But in the event this Bill was not proceeded with, so that only part of the original objective was achieved. A revised Book of Common Prayer was actually prepared which would, in the judgment of a contemporary, 'have bro't in two-thirds of the Dissenters'.[14] Had this occurred, 'few but Baptists and Quakers would have remained outside the Establishment',[15] and the whole future of religion in England might have taken another turn.

The Toleration Act did not do away with tests for civil office, and occasional conformity with the established Church became an accepted custom. Many dissenters held office by occasionally conforming and receiving the sacrament in the established Church. One can hardly imagine a more unfortunate misuse of the sacrament of the Holy Communion than merely as a test for holding office, and the general effect of the practice must have been to lower the proper understanding of what the sacrament should mean within a Christian church. Those who conformed did so from a variety of motives. Some certainly did so merely as a means of gaining office, although they did not in their hearts want to do it. But there were a good many others who conformed with a good conscience. Their point of view was that although they thought it right normally to support some other form of worship, there was every reason to recognise the Christian character of other churches and to conform occasionally in the established church was not only a permissible, but even a desirable, expression of Christian fellowship.

In the eighteenth century the bishops were for the most part Whigs appointed by, and expected to support, the Government both in its ecclesiastical policy and also in its politics by their votes in the House of Lords. The clergy, on the other hand, were mainly high church and Tory, and showed themselves opposed to attempts to placate dissenters. They were entrenched in key positions in the parishes, not only in their capacity as spiritual leaders but also in the rights which they held as incumbents in the parish councils and the apparatus of local government, which was based on the parochial system.

Nonconformists found themselves in the position of second-class citizens, not actually persecuted for their religious practices, but made to feel outside the organs of power, whether local or central, and having to touch their cap to the established church and its officers if they were to be entrusted with any position of responsibility. Such a condition, which continued in theory until the repeal of the Test and Corporation Acts in 1828, goes far to explain the deep-seated hostility and resentment which dissenters felt (and still to some extent feel) against the Church of England and all that it stood for.

Eighteenth-century religion is often described as being weak and inadequate, but it produced men of considerable gifts, both in writing and in devotion. It may have been his position as a nonjuror that enabled William Law to see the divisions among Christians with rather more detachment than many of his contemporaries. He clearly realised that most men's theological opinions were formed by the atmosphere in which they were brought up rather than by any deep convictions reached on their own account. 'If you ask why the great Bishop of Meaux (Bossuet) wrote so many learned books against all parts of the Reformation, it is because he was born in France and bred up in the bosom of Mother Church. Had he been born in

England, had Oxford or Cambridge been his *Alma Mater*, he might have rivalled our great Bishop Stillingfleet, and would have wrote as many learned folios against the Church of Rome as he has done. ... Ask why even the best among the Catholics are very shy of owning the validity of the orders of our Church; it is because they are afraid of removing any odium from the Reformation. Ask why no Protestants anywhere touch upon the benefit or necessity of celibacy in those who are separated from worldly business to preach the Gospel; it is because that would be seeming to lessen the Roman error of not suffering marriage in her clergy. Ask why even the most worthy and pious among the clergy of the Established Church are afraid to assert the sufficiency of the Divine Light, the necessity of seeking only the guidance and inspiration of the Holy Spirit; it is because the Quakers, who have broken off from the Church, have made this doctrine their corner-stone.'[16]

The verdict of religious failure in the eighteenth century is often exaggerated, for, although there is evidence to bear out such a conclusion, there is also evidence to counterbalance it. A study of *Eighteenth Century Piety*[17] avers that contemporary documents show that there was no spirit of complacency. It was, moreover, a century which produced in the Methodist movement a notable effort at deepening religion through personal holiness which met with a widespread response.

### Archbishop Wake and Roman Catholics in France

But before proceeding to take note of the Methodists, another singular correspondence should be recorded. During his tenure of the archbishopric of Canterbury, William Wake entered into extensive contact by letter with Roman Catholics in France on the subject of possible closer relations between their church and the Church of England. It will be recalled that the beginning of the eighteenth century saw doctors at the Sorbonne resisting the papal bull *Unigenitus*, which forbade national independence in the control of the church in France. Gallicanism, as it came to be called, continued through the eighteenth century, and it was an aspect of this national point of view which came out in the correspondence with Wake. Archbishop Wake had himself a close personal knowledge of the church in France, for in an earlier period of his ministry he was chaplain in Paris to the English ambassador from 1682 to 1684, and had indeed written an eirenic reply to one of Bossuet's works. When he became Archbishop of Canterbury in 1716 he took up connections with Paris and started a correspondence with Ellies du Pin and Piers Girardin, two doctors of the Sorbonne. The letters were exchanged during the years 1718–20, and the most interesting and significant document among them was a commentary on the Anglican Articles of Religion by Du Pin called *Commonitorium*. Wake thought that full communion between the churches did not need agreement in all details of belief and practice, though he held that there must be acceptance of the first four General Councils; his aim was union without uniformity, and he was ready to make some concessions to this end. Du Pin, in his work, made concessions in his turn, saying that tradition 'does not set forth new articles of faith, but confirms and illustrates those things which are contained in the sacred writings, and defends them with new securities against those who think otherwise'.[18] He was ready to consider purgatory, images, relics and the invocation of saints as minor matters which need not be accepted by all. On such subjects as transubstantiation and the sacrifice of the Eucharist he made statements which could be accepted by many Anglicans, and he was not ready to say that Anglican orders were invalid. On the subject of the papacy he defined the papal primacy as being 'this right, to watch that the right faith is everywhere kept and the canons observed, and as often as they are violated to act in accordance with canon law to repair the evil. This is the sole jurisdiction which we ascribe to the Roman pontiff.'[19] He restricted the spiritual jurisdiction of the papacy to the diocese of Rome.

Although this correspondence was conducted by the Archbishop of Canterbury, it was kept secret, and the *Commonitorium* was only rediscovered in the middle of the twentieth century by Dr. Norman Sykes. Wake did not consult anyone else, and it is extremely doubtful whether he could have carried his fellow-churchmen with him in any practical proposals, had they reached the stage of implementation. On the French side the Archbishop of Paris, although he knew what was going on, studiously refrained from giving any statement which could be construed as approval for the attitude of the Sorbonne doctors concerned. The exchange came to nothing at the time, but was a foreshadowing of discussions undertaken 200 years later.

## Methodism is Spread and Organised

The eighteenth century in England was, above all, notable for the rise and consolidation of the Methodist organisation, the first Christian division of any size which arose exclusively from within the Church of England, and which has persisted in large numbers all over the world since that time. John and Charles Wesley were devout brothers who took their religion seriously, so seriously indeed that the word 'Methodist' was coined to describe their disciplined and regular life of religion. John Wesley lived from 1703 to 1791, and like his brother was an ordained priest of the Church of England and never thought of himself otherwise. He experienced an emotional form of conversion in 1738, though this occasion only brought to new power the convictions and attitudes which he already possessed. His life was of great interest and extraordinary activity, but it lies outside our subject of church relations.

John Wesley undertook an immense work of preaching throughout the country and, later, overseas. He went from place to place drawing great crowds, convincing men of their sin and the need to put their trust in God for their salvation. His preaching had a great success and was attended by scenes of great emotion. For the most part he drew the middle and working classes to hear him, and gave them a religious experience which they had been unable to find in the worship of the established church. He travelled an average of 8,000 miles a year on horseback, preached constantly and wrote vast numbers of letters as well as keeping a diary of his experiences. He often found himself opposed by the official representatives of the Church of England, although there were many exceptions.

Frequently Wesley was forced to conduct his preaching in the open air because the parish churches were not open to him. Yet he had no intention of starting a rival organisation to the Church of England. On the contrary, the societies which he founded were intended to be the handmaids of the ordinary work of the parish churches throughout the land. For the most part, however, the bishops were hostile and tried to prevent him from preaching. There was in the eighteenth century a great suspicion of 'enthusiasm' as it was termed, a word used to cover almost any emotional form of religion to which the speaker happened to object. A tale is told of a missionary going to India who was given the advice to preach the gospel and to put down enthusiasm wherever he found it. The temper of the educated world of that century was somewhat cynical about religion, and religion itself often took a dry and impersonal form. It was the century of deism, which pictured God as a divine watchmaker who, having made the clock and wound it up, left it to run on or down on its own. No doubt many of the leading churchmen absorbed something of this intellectual attitude without being aware of doing so.

But even more influential in the negative attitude which most church people took towards Methodism was the 'establishment' mentality, a point of view which has been a curse to true Christianity whenever it has appeared or survived. Bishops and clergy disliked Methodists because they seemed to be trespassing on their preserves. Thus bishops objected to John Wesley preaching because he was not licensed to do so in their diocese, and the parochial clergy doubtless feared that their own influence in their parishes would be lessened if semi-independent, and certainly much more vigorous, centres of Christian prayer and practice were set up within them.

It has sometimes been asserted that the Methodists had close affinities with the Anglicans of an evangelical persuasion, and even that they were two horses out of the same stable. But historical evidence does not bear this out, and it seems that the evangelical clergy were quite as hostile to Methodist activities as their brethren of different views. Methodist religion was too vital and expansive to be contained within the bounds of established Anglicanism in the eighteenth century, and it eventually burst out of them because of its own nature. Some have thought that, if only the Anglicans of the time had been wiser, there need never have been a Methodist breakaway from the Church of England. But such a statement is misleading. In suggesting that the trouble lay chiefly in the tactics followed by the Anglican authorities, such a view completely misunderstands the situation. The real problem was that the sort of religion which the Church of England provided, and the very cast of mind of those who presented it, was unable to cope with such a phenomenon as the religious revivalism of Wesley's movement. The Church of England could not contain Wesley's followers just because it was the product of the historical circumstances and outlooks of the time which had formed it.

*Growing Division*

One is tempted to think that Methodists and Anglicans in the eighteenth century were to all intents and purposes the same as they are in the twentieth. But this is to misread history and to impose a false pattern upon it. The same tendency can be seen in some of the discussions about the ordinations by Wesley of ministers to serve the Methodists who needed them. Historians have occasionally interpreted this as an abandonment by Wesley of the traditional doctrine of the Church of England about the essential character of episcopacy for a Christian church. But again this is to put into his mind and the minds of his opponents ideas which had probably not occurred to them. They did not look at the doctrine of the ministry in terms which only became current half a century or more later. Episcopacy was seen as a desirable arrangement, but few if any thought of Wesley as abandoning 'Catholic order' when he ordained. Certainly he was defying the establishment and the regulations of the Church of England, but why should he be expected to observe them when he was being forced by circumstances to make provision for the spiritual needs of followers because the Church of England would not or could not do so?

A recent commentator has written: 'In fact, in his classic self-defence in the *Minutes* of 1766 Wesley established the foundation of his authority on the same basis as he had indicated in 1745: people willingly gave themselves up to his direction, either because he had converted them or because they hoped that he would convert them, and from this fundamental relationship there developed the ecclesiastical superstructure of the united societies. The power to ordain was the power to recognize what had already taken place.'[20]

The appeal of John Wesley was centred on personal holiness, and the organisation which was gradually formed was intended to foster the growth of personal holiness among those who had heard him and been converted as a result. In the Deed of Declaration of 1784, which was entered in the Court of Chancery, the basic identity and organisation of the Methodists was set up. It laid down that nobody should be put in charge of chapels for more than three years 'except ordained Ministers of the Church of England', a demonstration that at that date separation was not his intention. Wesley's words before his death were: 'I live and die a member of the Church of England; and none who regard my judgement will ever separate from it.'[21] Wesley himself could not see the whole problem, and for that reason his words did not correspond to the realities of the situation. In 1795, four years after his death, the Methodists formed themselves into a dissenting body by providing for the administration of the Lord's Supper by its ministers who had not been ordained in the Church of England. Nevertheless, they did not see themselves as separated from the Church of England as individuals, and continued to regard Methodists as members of the established church, following its customs. 'We agree that the Lord's Supper be administered among us, on Sunday evenings only; except where the majority of the stewards and leaders desire it in church hours. . . . Nevertheless it shall never be administered on those Sundays on which it is administered in the parish Church. The Lord's Supper shall always be administered in England, according to the form of the Established Church.'[22]

Methodists continued for many decades to regard themselves as members of the Church of England with the rights of parishioners. But the logic of developments eventually took command and, after clashes which grew in hardness and hostility, Methodists became a distinct body, separate from the Church of England like other dissenting church bodies. Unhappily this division was accompanied by further divisions within Methodism itself, the first being the Methodist New Connexion of 1797. But 'the early nineteenth century saw division after division in the ranks of the Methodists. The New Connexion, the Primitive Methodist Connexion, the Bible Christians, the Leeds Protestant Methodists, the Wesleyan Association, and the Methodist Free Churches', besides the personal followings of individual men, broke away from their fellow Methodists. Eventually these divisions were destined to be healed in the twentieth century in two important reunions among Methodists, the first in 1907 and the second in 1932.

The history of the Methodists points the observer to an important aspect of Christian division. It has been commonplace, following the pioneering work of Ernst Troeltsch (1865–1923), to divide religion into two types in western Christendom—the 'church' type and the 'sect' type. The former is typified by the concept of the *volkkirche* or church of the whole people, including within it all sorts of conditions of men, of an inclusive nature, containing as many as possible, even if their religious membership is merely nominal. The Church of

England was an example of this type, with its claim to represent the whole of the people, and its cooperation with government to persuade or force people to belong to it. It is not necessary for such a church to be established in any technical sense, though most of the churches of this character have had some official relations with the government of the country in which they exist. The other type is the sect which is exclusive, putting its stress on purity of doctrine, strictness of life and reality of membership in the form of commitment. The sect type of religious body has played a social rôle as the means by which a social protest has been made through religious movements. In many cases it can be seen how minority groups who have felt themselves deprived of their rights have found through their religious organisation a means of finding a social identity and influencing the society around them. In a classical study of the subject, H. Richard Niebuhr wrote: 'The denominations, churches, sects, are sociological groups whose principle of differentiation is to be sought in their conformity to the order of social classes and castes. It would not be true to affirm that the denominations are not religious groups with religious purposes, but it is true that they represent the accommodation of religion to the caste system. They are emblems, therefore, of the victory of the world over the church, of the secularization of Christianity, of the church's sanction of that divisiveness which the church's gospel condemns.'[23]

Professor Niebuhr saw Methodism as the 'last great religious revolution of the disinherited in Christendom'. As we follow events in the nineteenth century, the movements of revolt begin to follow a secular pattern and no longer express themselves in religious forms. This did not mean that they did not contain many elements which were parallel or similar to religious feelings and aims: evidently they had these. But when the new socialist movements began, they no longer allied themselves to the Christian religion and often expressly repudiated Christian views of man. If denominationalism was a sign of the failure of the Church to express within itself its own principles, then the abandonment of the Church by social reformers was the inevitable result of this failure, for the Church no longer exercised on men an influence which could only spring, not only from a conviction of the truth of its gospel, but also from the power and intention to put it into practice.

Denominationalism, in giving expression to deep-seated social needs, at the same time exhibited the force of religious ideas. For the fact that men's needs could be cloaked in religious forms and find through religious life an adequate outlet was an indirect tribute to the forceful character of religion itself.

## Moravians

Methodism had an interesting connection with another religious body, the Moravians, through the personal experiences of John Wesley. He was himself converted—or, more accurately, underwent the 'conversion' experience, since he was already a sincere Christian —through his presence at a Moravian meeting. He enjoyed a friendship with Peter Böhler, who convinced him of the necessity of 'that faith whereby alone we are saved', and in 1738 he had paid a visit to Herrnhut in Moravia, the headquarters of the Moravian Church (also called Moravian Brethren and *Unitas Fratrum*). This church derived from the Bohemian Brethren Church and underwent a renewal under the leadership of a remarkable man, Count N. L. von Zinzendorf. From 1722 he organised Protestants on his estate at Herrnhut, and five years later gave up all other activities for the purpose of caring for the community. He was strongly influenced by Pietism, a form of Protestantism which put all its stress on the importance of inner experience in the spiritual life and considered external matters to be secondary and relatively unimportant. Pietistic religion flourished in many parts of the Protestant world in the eighteenth century and counterbalanced the barren forms of rationalism with which it was much afflicted. The Moravian Church was particularly notable for its interest in Christian unity, and for the open-minded way in which it approached other churches, and, even more striking, the steadfast refusal of its members to try to promote their own church strength at the expense of other churches.

The Moravians were also of special interest because they retained an episcopate in their church which claimed to preserve the genuine historical apostolic succession of bishops. In spite of Zinzendorf's own hesitation and even objection at first, the church decided to revive the ancient episcopal succession of the old Unitas Fratrum, and in 1735 a new bishop (David Nitschmann) was consecrated by Daniel Ernst Jablonski, bishop of that church in Berlin. The authority of episcopal ordinations assisted recognition of their ministers in areas of the mission work of the Moravian Church, for which it was justly famed. It obtained for them a secular status which they did not otherwise have.[24] The fact that they possessed an episcopal order had the additional result of increasing Moravian interest in and influence upon relations between the various Christian churches. In 1737 Zinzendorf himself received episcopal consecration.

Zinzendorf spent much of his time travelling with a band of followers, trying to promote a deeper personal spiritual life and encouraging peace among the churches, especially after he was exiled from Saxony in 1736. In England several congregations were founded, but by a definite act of policy they were restrained from multiplying, for it was not thought right to start rival churches to the Church of England. The Moravians were welcomed by the Church of England, whose leaders fully recognised the episcopate of their church. The British Parliament recognised the Moravians as 'an ancient protestant episcopal church' with 'the approval of Anglican bishops and of the sixteen Presbyterian lords', an ecumenical act in itself.[25] But in spite of this promising beginning, no conclusion has been reached for union between Anglicans and Moravians, although it was pursued by several Lambeth Conferences into the twentieth century.

Zinzendorf worked in England from 1749 to 1755. He died in 1760 at his estate in Herrnhut, spending his last years in pastoral work there. His ideal was that the Moravians should not form a separate religious denomination but that they should see themselves as working equally in all Christian churches for a deeper religious life and for peace among the churches of God. In pursuing these aims he showed himself an exceptional man and a forerunner of future workers in the ecumenical field.

The bishop who consecrated him, Daniel Ernst Jablonski, also had close contacts with the Church of England at Oxford. He was counsellor of the Prussian king in Berlin and had made the acquaintance of William Wake in his earlier years. He was deeply interested in attempts to promote unity among the Protestant churches in Germany, and he had great admiration for the Church of England arising from his early acquaintance with it. He thought that the pattern of the Church of England would be the best way of uniting the Lutheran and Reformed churches in Brandenburg. Such a union might be based on a modified version of the Book of Common Prayer and on the introduction of episcopacy into Prussia.

Jablonski had corresponded with Archbishop Sharp of York

about reunion during the reign of Queen Anne. But political events made the advancement of the project impossible then. He took the matter up once more when Wake became Archbishop of Canterbury in 1716, for in Wake he found someone as enthusiastic about better church relations as he was himself. The plans for a close alliance eventually foundered once more on the rocks of political interest. Jablonski's reasons for valuing the Church of England in the matter of church unity between Lutheran and Reformed churches was that 'she might be regarded and received by both parties as a mediator. She has something in common with each. In the doctrine she comes nearer to the Reformed; in some ceremonies to the Lutherans. She is loved and esteemed by both sides; and by her means the kingdoms of Sweden and Denmark might in time be so much the easier disposed to concur in this holy work.'[26] Wake in a letter of 17 June 1719 summed up the reasons why the unity plans failed so far as England was concerned. 'I am sorry to end with an indifferent account as to my present hopes of a union, concerning which I lately wrote in a more sanguine manner to Mr. Jablonski. But the unhappy difference between our court and that of Berlin, which I reasonably hoped Mr. Whitworth would have been able to make up, and which I fear there is but little hopes of doing at this time, will for a while retard this affair.'[27]

Dr. Norman Sykes averred that ecumenism was part of the *Zeitgeist* of the eighteenth century.[28] There were certainly signs of new outlooks which would draw churches together instead of apart from one another, though, as we have seen, they were limited in scope and did not penetrate much beneath the surface of doctrinal and national differences. But they kept alive the vital truth that Christians could not regard with indifference a state of hostility between those who professed to follow a master who preached the opposite virtues.

[1] David Mathew, *Catholicism in England*, London, Longmans, 1937, p. 68.
[2] Mathew, *op. cit.*, p. 69.
[3] Bettenson, *op. cit.*, p. 345.
[4] *Kyrillos Loukaris*, London, 1951.
[5] Cited J. B. Dockery, *Christopher Davenport*, London, Burns & Oates, 1960, p. 84.
[6] *Op. cit.*, p. 148.
[7] *Ibid.*
[8] Cited J. Minton Batten, *John Dury*, Chicago, 1944, p. 47.
[9] G. R. Cragg, *The Church and the Age of Reason*, Pelican Books, London, 1960.
[10] Robert S. Bosher, *The Making of the Restoration Settlement*, 1649–1662, London, 1951.

[11] Bosher, *op. cit.*, p. 282.

[12] *Anglo-Russian Theological Conference*, ed. H. Waddams, London, 1958, p. 2.

[13] *Old Priest and New Presbyter*, Cambridge, 1956, p. 118.

[14] Edmund Calamy, quoted in *From Uniformity to Unity*, by Ernst A. Payne, London, 1962, p. 260.

[15] *Ibid.*

[16] *Some Animadversions upon Dr Trapp's late reply, Collected Works*, London, 1893, p. 183.

[17] W. K. Lowther Clarke, *London*, 1944.

[18] N. Sykes, in *The English Church and the Continent*, London, 1959, p. 87.

[19] *Ibid.*

[20] John Kent, *The Age of Disunity*, London, 1966, p. 172.

[21] Bettenson, *op. cit.*, p. 359.

[22] *Ibid.*

[23] *The Social Sources of Denominationalism*, Living Age Books, New York, 1957, p. 25.

[24] A. J. Lewis, *Zinzendorf*, London, S.C.M., 1962, p. 112.

[25] *Op. cit.*, p. 155.

[26] Quoted: Sykes, *William Wake*, II, Cambridge, 1957, p. 65.

[27] *Op. cit.*, p. 69.

[28] *The English Church and the Continent*, p. 92.

# 9

## The Modern Formation of the Churches

### Orthodoxy under the Ottomans

THE fall of Constantinople signalled the complete victory of the Turks over the Byzantine Empire. Most of the Empire had already fallen before 1453: the capture of the capital was the final stroke. Of the Orthodox Christians, only the Church of Russia remained outside the power of the Turks. We must now observe the fate of the Christians who found themselves within the Ottoman Empire and try to note some of the influences which have affected the outlook of the Orthodox churches.

All the Greek-speaking churches and most of the other churches (viz. Serbia, Bulgaria and Rumania) were governed by the Ottoman Sultans for between 300 and 400 years. The experiences which they underwent produced certain inevitable characteristics. They entered a sort of tunnel, during the period of which the survival of their religion depended on certain qualities. One of these qualities was an unbending conservatism, which strengthened a tendency already manifest. If a religion is to survive in a hostile environment it is plain that it must not be weakened by internal strife about the central tenets or practices of the faith. In such adverse circumstances religious attitudes tend to cling to the state of affairs which existed at the start of the new conditions. In this way members of the Church can more easily stand together without dispute. From a religious point of view this has dangers, since it makes spiritual adaptation more difficult, but those dangers do not seem as serious as the breakdown of the religious system altogether. It is interesting to see that in modern Russia and other Communist countries the same conservatism in religious matters is again strongly entrenched, for the same reason as under the Ottoman régime. Christians who have not had to suffer similar conditions of oppression under an alien religious or irreligious power do not always understand this reaction.

Within the Ottoman Empire the position of the Ecumenical Patriarch of Constantinople became even more important than it had been earlier, for he became the instrument through whom the Turkish authorities ruled their Orthodox subjects. The fact that the Government was now opposed to Christianity made no difference to the method by which Patriarchs were appointed or deposed. The deplorable practice of making or unmaking Patriarchs, which had become common form in the Byzantine Empire, was continued by the Ottoman rulers. Their system of rule went further: it made the Patriarch personally responsible for the good behaviour of his flock, and his position was given or taken away according as he was or was not successful in the task the Government had given him to do.

Another sinister element in the situation was that the Patriarchate of Constantinople came to be looked upon as a highly desirable post, both for its influence and for financial reasons, and appointments were made as a result of bargaining with those responsible, by bribing officials who had influence, as well as by direct payment into the hands of the Sultan. The Greeks of the Empire were largely engaged in commercial pursuits and controlled much of its wealth. Thus the patriarchate was bought and sold by unworthy men; and eventually there was a regular payment attached to it, an entrance fee and an annual subscription payable to the Sultan. Some Greeks were as ready to enter into this sordid simony as the Turks were to profit by it, and the result was inevitably to lower the status of the Ecumenical patriarchate in the eyes of all serious Christians.

'Vacancies could be arranged: and the tenure of each Patriarch was precarious and short-lived,' wrote B. J. Kidd. 'So rapid were the changes that many Patriarchs secured the throne, lost it to a rival, and regained it: while some lost and recovered it as many as five or six times. Out of 159 Patriarchs who held office between the fifteenth and the twentieth century, the Turks have on 105 occasions driven Patriarchs from their throne; there have been 27 abdications, often involuntary; 6 Patriarchs have suffered violent deaths by hanging, poisoning or drowning: and only 21 have died natural deaths while in office. No succession of rulers could maintain its prestige under such conditions; nor is it matter for surprise that few of the Oecumenical Patriarchs have been men of any distinction.'[1]

*Nationality and Religion*

The Turks considered themselves infinitely superior to the subject races of the Empire, many of whom were Christians. They prided themselves on their military qualities and despised commercial activities as being contemptuous and fit occupations only for the Christian communities of the Empire. Nor did the Turks have any desire actually to govern beyond maintaining themselves in the seats of power. Partly from laziness, and partly from a sense of superiority, they did not wish to embroil themselves in the petty details of running the Empire, and were perfectly content to make others do it for them. They continued to use the *millet* system for the government of the religious minorities throughout the Ottoman Empire (see p. 47). A *millet*, often translated 'nation', was composed of all those subjects of the Empire who belonged to one particular church. Thus the Greek Orthodox formed one *millet*, the Armenians another. The system of ruling was simple: the head of the church, in the case of the Orthodox the Ecumenical Patriarch of Constantinople, was made the head of the *millet* as well. He was thus not only the spiritual head but also the political or secular head, of his people, and he was personally responsible to the Turkish Government for their good behaviour. The Orthodox Christians belonged to the *Rum millet*, that is the 'Roman nation', because they were the Christian body identified with the Byzantine or Roman Empire which the Turks had conquered.

The psychological effect of this method of rule during several centuries was deep. In Byzantine times there was a close connection between Church and State, as we have seen, and from the time of the early eastern schisms churches were often closely linked with national causes. The Syrian and Egyptian national causes became linked with the Monophysite heresy: the Armenian nation and church were indistinguishable. So Orthodoxy became linked to the Greeks, and the customs of Turkish rule made this identification of religion and nationality even more pronounced. It is true that Orthodoxy comprised other nations besides the Greek, but the curious fact is that they, too, took over the religio/national outlook. It was assumed that a Greek or a Russian was Orthodox, and that a Pole was Latin. The two elements of religion and nationality became so intermingled as to make it impossible to distinguish where one ended and the other began.

The general condition of the Christians in the Ottoman Empire was by no means bad, if they did not indulge in any rebellious activities. There was a respect on the part of the Christians for the military virtues of their conquerors, while the Turks often secretly admired the skill which they themselves did not possess in debate and commerce. Christians enjoyed certain privileges which gave them considerable independence. They had liberty of worship and separate schools for their children. Together these two privileges made it possible for Christians to maintain their own religious traditions, and to keep alive their own language and something of the historical sense of nationhood and patriotism. They were also given their own courts of law in those personal matters which impinged on their religious belief and practice. The Turks had two sets of courts— *Nizām* or civil courts, and *Sheri'* or ecclesiastical courts. Christians were allowed their own ecclesiastical courts, an important concession in such questions as marriage and divorce and the internal discipline of their churches. In addition, Christians had exemption from military service. This was granted because the Turks thought the *rayahs*, as members of subject *millets* were called, to be unworthy of bearing arms. But it was a privilege of the highest value to those concerned, who had to pay but a small sum in compensation for their freedom from the Army.

## Greek Influence

The Greeks in the Empire found themselves, therefore, relatively free. Indeed, their condition compared favourably with the treatment meted out in the West by Christians to Christian minorities. On another side of the Empire's life Greeks played an important part in governing Orthodox Christians who were not Greek by race, for example, Serbian and Bulgarian Christians. The Greeks who were centred at Constantinople were often very rich, and, as we have noticed, were not above engaging in unsavoury practices. They considered themselves superior in tradition, breeding and intelligence to other members of the Orthodox Church, whom they were employed by the Sultan to control. They reimbursed themselves for the money simoniacally expended in Constantinople by squeezing it out of the parishioners through the bishops. This made bad blood between Greek and Slav Christians in the Balkans which still has results today, for it bred a tension which has by no means disappeared. It also encouraged the Balkan churches which were not Greek to look to the Church of Russia as the church which would not only save them from the Turkish yoke but would also rid them of their rapacious Greek ecclesiastical superiors. The Greeks who were engaged in these activities were known as Phanariots, because they were connected with the *Phanar*, the name of the Patriarch's headquarters in Constantinople.

But even when the black sides of history are frankly recognised, it must not be forgotten that there were many sincere Christians who kept alive their faith in most unfavourable circumstances. The Ecumenical Patriarchs themselves provided during this period examples of steadfastness in the face of mutilation or death.

During the Ottoman period the patriarchates of Antioch, Alexandria and Jerusalem were subject to Constantinople. Their Patriarchs for many hundreds of years were invariably Greeks, although in the patriarchate of Antioch the people were Arabic speaking. It was not until the beginning of the twentieth century that a Patriarch who was an Arab ascended the throne of Antioch. Anyone appointed to one of the patriarchal thrones had to receive the Sultan's *berat*, or certificate of approval, before he could hold his position. We may also note that it was in the *millet* system that its head acquired the title *ethnarch*, ruler of the people. The Archbishop of Cyprus, leading the island's struggle for independence in the twentieth century, used this title which for centuries had expressed the unity of his church and people.

The Turkish conquest largely isolated eastern Christendom from the West. Russia, it is true, was nominally free to have contacts with the western world, but these were limited because of historical factors which we shall note later. One most important effect of this isolation was to seal off the Orthodox from the movements of the Reformation. The East was certainly affected by the Reformation in various ways, but these effects were external: the Christian East never wrestled internally with the problems of doctrine and order which faced the West in the years of the Reformation and after.

Some of the difficulties which the Orthodox in the Ottoman Empire had to meet came from the intrigues of foreign powers with the Porte, as the Sultan's government was called. Roman Catholic interests were promoted through the French ambassadors for the most part, whereas Protestant interests were supported by England and other Protestant powers, notably the Dutch. Outside the Empire under the direction of the Jesuits the Roman Catholic Church was conducting a spiritual war of aggression against the Orthodox, in which every sort of political and diplomatic influence was used to try to gain the obedience of the Orthodox for the Pope. The formation of the *Unia* and of Uniate churches in 1596 has already been noted elsewhere. The influence of the Protestants was seen in the career of Cyril Lukaris.

Under the Ottoman Empire Jerusalem continued to be a place of importance for pilgrims, and, as such, attracted the interest of the secular powers. When the Russian Church built up its strength the number of Russian pilgrims became vast, and this inevitably engaged the interest of the Russian tsars, who began by caring for the welfare of their own subjects and visiting the holy places for reasons of piety, and ended by seeing Jerusalem as a centre through which Russian imperial influence could be extended within the Ottoman Empire to the disadvantage of Turks, Greeks and Roman Catholics. Russia was the Orthodox power which cast its protective mantle over the Orthodox people and causes: the French did the same for the Roman Catholics.

At the beginning of the nineteenth century the Ottoman Empire was at a low ebb and ready to crack. Independence movements were not slow to appear in the Balkans. The Serbs revolted in 1804 and again in 1815, and in 1830 they were granted some independence by the Turks, and in the following year they gained autonomy in church affairs and release from the rule of the phanariot Greeks. A revolution secured a liberal constitution for Wallachia, which in 1862 fused with Moldavia to make Rumania.

Greece rose against the Turks in 1821, and independence was eventually secured in 1833. When the news of the Greek rebellion reached Constantinople the Oecumenical Patriarch and about 30,000 Greeks there were murdered. Subsequently, the Patriarchs of Constantinople refused to allow the Church of Greece to have autocephalous or independent status, and the structure of the church was weak until a change was made in 1852 and the dioceses were reorganised.

In all these independence movements churchmen took a leading part as national leaders. This was one result of the identification of nationality and religion, for the churches had for centuries been the only places where the feeling for national language and sentiment could be nurtured. The leader of the Greek fight for independence was the Metropolitan Germanos of Patras. Such a national rôle is considered by the Orthodox to be a duty of a bishop, and a striking example of the persistence of this idea was the part played in securing the independence of Cyprus by Archbishop Makarios, the first president of the island. During and after the Second World War a similar rôle was performed in Greece by Archbishop Damaskinos, who led his people in resistance to the German occupation, and afterwards in a struggle against armed Communist revolt.

The Bulgarian Church was the last in the Balkans to gain independence (1870), and soon after doing so it found itself in a dispute with the Patriarchate of Constantinople, which resulted in a breach of communion from 1872 to 1945. The quarrel concerned jurisdiction over Bulgarian Christians in Constantinople, which the Bulgarian Church claimed against the Ecumenical Patriarch. But, although the Bulgarian Church was not in communion with the Greek-speaking Orthodox churches, it remained in communion with the rest.

## The Russian Church

After the fall of Constantinople the Church of Russia was the only free Orthodox church in the world. Although it was not the first Slav church, it soon became by far the largest in numbers of the Orthodox churches, and has remained so ever since. In spite of persecution and repression under Communist rule, it outnumbers all other Orthodox Christians throughout the world.

Something has already been said about the early years of the Russian Church. Its relations with the West were deeply affected by the fact that invasions of Russia from the West were accompanied by attempts to Latinise its Christianity. From historical tensions of this kind arose the deep enmity between the Roman Catholic Pole and the Orthodox Russian, which confused religion and nationality in eastern Europe.

Many Christians in Russia thought that the fall of Constantinople was the direct act of God, who was punishing the Greeks for their treachery to the Orthodox faith in accepting the union of Florence. With the idea of Moscow as the third Rome the Russian Church saw itself as the sole defender of the true faith—'Holy Russia'—with a special Christian task and destiny. When Ivan IV in 1547 first adopted the title of Tsar (a form of Caesar), he obtained the approval of the Patriarch of Constantinople, thus reinforcing the concept of the third Rome. The Council of the Hundred Chapters held at Moscow in 1551 endorsed the superiority of Russian over Greek Orthodoxy.

As the self-consciousness of church and nation developed, it became natural that the head of the Church should desire a status higher than that of Metropolitan, and in 1589 the Metropolitan of Moscow acquired the title of Patriarch. But the office lasted little more than a century, for it was abolished by Peter the Great in 1700. By being raised to this rank, Russia became the fifth eastern patriarchate: it was the second patriarchate to be created since the four ancient eastern centres of Christendom, but the patriarchate of Serbia had lapsed. It was thought by some that the Moscow Patriarchate replaced that of Rome, which had fallen away and was no longer in union with the true Church.

During the seventeenth century one of the most famous of Moscow Patriarchs, Nikon, was the storm centre of a bitter dispute whose echoes still resound in the religious world of Russia. He was noted for his pastoral zeal, his preaching and his work for reform. With reluctance he gave in to the Tsar's insistence that he should become Patriarch, and he ascended the patriarchal throne in 1652. For some years he enjoyed the Tsar's confidence, though he made himself unpopular with many others by his tactlessness and ruthless determination. The language of the church services in Russia was and is Old Slavonic, and a lack of scholars and the weakness of the links with Greek Christendom had resulted in a number of mistakes and mistranslations from the Greek. There were also minor differences of custom between the Greek and Russian churches, the best known of which was the difference in the way of making the sign of the Cross. In Greece and the churches of the East the sign of the Cross was made with three fingers, and in Russia with two only. Nikon was encouraged to enter upon a programme of reform by visits from eastern Patriarchs. A synod of 1655 revised the liturgy, and Nikon also resisted the introduction of Latin ecclesiastical art, which had crept in and tried to encourage the true Byzantine tradition. But his attempts to put these reforms into practice and to enforce them by severe punishment led to a popular revolt against him. His decisions were upheld after his removal, but they had resulted in a permanent schism of the more extreme conservatives from the Russian Church:

they formed themselves into the sect of the Old Believers and continue at the present day.

Peter the Great became sole occupier of the Russian throne in 1696 on the death of his half-brother. He was an autocrat with ideas of his own, many of which he had acquired in the course of visits to western Europe. Sir Bernard Pares[2] averred that Peter was a religious man. He apparently founded this judgment on the fact that Peter liked singing in the choir—an uncertain basis for such a conclusion. Moreover, he described Peter in his bouts of drunkenness blasphemously parodying the priests and ceremonies of the Church. It seems more probable that Peter was interested in the Church mainly as an instrument of his general policy for Russia, but ready to give lip-service to its beliefs, where they did not conflict with his own wishes. When the Patriarch Adrian died in 1700 Peter nominated a locum tenens instead of appointing a successor, giving him the title of Exarch and administrator of the patriarchal throne. At that date he had probably already made up his mind to do away with the office of Patriarch, but that he planned a period of waiting before he instituted the régime which he favoured. A forceful Patriarch was too dangerous a rival for power to be supportable to one of Peter's temperament.

In 1721 Peter set up the Holy Synod as a permanent replacement for a Patriarch. The synod was a body of bishops, some of whom came and went in rotation, but with them on the synod was a layman appointed by the Tsar and called the Over-Procurator. The synod was the central committee of a lay civil service which ran the church, of which the head was the Over-Procurator, who was the 'eye' of the Tsar in the synod and also controlled the way in which the civil service worked throughout the country. The officials in the church offices were far more permanent than the bishops who were their titular heads. A simple device to ensure control of what went on throughout the Church was to move the bishops fairly frequently from one diocese to another, so that the reins of power inevitably fell into the hands of the administrative permanent civil servants who were directly responsible for their jobs to the Over-Procurator. There is little doubt that the idea of State control of the Church in this way was derived from what Peter had seen in the countries of western Europe.

The position has been summed up like this: 'Through the Synod Peter's hand was laid upon the whole church, for in his *Religious*

*Regulation* creating the new body it was granted wide powers: over the dogmatic correctness and the ritual of the church, over its education, over the diocesan administration, over church property, and over the discipline of the monastics and of the parish clergy.'[3]

At the same time as the Tsar was consolidating his control over the Church a semi-religious adulation of the Tsar was much encouraged, and the authorities of the Church did not hesitate to extend it in a way which can hardly be thought short of idolatrous. 'In the seventeenth century Otrep'ev, Akimdov, Stenka Razin, and Mazeppa had been so singled out (that is, as enemies of the state), and even though the ritual was revised and shortened in 1766, once a year until 1869 the following curse was proclaimed in all Orthodox churches: "To those who do not believe that the Orthodox monarchs have been raised to the throne by virtue of a special grace of God—and that, at the moment the sacred oil is laid on them, the gifts of the Holy Ghost are infused into them anent the accomplishment of their exalted mission; and to those who dare to rise and rebel against them, such as Grishka Otrep'ev, Ian Mazeppa, and others like them: Anathema! Anathema! Anathema!"[4]

The Russian State, like other states, tried to use the Church as an instrument of cultural control, and at the same time to prevent it from independent action. The Church of Georgia, for example, was forcibly subordinated to the Church of Moscow, and did not regain its independence until the twentieth century. But the heavy hand of the State could not, and did not, prevent movements of spiritual power in the church, especially under two great nineteenth-century Patriarchs Platon and Philaret, who together led the church for almost a century, 1775–1812 and 1821–67. There were notable lay theologians also. Siberia, China, Japan and Alaska became territories for missionary work; and from Alaska missions went south into the United States of America. There were also deep currents of spiritual life led by outstanding men of prayer and holy life. But efforts to reform the church from within were not successful, and it needed political revolution before the church was able to reorder its own life.

It was such historical backgrounds which gave to the Orthodox churches their own particular attitudes towards other Christians. The isolation which cut them off from the West was never complete, and during the nineteenth century it began more and more to be broken down. New friendships became possible between eastern and western Christians and between their churches. But in the process of creating such new connections the outlooks formed by history proved formidable obstacles to understanding, for they had assumed fixed patterns which could not be abandoned without forsaking the security which they provided and seeming to question the authority on which they rested.

## The Explosion of New Ideas

The period between the French Revolution of 1789 and the outbreak of the First World War in 1914 provides material of bewildering richness and variety both inside and outside the churches. The Industrial Revolution was changing the face of Europe, creating new social conditions and out of them new political power and new ideas. Intellectual life was exploring new avenues; and traditional outlooks and practices came more and more under attack, both in secular and ecclesiastical life. The relations of the churches were continually affected by forces which were pulling in different directions, and which produced reactions which were difficult to combine with one another.

The psychological effect of the French Revolution was in its day parallel to that produced nearly 140 years later by the Bolshevist success in Russia. It seemed to threaten the stability of European civilisation, and it aroused horrified protest and alarm in the minds of churchmen and conservatively minded people. There was a direct threat to religion, and England housed many religious refugees from France. Stability began to return when Napoleon Bonaparte took over control, and his agreement with the Pope in 1801 enabled church life in France to function more normally.

The nineteenth century was a bridge from one sort of world to another, in religion, in politics, in international affairs, in science. Revolutionary changes took place, many of which made direct impact on the life of the churches, in addition to the hidden pressures which also affected men's religious attitudes. In the political realm the French Revolution began a process which gathered momentum as the century went on. 1848 was the year of the Communist Manifesto, drafted by Marx and Engels. This was not the only manifestation of socialism—there were a number of others based on different principles. Robert Owen had tried to start communities on socialist principles, both in Lanark in Scotland and in New Harmony, Indiana, U.S.A. But the Communist Manifesto marked a new departure in its rigorous hostility to the established order on all fronts. The questionings and new departures which this and other movements represented meant that old structures were being attacked and replaced by new when possible.

Liberal trends in government were also growing. No longer were men content to continue under the power of the traditional ruling classes. Trade and manufacture were giving new power into the hands of men who had no connections with the families which, in England, for example, had ruled the country for so long. A liberalisation of government was proceeding which was making democracy more of a reality than it had ever been before. Although the grip of the aristocratic tradition of government continues even in the middle of the twentieth century to some degree, it began to be threatened with the new developments of the nineteenth century.

## Changing Religious Patterns

The religious world reflected similar changes. The establishment of religion in England was being weakened by the growing strength of the dissenters, on the one hand, especially the Methodists, and on the other, by that of the Roman Catholics. The latter were particularly increased by the great influx of men and women from Ireland, who came over to find employment in the industrial centres of England. They brought their religion with them. This was not only a source of great spiritual and social strength to them but it also identified them in contradistinction to the English among whom they had to live, and to whom they were beholden for their livelihood. Not only did the presence of the Irish in England affect the position of the Roman Catholics in the country, but by their political presence it also brought the problems which were a constant source of difficulty for English governments in Ireland itself. Such problems became far more urgent when hundreds of thousands of Irish people had their homes in England, and pressed the affairs of their country upon the attention of their neighbours by their presence.

These events bred in the new Roman Catholic leaders a sense of growing power. At the same time the Church of England was having trouble within its own borders. The Oxford Movement, usually dated from 1833, brought back to the Church of England a sense of the importance of its Catholic past and its claim to be the Catholic

H

church of the country, as distinct from Christians of the Roman obedience who were looked upon as a foreign mission. The movement tried to return to traditional sacramental practices, and as time went on it began to reintroduce ceremonial practices which were common on the continent of Europe, but strange to the Church of England. The furore aroused by this movement resulted in a crisis of conscience for some of its leaders, the most famous and distinguished of whom, John Henry Newman, joined the Church of Rome in 1845, together with a number of other men of standing. Roman Catholic leaders were encouraged by such defections to believe that they had only to keep up the pressure to make heavy inroads into the Church of England by converting many of its best adherents to their own obedience. Their hopes proved to be exaggerated, although a small but steady stream of converts did in fact continue.

The effect on the psychology of the Roman Catholic leaders was to encourage them in an attitude to which they were already prone, namely to claim that they alone were the true church of Christ, that all others were heretics and schismatics whose sacraments were invalid and whose ministries were worthless, and that salvation could only be found under the jurisdictional umbrella of the papacy. In England Roman Catholics were a minority and exhibited many attitudes which are associated with minorities, being bitter and aggressive towards the Church of England and its members. These points of view were not discouraged by the fact that the majority of the Roman Catholic flock consisted of Irish people cared for by Irish priests, none of whom had reason to be anything but hostile to the English Church and people. The history of Ireland's misgovernment by Englishmen was a sorry story which abounded in scandalous oppression from one side and great suffering on the other.

In Ireland the English rulers were identified with the English Church: both of them enjoyed the fruits of an occupying power and the wealth of the country, while the native peoples lived in poverty without influence. The United Church of England and Ireland was given the ancient church buildings of Ireland, a state of affairs which is perpetuated in the continuing ownership by the Anglican Church of Ireland of the only two ancient cathedrals in Dublin, St. Patrick's and Christ Church, whereas the great majority of Dublin Christians, who are Roman Catholics, have to be content with an inferior modern construction for their own worship. When the Church of Ireland was disestablished in 1871 it retained these ancient medieval buildings, although it contained only a tiny minority of Ireland's Christians.

## Roman Catholic Advance in England

Roman Catholics in England had reason to be thankful to their coreligionists in Ireland for the assistance which they brought to those living in England; for their gradual emancipation from legal disabilities owed much to the need for placating the Irish. Various reliefs were afforded in the concluding decades of the eighteenth century; but the most important measure was the Roman Catholic Relief Act of 1829, which removed almost all remaining disabilities. The transformation of the position of the Roman Catholic Church in England during the course of the nineteenth century was startling. In 1850 the Pope re-established the English hierarchy and the church reorganised itself along traditional lines, adopting territorial titles for its sees but avoiding those used by the Church of England. Since that time there has been some duplication. The official policy of aggression and denigration of the Church of England, its doctrines and its practices, inevitably made for bad relations, but in spite of this fact, there were contrary movements aimed at better understanding and closer contacts.

Problems in the field of belief also increased during the century, two new dogmas being added to those which had to be accepted *de fide* by the faithful of the Roman obedience. In the bull *Ineffabilis Deus* of 1854, the Pope enunciated the dogma of the Immaculate Conception, which held that from the moment of her own conception in the womb of her mother the Blessed Virgin Mary had by a special providence been kept free from all stain of original sin. (This dogma has nothing to do with that of the Virgin Birth, which concerns the birth of Jesus without the intervention of a human father.) For many Christians the dogma of the Immaculate Conception, lacking any scriptural basis, was unacceptable, and to many it also appeared to remove the Virgin Mary from the category of ordinary humanity. It was a belief which in the thirteenth century had been rejected by St. Thomas Aquinas, the greatest of Roman Catholic theologians.

The divisive effect of this doctrine was, however, much surpassed by the Vatican Council of 1870 in its promulgation of the doctrine of papal infallibility. The definition of this dogma stated that when the Pope spoke *ex cathedra* on a matter of faith or morals he was infallibly guided, and that such definitions are irreformable of themselves, and not from the consent of the church. The announcement of this dogma caused severely adverse reactions among the other churches of Christendom, and was the cause of a schism, small but significant, within the papal obedience. A group of Roman Catholics, headed by the famous scholar Döllinger, left the Church because they were unable to accept the new doctrine. He and those with him associated themselves with the Old Catholic Church of Holland and set up new branches of the Old Catholic Church in Germany, Switzerland and elsewhere, though their numbers were never large.

Evangelical strands were important during the century in promoting united action among Christians, but before examining them it would be convenient to follow the more 'catholic' side of unity movements in England, since they belong to the Roman Catholic aspects which we have just now been examining. The 1830s saw the rise of the Oxford Movement, which placed stress on the recovery of the catholic and traditional elements in the historical practice and thought of the Church of England. True, the defection of some of its members to the Church of Rome seriously compromised its influence, causing many Anglican people to react more strongly against Rome and to reject the Tractarians, as its adherents were called, as dangerous to the independence and the Protestant heritage of their church. But the movement had a strong devotional appeal, especially to those who wished to lead a life of discipline in accordance with the teaching and experience of fellow Christians elsewhere. Roman Catholic books from Europe began to be translated and widely used, though sometimes amended to temper the wind of papal authority to the shorn lamb of Anglican independence and liberty. The depth of this devotional spirit was shown in the revival within the Church of England of religious communities living under a rule which, although often specially composed for the purpose, reflected faithfully the best elements in the religious life of traditional Catholicism. Monks and nuns once more began to take their place as a natural and legitimate part of the life of the Church of England.

Relations of members of the Church of England with Roman Catholics in England were much less friendly than those with continental Catholics for obvious reasons: the former represented a threat to the Church of England which the latter did not. An increasing sense of catholicity, on the one hand led Anglicans to resent

Roman Catholics in England more, and at the same time led them to welcome contacts with Catholics elsewhere. This ambivalence was quite logical, for if the Church of England were the true catholic church of the land, Roman Catholics were interlopers disturbing catholic order, whereas on the Continent Catholics were the true counterparts to Anglicans in England. Many Anglicans adopted the 'branch' theory of the church, holding that the catholic church continued to exist in three branches—Romanism, Orthodoxy, and Anglicanism. The theory has not stood the test of time and is no longer held, but while it lasted it encouraged closer contacts between Anglicans and members of the other two groups abroad.

There also appeared during the nineteenth century a group of Anglicans who can best be described as 'papalist'. Its members professed to accept all the teaching of the Roman Church, but thought it their duty to remain Anglicans until such time as the whole of their church was ready to return to the papal fold. The inconsistencies of such an attitude were glaring, but its adherents appear to have held it with sincerity, and they still exist within the Church of England. Various attempts were made to promote reunion on these principles, one of which was the Association for the Promotion of the Unity of Christendom founded in 1857. It originally included Anglicans and Roman Catholics, but the latter were compelled to leave it when it was condemned by the Holy Office in 1864.

The ecclesiastical aspect of relations between the Church of England and Rome may be pursued until the end of the century. Through a personal friendship with a French priest, the first Lord Halifax towards the end of the century spent efforts in trying to secure from Rome some sort of recognition which would be a means of bringing the two churches closer together. He was the leader of the Anglo-Catholics, as that group within the Church of England came to be called, and he was convinced that the best way of proceeding would be to get from Rome an official decision which would recognise the validity of Anglican ordinations, thus acknowledging the status of Anglican orders, even though they would be regarded as irregular and schismatic. There seemed good reason to expect a favourable outcome to his efforts, but in the end they were frustrated, largely through the influence in Rome of representatives of the English Roman Catholic hierarchy, who realised clearly enough that the invalidity of Anglican orders was one of the most powerful

H2

weapons in their propaganda armoury against the Church of England. In 1896 in the bull *Apostolicae Curae* Anglican orders were declared to be invalid, though the grounds on which this decision was taken have been shown to be insufficient, even on the principles of Rome itself. The decision was a damaging blow to hopes for better understanding. It elicited from the two Archbishops of Canterbury and York a *Responsio* setting out a cogent presentation of the Anglican position.

## English Dissent

At the beginning of the nineteenth century the most active elements within the religious life of England were to be found among Evangelicals and Methodists. Relations between the two were not always good, and their interconnection has sometimes been exaggerated. From a religious point of view there was much in common between them, but the Methodists with other dissenters found their chief opponents to be those who were defending the position and privileges of the establishment, rather than theological critics. Questions of education, church rate, repair of churches, right of burial and similar practical matters constantly provided occasions of dispute and bad feeling. As the century went on there was a growing sense of political power among the rising classes, and dissenters who shared this sense wished to establish their position against those who had oppressed them, or at least regarded them as inferior and acted accordingly. They wanted to rid themselves of the impositions which forced them to pay their money in aid of repairing churches in which they had no desire to worship. But at the same time it must be remembered that many Methodists continued to regard themselves as members of the Church of England for a long period, and that many of them valued their rights to be buried in the churchyard and to receive other ministrations when desired. Moreover, when the problem of education according to the principles of the Church of England and its support by public money arose and when dissenters had no option but to send their children to schools where these principles were taught, it is well to remember that the Church of England schools were built by the personal contributions and sacrifices of church people, and that the Methodists, when they had the chance, did not always think it worth while to contribute in the same measure to building their own schools.

Dr. Owen Chadwick[5] recounts that in 1834 relations between church and dissenters showed unparalleled bitterness, and dissenters and Irish Roman Catholics came together in the House of Commons to attack the established church. At the beginning of Queen Victoria's reign schismatic tendencies were more evident in the churches than understanding and unity. 'The early Victorians witnessed a schism or two among the Methodists, schism among the Quakers, schism on the grand scale among Scottish Presbyterians, secession from the Church of England so grave as to amount to a schism, a Baptist body divided over open communion and Calvinism, a Roman Catholic body divided over everything but the necessity for not being divided. Because the armies not seldom wheeled into this battle under the generalship of bigots or fools, we may forget that in some form the battle was necessary to health, an unavoidable pace in the march towards free churches in a free state.'[6]

That judgment sounds mainly negative. But it must be put against the undeniable fact that these divisions were from one point of view a mark of religious vigour. It is true that some of the vigour was misplaced and that wider horizons were often obscured. Nevertheless, it was because men took their religion seriously and were prepared to sacrifice themselves for it that these differences of conviction became so important as to divide men from one another. And there is some substance in the accusation made against the movement for Christian unity that such a movement is only possible because men have ceased to care enough for their religious principles to maintain them. Certainly this accusation cannot be accepted in its simple form, for the matter is far more complicated than that. Yet there can be little doubt that feebleness of conviction, as well as changes of conviction, can and do play a part in movements towards closer unity.

*New Cooperation*

The nineteenth century was rich in its vigour and its variety, of which merely one or two aspects can here be mentioned. In the life of the evangelical groups Christian cooperation increased considerably through the century. Evangelicals showed themselves anxious to ally themselves with other like-minded Christians in causes of practical concern and in the spreading of the Christian message. The London Missionary Society, for example, was the outcome of such cooperation: it was founded in 1795 by a group which contained

Anglicans, Congregationalists, Presbyterians and Methodists, and it established missions all over the world, leaving it to the missionaries themselves to decide what form of church government they would prefer. Later the YMCA and the YWCA sprang out of similar joint efforts among Evangelicals, and in 1846 the Evangelical Alliance was formed. These efforts were those of individuals rather than of church groups, and they continued to exhibit the power of evangelical earnestness throughout the century, as was later seen in the Christian Endeavour Union, begun in Maine, U.S.A., in 1881, and the organisation on a world scale of Christian students at the end of the century.

From evangelicalism came also important movements of social reform, such as the abolition of the slave trade. The conversion of William Wilberforce to evangelical religion had widespread consequences. He determined to serve the Christian cause in Parliament, and he became a prominent member of the Clapham Sect of evangelical laymen. He was foremost and best known for his work to abolish slavery, which reached its climax with the Emancipation Act of 1833. He was active in many other social causes as well as in religious endeavours such as the Church Missionary Society and the Bible Society (founded 1804). He was also a supporter of Catholic emancipation. When he died in 1833 he had made an enduring mark on the history of his country's moral progress through the earnestness of his own evangelical persuasions.

The growing chaos of the Industrial Revolution produced social conditions of appalling misery. From some of the clergy this called forth efforts to improve the lot of the working classes, conditions resulting not only in severe hardship but in the moral degradation of many who had to live in circumstances of utter poverty. Temperance movements were part of the attempts to combat social evils, but these and other moral campaigns could be no more than palliatives without fundamental changes in the conditions which gave rise to these moral problems. Some clergy, such as Stewart Headlam, adopted a revolutionary attitude and launched a movement of Christian socialism, for example by the foundation in 1877 of the Guild of St. Matthew. He identified Christianity with socialism, and gained immense unpopularity among most of his fellow churchmen, but he pointed to the things which really mattered, namely the need for social action at the roots of men's lives. Christian socialism had better-known leaders than Headlam—F. D. Maurice, Charles Kingsley and Thomas Hughes—who had earlier tried to bring Christian insights and principles to bear on social problems, though their success was limited. But they were the forerunners of others and brought into being ideas and organisations which would later be further developed.

In 1889 a volume of essays entitled *Lux Mundi* took up the cause of Christian socialism and led to the formation of the Christian Social Union 'with Westcott as President and Gore and Scott Holland as leaders'.[7] These men were passionately convinced of their cause, but they came from aristocratic and learned backgrounds and had little in common with those whom they were trying to help. Nevertheless, the ideas which they propagated did much to rescue the Church of England from a blindness to these social problems and to defend it against an accusation of total lack of interest. Part of the efforts made in this field was concerned with bringing the universities and the working men into contact with one another, a living memorial to which still exists in Toynbee Hall, founded in Whitechapel in 1884, which was the pioneer of the university settlements which played a valuable part in subsequent decades in the poor parts of London and elsewhere. They became centres of Christian work in a common cause and attracted to themselves young men of different religious traditions. The Workers Educational Association was also an influential factor in bringing opportunities to working people of study under university teachers.

On the continent of Europe movements towards closer unity among the churches in the nineteenth century were not numerous. The Catholic movement in England was matched within Lutheranism by a high-church movement of its own. For the most part the tendencies were for unity to be set forward within confessional groups rather than between them. Thus the Scandinavian Lutheran churches began to have meetings together in 1857, a habit which since then has grown into close and regular consultation and cooperation. In 1868 the Lutherans in Germany started to come together and set up the *Allgemeine Evangelisch-Lutherische Konferenz*, the forerunner of the present-day close cooperation among the German Protestant churches, which continue to be organised on a regional or *land* basis. And after the first Vatican Council and the tensions which it aroused the Bonn Conferences from 1874 onwards brought together the Old

Catholics, and in consultation with them representatives of the Orthodox and Anglican churches.

## Dangers and Counter-measures

The growing power of liberalism in politics and religion seemed to many Christians to be direct threats to the stability of their faith and tradition. Added to these were new outlooks beginning to be formed by men of science. The Bible was more and more subjected to critical examination in the same way as, and even more minutely than, other historical documents. In response to these various challenges, churches reacted in different ways. The Church of Rome became more authoritative and resistant to any outside pressures. The Ultramontanes, who were trying to exalt the absolute authority of the papacy, grew in power and influence. The official reaction of the Church of Rome to some of the tendencies of the times can be seen in the Syllabus of Errors of 1864. In it Pius IX condemned a large number of theses with appropriate censures, and ended by ana-thematising the view that the 'Roman Pontiff can and ought to reconcile and adjust himself to progress, liberalism, and modern civilization'. In doing this there is little doubt that he expressed the views of many Christians outside his church as well as within it.

In 1859 Darwin published his *Origin of Species*. In it was first put forward his theory of evolution, which caused deep shock to many Christian minds. Hitherto the generally accepted view of the Bible was that it was completely reliable, not merely as an account of the way in which religious knowledge had been received and God's truth revealed but also as an historical account of what had actually happened, a sort of manual of history of the past. A theory of evolution was plainly incompatible with any such view of the Bible. At the same time biblical scholars were questioning the generally accepted view and dissecting the documents of the Bible, showing that they were made up of many different elements, and that their origins were not what had been generally supposed. The authorities of the Roman Catholic Church rejected these findings and forbade its members to have anything to do with such speculations, but gradually other churches began to accept them. The publication of the volume *Lux Mundi* was an important landmark because of the essay by Charles Gore, in which he broke away from the static conservative views of the Bible hitherto held by his contemporaries.

The importance of new thinking, independent of the official church authorities was that a new state of affairs began to appear within the churches, in which differences between Christians no longer corresponded to the boundaries of churches, but cut across them. It took a long time for this process to spread, but in the middle of the twentieth century a position was reached in which every church, except those of the strict 'sect' kind, reflected within itself important divergences of belief and outlook which were not identical with the official formularies or doctrines of the churches themselves. This development had an important bearing on the question of unity, for it made still more irrelevant the structures of churches which have remained virtually the same for several centuries, having originally been formed because they stood for principles which are no longer considered important in their original form.

The nineteenth century therefore provided a number of conflicting tendencies, some ecclesiastical and internal, and some external and deriving from the advance of knowledge in science, politics, critical research of documents or social development. Within the churches themselves there were those who withdrew into a defensive posture of authoritarianism, like the Roman Catholic Church, though the mental attitude was by no means confined to its members. Resistance to new ideas was strengthened by the widespread romanticism of the century, much of which looked back to medieval models. This reinforced a backward-looking mentality, even though it gave rise to artistic and religious achievements of distinction.

## Movements Towards Unity

But when allowance has been made for outside pressures of one kind or another the century gave much evidence of a growing desire for Christian unity for the sake of religious and theological principle. Societies sprang up with the aim of furthering Christian understanding—the Eastern Churches Association, the Church Unity Society (in the United States of America), the Anglo-Continental Society. In England, where many of these movements originated, the Lambeth Conferences, normally held at ten-yearly intervals, beginning in 1867, brought together Anglican bishops from all over the world in a new attempt to reach a common mind and common policies. In doing so it assisted and foreshadowed to some extent growing consultation within the British Commonwealth. The conferences themselves took an interest in Christian unity from the first, and at the end of the century were making specific advances to other churches to create closer relations. Bishop Tottie of Sweden attended the Lambeth Conference of 1908 as a visitor, and the Old Catholics and the Orthodox also figured in considerations of growing Christian contacts.

The increase in travel possibilities and the wealth of England in the nineteenth century greatly facilitated personal contacts between English Christians and those of the continent of Europe. In the light of the difficulty of better relations with Rome, many Anglicans looked to the Eastern Orthodox churches to provide a fellowship of non-papal catholicism of unquestioned pedigree. The Russian Church, then at the height of its influence, aroused special interest, and authors such as John Mason Neale wrote books about Orthodox history, translated its hymns and brought eastern christianity to the attention of a wide public. Anglicans from the United States also began to interest themselves in Orthodox relations and approached the famous Metropolitan Philaret of Moscow.

During the century more and more English people went to Europe for holidays, education or health, and the English 'colonies' which were set up in various continental centres were followed by chaplains to provide them with spiritual ministrations. In the south of Europe these chaplains came under the jurisdiction of the bishops of Gibraltar from 1842 when the bishopric was created, while north and central Europe remained under that of the Bishop of London. Much was done to encourage understanding with the Orthodox by the bishops of Gibraltar, who adopted a policy which avoided proselytisation in any form. Bishop Sandford, Bishop of Gibraltar from 1874 to 1904, followed a policy which has been described as follows by one of his successors. 'From the opening to the end of his episcopate he set his face against proselytism, direct or indirect, in all forms. To detach members of the Greek and Roman Churches from the churches of their baptism he held to be inconsistent with the principles of the Church of England ever since the Reformation; to be a mistaken policy; to be a direct hindrance to internal reform; to be an act of intrusion and schism; to be a violation and outrage of the courtesy increasingly accorded to the Church of England; the creation of fresh wounds in Christendom instead of healing the old.'[8] A cynic might comment that naturally bishops of Gibraltar took this view, for it was the only attitude which was consonant with the pursuit of their particular task, namely the care of Anglicans living among Christians of a different persuasion, who might easily influence their governments to keep out Anglican chaplains unless they behaved themselves discreetly. But there is no doubt that it went much deeper than this, and witnessed to an important principle, namely the ready recognition of the sincerity of other Christians who differed from oneself. In the field of ecumenical relations and church unity the importance of this principle can hardly be exaggerated, for mutual recognition and respect is a *sine qua non* of civilised, and still more of Christian, relationships between people of different beliefs and backgrounds.

The attitude of non-proselytisation was that officially adopted by the leaders of the Church of England, but it was not always followed by Anglican evangelists and missionaries. In the Middle East, for example, missions meant for the Muslims sometimes turned their attention to fellow Christians of the eastern churches, who appeared to evangelical missionaries to be almost as much in need of conversion as the heathen. The small Anglican Arab communities of the Middle East were in origin almost exclusively Christians of one of the eastern churches, who had been induced to abandon their own church for the reformed religion provided by the Church of England sometimes not for religious reasons, but for the political protection of a great power, or for business connections. A similar policy in South India, where there were ancient eastern churches, had the effect of creating an additional schism. Under the influence of British missionaries the 'Mar Thoma' Church broke away from its fellow Syrian Orthodox Christians and adopted a liturgy which was 'reformed' by the omission of prayers for the dead and the invocation of the saints, which were repugnant to the evangelical conscience (see p. 72).

## Bishopric in Jerusalem

We earlier noted eighteenth-century efforts in Germany to bring together churches of the Reformed and Lutheran traditions, and to use the Church of England in this purpose. In the nineteenth century the Church of England was again concerned in a unity enterprise with the churches of Germany, centred on a plan to create a bishopric in Jerusalem which would be a joint operation alternately providing an English and a German bishop to care for the English and

German Christians of the area. Promoted by an energetic tutor to the crown prince of Prussia, a certain Dr. Bunsen, the plan envisaged a bishop who would always be episcopally consecrated according to Anglican requirements. Ecclesiastically, therefore, its character was that of an Anglican bishopric with German Lutheran congregations attached to it, and parliamentary approval was given to this scheme in 1841. As an act of Christian cooperation it did not survive. Much heart-burning and opposition to the scheme came from the Tractarians, and Newman is said to have been influenced by it in submitting to Rome in 1845. Eventually it was revived as a normal Anglican bishopric in 1886 after it had been suspended for five years. Three bishops had been appointed under the original plan.

When the bishopric was set up as an exclusively Anglican operation particular care was taken not to infringe the rights of the Orthodox Patriarch of Jerusalem, who was regarded as the rightful bishop of the holy city: for this reason the Anglican bishop (and later the archbishop) has always been known as the bishop *in* rather than *of* Jerusalem. At the time the Archbishop of Canterbury described the policy of the Anglican bishopric as being to 'establish and maintain, as far as in him lies, relations of Christian charity with other churches represented at Jerusalem, and in particular with the Orthodox Greek Church; taking special care to convince them, that the Church of England does not wish to disturb, or divide or interfere with them; but that she is ready, in the spirit of Christian love, to render them such offices of friendship as they may be willing to receive'.

The many activities of the Church of England in building up good relations with the eastern churches was a pioneer work of importance in bringing them back into living contact with western Christendom. The success which was achieved was not entirely due to ecclesiastical or religious causes, though it was the labours of Christians which achieved it. During the period up to the First World War Great Britain exercised the greatest power in the world, and the close connection between the leaders of the Church of England and those who wielded the power of the British Empire was a strong magnet in encouraging closer friendship on the part of other churches, especially when they were minorities in their own country. It enabled the Church of England to extend its activities in advantageous circumstances.

*Questions of Validity*

Once discussions began to take place between churches, differences of theological principle and practice came to the fore which earlier had been ignored. Among these the question of validity of orders was an important element in relations between those churches which belonged to the 'Catholic' or traditional group and those who had abandoned the traditional form of ministerial orders in their churches and had not retained bishops or, if they had done so, retained them merely as titular offices without serious theological significance. There is little doubt that the question of validity has bulked larger than it ought, and it has therefore seemed to draw to itself a more important place in discussions about Christian unity than it deserved in its own right. The general attitude of the Roman Church has been to lay its main stress on the need to fulfil certain external and identifiable conditions which alone can make ordinations 'valid'. In doing so they followed the point of view of St. Augustine. The idea of validity is a legal concept, and in the case of ordinations validity could be achieved only if an ordination was conducted by a person qualified to do so, who had a right intention, and who used a rite which was itself adequate in form and matter. The 'form' of a sacrament is its verbal content, and the 'matter' is the outward action accompanying it and the materials (if any) used in it. In the case of an ordination this meant that the minister must be a bishop, himself duly ordained in the historic apostolic succession of bishops; he must have the intention to ordain to the priesthood of the Catholic Church (or to the episcopate as the case might be); the rite must express this intention, and it must be accompanied by the laying on of hands.

It is not possible here to enter into all the details of how these things may be tested. It is relevant to note, however, that the Roman Catholic attitude made the sacrament almost independent of the Church itself (see p. 53). An ordination could be fully valid according to these principles, even if the bishop in question was doing something of which the Church disapproved, so long as the external requirements were satisfied. Such an ordination would be irregular, and the persons concerned might never be able to exercise their orders within the Church, but neither of these drawbacks would affect the intrinsic validity of an ordination which had met the necessary conditions.

One result of the condemnation of Anglican orders was to encourage Anglicans to seek support for them from other sources, the Orthodox churches being a natural place to look for such support. During the first half of the twentieth century considerable efforts were expended on trying to secure 'recognition' of Anglican orders by the Orthodox Church authorities. The word 'recognition' is put in inverted commas because the attitude of the Orthodox churches about orders differs in an important respect from that of the Church of Rome. The Orthodox require that the succession be maintained, just as the Romans do, but they do not stress the legal concept of validity: when they use the word they usually mean something different. The Orthodox are mainly interested in authenticity or canonicity, that is to say, their stress is laid on the fact that any ordination must be one which has the proper living church authority. Outward circumstances of the rite may be perfectly correct, but if the ordination is not authorised by the church of which the bishop is a member it is not a true ordination. A man who has been irregularly ordained may therefore be reordained, if he is admitted to the church, or he may be accepted without reordination if he submits to its authority, but in this case it is the acceptance which provides the authenticity of his ordination rather than the original rite.

When, therefore, Anglicans approached the Orthodox churches to discuss with them the question of Anglican ordinations the matter was conducted on different presuppositions from the discussion with Roman Catholics. It was assumed by the Orthodox that, as Anglicans were not members of the Orthodox Church, their orders could not be fully authenticated until they were. So the issue was narrowed to the question as to whether, if Anglicans were to become members of the Orthodox Church, the other aspects of their ordinations would be considered as satisfactory. The question was whether the Orthodox churches were satisfied that Anglicans had preserved a proper historical succession in the episcopate, and other necessary elements of the rite.

As a consequence of discussions, recognition was given by the Ecumenical Patriarchate to Anglican orders, and subsequently by the Patriarchates of Jerusalem, Alexandria and Rumania, and by the Church of Cyprus. But the limitations must once more be stressed, for in effect these decisions only stated that the Orthodox recognised Anglican orders as being as good as any other orders outside their own church, specifically stating that they were on the same footing as the orders of the Roman or Armenian churches.

The Roman Catholic decision of 1896 against Anglican orders was not an infallible utterance of the Pope, and many Roman Catholic theologians believe that it was mistaken. It may yet be modified or reversed, but, if so, it is likely to be through some kind of reinterpretation and not by a direct repudiation of an earlier decision. This may not be as difficult as was once thought.

The question of episcopacy has become particularly important for Christian unity in the twentieth century, and Anglicans have been especially concerned with it because they have links both with the churches of reformed tradition and with those who did not accept the Reformation. The problem of the unity of Christendom raises in an acute form the need to find a common ministry which can be accepted by all Christians, and episcopacy has been the only form of ministry generally considered able to fulfil such a rôle.

### North America

The settlement of North America at first reproduced in separate compartments the religious beliefs of those who made their homes there. Many of the emigrants went there partly to find freedom to practise their own religion, but in doing so they did not always allow the same freedom to others. They carried with them intolerance as well as conviction. Certain areas of North America became identified with specific religious local establishments. New England became largely the preserve of Congregationalism; Virginia was a stronghold of Anglicanism; Pennsylvania exhibited a Quaker spirit of tolerance; and Maryland gave a home to a tolerant Roman Catholicism under the inspiration of Lord Baltimore. It was natural that new emigrants should settle together with people of their own country and religion, for reasons of self-help as well as for reasons of language. The first immigrants therefore formed distinctive patches of religious affiliation in many places.

But this state of affairs did not last long, for the successive waves of settlers and the expansion of the frontier westward made more and more intermingling inevitable; and although blocks of people of the same place of origin continued for many years and can still be recognised today, the general religious situation became 'pluralistic'. The attachment to home churches, which in most cases used the original home language, gave an important psychological security to the settlers, and it still does so in the twentieth century for new groups who come in large numbers. The familiarity of the old church, and the chance of speaking and hearing the old language, provided great comfort. But it had its dangers and risks. The continuation of old religious traditions had negative as well as positive aspects. On the one hand, it helped people to be content in new surroundings just because they were not entirely cut off from their previous existence. On the other hand, it hindered a ready adaptation to their new society, because it cut them off to some extent from other settlers who had a different religious and linguistic background. Moreover, the persistence of the use of their old customs tended to identify them as separate ethnic groups, and this in turn put temptation in the way of foreign governments to try to exploit such ethnic groups in order to increase their internal influence within North America itself.

Fragmentation is a mark of North American religion much more in the United States than in Canada. (It will be convenient to refer to the United States, even if it leads to the anomaly of using the title before the States were in fact united. The word 'America' is not suitable, since it includes Canada and South America, and even North America includes Canada. 'United States' is therefore the most convenient way to describe the territory which that country now comprises.) The large number of different churches in the United States was due in the first place to the importation of all the divisions of the immigrants from Europe. Not only were these settlers divided into different denominations but they were divided into different groups within the denominations, each of which organised its own church. There were therefore separate groups of German, Swedish, Danish, Norwegian, Finnish and Icelandic Lutherans, different sorts of Baptists, Presbyterians and others. So that in the year 1890 there were 143 denominations.[9]

But in addition to these, which were conservative in outlook, new sects sprang up in great profusion in order to meet the spiritual needs of the frontier. These were for the most part of a revivalist nature, and they did not fit in easily with the conservative elements of the older churches. They therefore formed their own religious groups. As the history of sectarianism shows, the new enthusiastic religious groups in the second or third generation themselves often turn into respectable unadventurous churches rather like those from whom they originally broke away. Then they are inadequate to cope with the new revivalism of their successors.

There were also social strains causing further church division in the United States. The civil war split the churches as well as the country, and the tensions engendered by the slavery question, the fighting and the question of states' rights divided many of the Protestant churches into a northern and a southern branch which were at enmity with one another. Meanwhile specifically Negro churches were formed in the south and gathered strength. The situation was one of great complexity, and the divisive tendencies were evident, but against them there gradually formed a contrary current which was to counteract them and to mend the links which had been broken. The most important of these influences was what may be termed 'Americanisation', that is, the need to find a specifically American form of religious practice which would correspond to the social needs of the developing country.

Conformity to a standard of convention and method of life has been a marked feature of settlement in the United States. The extreme variety of background of the immigrants has made such conforming pressure essential: the size of the country made local tensions damaging, and made more acute the difficulty of creating a sense of common nationhood. The churches played an important rôle in integrating newcomers into the local community, especially when the pattern of church life was American rather than European. As soon as 'Americanisation' began to affect the outlook of the younger generation, a growing tension became apparent between them and their parents. The young Americans soon lost the ability and the desire to speak the mother tongue of their parents, and religious bodies which conducted services in a foreign language and preached sermons in it began to alienate the younger groups.

Successive waves of immigration have faced the same problem, and it has by no means been solved. In the United States in the mid-twentieth century the Orthodox churches, for example, continue to be organised by their European origin, Russians, Greeks, Serbs, Bulgarians, etc. The fact that there have been several different immigrations has kept the old language alive, but most of the second and third generations have found these religious habits unwelcome and irrelevant for them. Moreover, the Orthodox principle is to have one church in each country using the language of the inhabitants, so that the present separations in the United States deny their own basic standards. The persistence in the use of European languages has often led the younger generation to attach itself to a different church.

## The Disciples of Christ

At the beginning of the nineteenth century two members of the same family, named Campbell, tried to overcome the divisions which kept Christians apart and to start to reconcile warring sects. Campbell attempted to abandon the traditional outlooks of denomination- alism and to persuade Christians to give up human creeds and unite on the basis of the Bible. But his efforts made one more denomina- tion, even though committed to a programme of Christian unity, which has come to be known as The Disciples of Christ. The methods used showed a tendency which grew among American Protestant churches, namely to weaken the stress placed upon doctrinal ortho- doxy, or doctrinal formulations of any kind, and to put their stress on social aspects of Christianity.

An examination of the history of religious life in the United States shows how the divisions of the churches, of which there are more than 200 different organisations, were affected by the conditions of the growing country. North and South, as we have seen, provided one cause of break: the spread of the frontier westward produced a different kind of religion, revivalist and emotional, from what was found in the East. Different churches became attached to different classes. The Anglicans, the Protestant Episcopal Church to give their church its right title, were identified with the earlier settlers and the 'establishment' in the modern loose sense of that word. They were not prepared to follow the frontier with its rough conditions, im- maturity and lack of culture. Methodists and Baptists therefore did the Evangelistic work and set up their churches among those who were facing the severest struggles. Anglicans or Episcopalians still continue to be the church of the privileged, to the extent even of drawing recruits from other churches as a sign of their rise in the social scale. But many of the churches which were close to the pioneers and were originally adaptable and individualistic have now become organised in the typical American church pattern, with central administration and large local parishes and budgets. The

Methodists, for example, became as respectable and 'established' as any other church—the Presbyterians too.

No church in the United States has any special relationship to the State: all are free churches. Among Protestants the importance of the individual tenets of the church in many cases became of little or no importance, and it has been said with some truth that Protestants in the United States change their church as readily as they change their grocer. They take the church which gives them the best service, usually in the form of the most convenient Sunday school for the children or the most efficient and socially agreeable church organisations. But there are still traces of ancient animosity, as in Canada, for example, where Roman Catholics have separate parishes with churches close to one another, but divided into those of French, Italian and Irish origin.

*Canada*

In Canada the religious map was formed by a few main denominations and is far less variegated than the United States. The French-speaking part of Canada was, and is, almost exclusively Roman Catholic, while the English-speaking part was chiefly divided among Anglicans, Methodists, Presbyterians and Congregationalists. These groups corresponded to the national origins of those who composed them, the Anglicans including empire loyalists who had migrated across the border from the United States rather than give up their allegiance to the crown. In 1925 a notable union was achieved in Canada by the merging of Methodists, Congregationalists and Presbyterians to form the United Church of Canada, which thus became the second largest church in the dominion. But the union aroused great bitterness and did not succeed in uniting all the members of the constituting churches. About a third of the Presbyterians declined to go into the United Church and continued separate. The new United Church was set up by special legislation and the transfer of property governed by the voting of the various congregations. The difficulties which then arose were a salutary warning of troubles which may arise in attempts of this sort. In one village, for example, a minority of Presbyterians refused to join the United Church: the majority, however, agreed to do so, and the new United Church was set up in the village in the Methodist building, which was the better of the two available. The former Presbyterian church was then shut down. The minority, which had worshipped there all their lives, then asked if they could buy it, and were refused. The church was sold and pulled down, and the Presbyterian minority were forced to worship in the Anglican church, which offered them hospitality as a temporary measure. They then had to find money to build for themselves a new Presbyterian church, and this they eventually did. Such events, which were not uncommon, left a legacy of bitterness and ill-will which were still evident nearly forty years later.

Conversations have begun in Canada between the Anglican Church of Canada and the United Church with a view to future union. In the United States there have been a number of mergers, almost all between churches of the same confessional groups, such as different branches of Presbyterianism or Lutheranism. The Episcopalians have agreed with the Polish National Catholic Church on a relationship of full communion without any change in the organisational structure of their churches, each retaining its full independence. Other churches of different traditions are engaged in discussions with a view to unity on a wide scale, and these include many of the larger Protestant groups.

In the United States the National Council of Churches, formerly the Federal Council of Churches, has played a large part in fostering better understanding and practical cooperation among the churches. It has included Orthodox churches as well as Protestant groups, although its general tone is more to the liking of Protestants than of Orthodox, and there are tensions between the two. The Council is active in social and international affairs, but does not succeed in carrying all its members in support of its policies. Abroad it has set up American community churches in centres where Americans were to be found in substantial numbers in Europe and elsewhere, and in doing so has betrayed a tendency of American Protestants to value what is called 'the American way of life' more highly than the doctrines of the churches themselves. Whereas this may be a healthy corrective to some church divisions, it exacerbates the tensions which divide Americans from the foreign people among whom they live and work.

Since the Second World War Christian leaders of the United States have played a large part in efforts towards ecumenical action, especially in the promoting of world confessional organisations and in the support of the World Council of Churches. It is interesting to note how the expansion of these activities coincided with the increase of responsibility of the United States in international political affairs. Moreover, the vast wealth which the United States owns, both corporately and privately, has enabled its church leaders to promote those international organisations which appeal to them. The rôle which the Lutheran World Federation, for example, has played in the second half of the twentieth century owed its effectiveness and influence exclusively to American organisation backed by American money.

[1] *The Churches of Eastern Christendom*, London, 1927, p. 304.
[2] *History of Russia*, p. 207.
[3] John Shelton Curtiss, *Church and State in Russia*, New York, 1940, p. 24.
[4] Curtiss, *op. cit.*, p. 28.
[5] *The Victorian Church*, Part I, London, 1966, p. 61.
[6] Chadwick, *op. cit.*, p. 570.
[7] J. R. H. Moorman, *A History of the Church of England*, Edinburgh, A. & C. Black, 1953, p. 392.
[8] Bishop Knight, *The Diocese of Gibraltar*, London, p. 164.
[9] Neill and Rouse, *History of the Ecumenical Movement*, London, S.P.C.K., 1954, p. 221.

# 10

---

## Present and Future

### The Twentieth Century and After

THE First World War was a watershed in human relations in all fields, and the churches were deeply affected by its conduct and aftermath. Before the war there were, as we have seen, many different trends affecting Christian relations, and at the beginning of the twentieth century a number of strands towards greater Christian cooperation and understanding seemed to be drawing together. Organisations specifically aimed at Christian service in social matters had grown in strength. The missionary movement was finding it necessary to concert its various activities and to reach agreement which would do something to counteract the worst effects of Christian division in the mission field. There was a growing Christian movement for peace, and an important conference at the Hague in 1907 gave birth to the World Alliance for International Friendship through the Churches, set up at Constance in 1914. It is ironic that it should have come into being in the very year of the outbreak of the First World War. In 1914 another event occurred which was to affect Christian unity—Nathan Söderblom was appointed and consecrated Archbishop of Uppsala in Sweden.

The modern ecumenical movement is usually dated from 1910, for in that year was held the first official international inter-church conference on a world scale, which by its success and achievements set a pattern later to be followed in other fields. This first conference at Edinburgh was organised to deal with mission affairs and to face the problems which world evangelisation was posing for the churches and for the missionary societies. As in all such pioneer efforts, there was opposition, but in spite of the reservations of some, the conference clearly showed the advantages of such a wide forum of discussion and debate. Moreover, it represented an important change in outlook, for at Edinburgh those who came were the official represent- atives of their churches or societies, and this meant a decisive change from the previous state of affairs, in which all such efforts had been left to the initiative and enthusiasm of those individuals who hap- pened to be interested in closer Christian relationships.

## International Efforts of the Churches

The tragic suffering and slaughter of the First World War brought home to Christians the ineffectiveness of their own efforts to bind men together, and the spectacle of Christians on different sides of the firing line condemning the other side was one which could not fail to be a scandal to all who took the Christian faith seriously. Archbishop Söderblom, to whom reference has been made, determined to do all that he could to redress these faults by bringing Christians together across national boundaries in work of practical cooperation for the good of mankind. Largely owing to his efforts, a great international conference was held in Stockholm in 1925, representing all major churches except the Roman Catholics, concerned to create coopera- tion in 'Life and Work', a title which became attached to this move- ment. A second world conference was held in Oxford in 1937.

Parallel to this movement was another, of which the leading spirit was an American Anglican Bishop, Charles Brent, trying to bring the churches together to discuss their differences on the fundamental problems of 'Faith and Order'. Its first great world conference was held in 1927 at Lausanne: its second at Edinburgh in 1937. At the two conferences of 1937 decisions were taken to merge the two movements into one, and to form a World Council of Churches to which the delegates would be officially appointed representatives of the churches, and of which membership would be by churches them- selves. A preparatory commission was set up, but before action could be taken the Second World War broke out in 1939. It was therefore impossible to establish the council until afterwards, and the con- stituent assembly was eventually held in Amsterdam in 1948. World assemblies have been held elsewhere since that date, and the perma- nent secretariat of the council is situated in Geneva. One effect of the work for Christian unity between the wars was seen in the absence of some of the more deplorable features of the First World War, and the

I

links which were kept during the Second World War between Christians of the warring nations in spite of their national enmity.

The Edinburgh Conference of 1910 set up the International Missionary Council to act as a permanent organ of consultation among those responsible for Christian missions. It continued its separate existence until its integration with the World Council of Churches at the third assembly in New Delhi in 1961.

The mission field continued to exercise pressure on the Christians of the old world to do something effective about Christian unity. Disunity in countries where the vast majority of the population belonged to a non-Christian religion was not only a scandal, it was also a serious hindrance to the preaching of the gospel. Moreover, the divisions imported by missionaries into foreign lands were those which had been made in Europe and bore the marks of European history of several centuries earlier. They had no relevance to the conditions or experience of the countries to which missionaries had taken the Christian message. During the twentieth century most of the churches in the mission field have progressed, like their countries, from dependence on European control to independence and management of their own affairs. The paternalism which was taken for granted for so long by the younger churches now became obnoxious to them, and they were no longer ready to allow European Christians to manage their affairs, except as agents of the churches in which they were working and under their local leadership. A number of schemes of unity have been put forward among these younger churches, the most notable of which was the creation of the Church of South India in 1947 from a union of Anglicans, Methodists, Congregationalists and Presbyterians in that area. But even this was not achieved without trouble, and a small schism resulted from it. Moreover, a number of leading churches in the area were not included in it, important among them being the Roman Catholics, Lutherans and Baptists.

### Individual Churches Act

In Europe the movement towards unity after the First World War gathered pace and was supported by many independent activities on the part of various churches. In 1920 the Oecumenical Patriarch of Constantinople issued an encyclical letter calling for closer Christian cooperation. In the same year a Lambeth Conference was held at which the Anglican bishops issued 'An Appeal to All Christian People' of some importance. In it the bishops stated that they were prepared to undergo a form of ordination if it would create the unity which could not be achieved in any other way.

One of the main problems of unity, already noticed, was the difference of ministry between episcopal and non-episcopal churches. In the Church of South India the gap was bridged by an agreement that the church should be episcopal and that all new ministers should be ordained by bishops, while permitting those ministers already serving in the church to continue without reordination. The main problem of reconciling ministries so that all can accept them is that of securing episcopal ordination for ministers already ordained by some other means without implying that their former ordination was in some way incomplete or invalid. It is on this rock that many of the efforts have foundered, although Free Church leaders have publicly acknowledged that only an episcopal ministry has any chance of being universally recognised, and Anglican leaders have paid tribute to the spiritual power of non-episcopal ministries.

The Lambeth Conference of 1920 approved four points, known as the Lambeth Quadrilateral, to serve as the minimum basis for any agreement between churches which would result in full communion or unity between them. They covered: (a) acceptance of the Bible; (b) the two sacraments of Baptism and the Lord's Supper; (c) the Nicene creed; and (d) an episcopal ministry which it described as 'a ministry acknowledged by every part of the Church as possessing not only the inward call of the Spirit, but also the commission of Christ and the authority of the whole body'.

Between the two world wars the Church of England pursued discussions with the Orthodox, the Old Catholics and certain Lutheran churches. It established full communion with the Old Catholics on the basis of the complete independence of both bodies, coupled with a recognition of each other's doctrine and practice in essential matters. Although the agreement affected only small numbers, the principles have wide application. They were as follows:

'1. Each Communion recognizes the catholicity and independence of the other and maintains its own.

'2. Each Communion agrees to admit members of the other Communion to participate in the sacraments.

'3. Intercommunion does not require from either Communion the acceptance of all doctrinal opinion, sacramental devotion, or liturgical practice characteristic of the other, but implies that each believes the other to hold all the essentials of the Christian Faith.'

These principles also served as the basis for intercommunion between Anglican churches and the Spanish Reformed Episcopal Church, the Lusitanian Church of Portugal, and the Philippine Independent Church.

Anglicans and Old Catholics come into daily contact with each other mainly in the United States of America, and there the agreement has not made much difference to the daily lives of those members of the churches to whom it applied. But it removed a scandal of division and allowed mutual help to be given whenever that is convenient. In some ways the agreement would seem to be the application to different circumstances of the principles which apply to the Uniates in the Roman obedience, full communion being combined with different rites and customs in secondary matters.

Between the two wars the Roman Catholic Church did not take part in the common activities of other Christians, although it was invited to do so. It particularly stressed the danger of 'indifferentism', that is, the encouragement of a notion among the faithful that it does not matter much which church one belongs to, as they are all on very much the same level. Efforts were, however, made to improve relations; and the second Lord Halifax was the moving spirit behind informal discussions between Anglican and Roman Catholic theologians which took place at Malines in Belgium between 1920 and 1925. The Archbishop of Canterbury and the Pope were cognisant of what was going on, but both were cautious and unwilling to give official support. The Roman Catholic hierarchy in England had not been consulted, and strongly disapproved, being of the opinion that continental Roman Catholics knew far less about the Church of England than they themselves did. One interesting suggestion made from the Roman Catholic side during the conversations was that the Church of England might become a sort of Uniate church retaining its own customs, rite and government. No immediate practical result came from the talks, although they certainly played some part in preparing the way for better future relations. The closure was put upon such efforts by the encyclical *Mortalium Animos* of 1928, by which Roman Catholics were forbidden to take part in ecumenical activities.

The pressure on the churches from the world outside had been dramatically increased by the success of the Bolshevik revolution in Russia in 1917, through which the largest of all Orthodox churches found itself under a régime which was not merely hostile but actively persecuting and trying to break up the Church. The Church survived, and during the Second World War played a part of no little importance in supporting Russian morale in the desperate struggle against German invasion. As a consequence, the Russian Church began once more to enjoy a certain freedom, and it was able to resume contacts with Christians abroad. The Church of England was the first foreign church to be able to send an official delegation to the Russian Church after the revolution: Archbishop Garbett of York visited Moscow in 1943 as the tide of war was beginning to turn in the Russians' favour.

Since that time many contacts with foreign churchmen have been permitted to the Russian Church leaders by the Communist government, and for some years after the Second World War the Russian Church enjoyed a relative freedom in which it flourished. But in the 1960s oppression once more became the order of the day, and its life became more and more difficult.

## Second World War

One result of the Second World War was that all the Slav countries fell under Communist rule, for the most part without the consent of their peoples. The churches of these countries, when they were Orthodox, took their cue from the Russian Church, and tried to maintain as much independence for their church life as possible without falling out with the Communist authorities. In this tricky situation the leaders of some of the Orthodox churches have been accused of being too friendly to avowedly atheist governments, though it is difficult to see how they could have avoided such an accusation and survived. There were, however, some events where this cooperation left a bad impression, in particular the liquidation of the large Uniate churches in Russia, Poland and Rumania. There can be no reasonable doubt that some Orthodox willingly allowed themselves to collaborate with the Communist governments in destroying these churches, which had been a running sore for them for so many years. No attempt can be made to justify acting in this way, but it has to be remembered that in some cases these Uniate churches were originally set up as the result of equally disagreeable intrigue on the part of those concerned.

Under Communist rule are also many millions of Roman Catholics, chiefly Poles, Hungarians, Czechoslovaks, Slovenes and Croats. Their resistance to Communist pressure has been heroic, and, whatever their past, since the end of the Second World War they have undoubtedly been the protagonists of freedom against improper and illiberal tyranny.

The actual pursuit of atheist policies and propaganda under Communist rule has been accompanied in western Europe since the war ended in 1945 by a growing alienation of intellectual circles from the Christian churches, and by increasing pressures of secularism and hostility to the churches. When the war ended the churches had an opportunity once more to give moral leadership to Europe, but they did not take it. It is indeed somewhat depressing to note throughout history how slow the churches have been to read the signs of the times. Too often they have failed to act until they have been forced to do so against their will.

## Pope John XXIII

A dramatic change came over the situation of Christian relations with the pontificate of Pope John XXIII. He was elected in 1958, already an old man in his late seventies. There seems little doubt that he was put in as a stop-gap who would hold the fort until some commanding figure could be found. But his own personality became the most commanding of all modern Popes, and his appeal to the world changed public sentiment to an astounding degree. He was simple, straightforward and animated by a Christian spirit of love which men could not but recognise, and early in his reign he announced that he was intending to call an 'Ecumenical Council' of the Church. The phrase 'Ecumenical Council' in this connection meant a council of all the bishops of the Roman Church; but from the beginning Pope John clearly showed that he intended it to be a council which would pay great attention to Christian unity. The announcement of his intention was carefully timed on the last day of the week of prayer for Christian unity, and thus was linked with this cause.

His plan met with much opposition, and in conservative circles it was thought to be ill advised and badly timed. But nothing could withstand the impetus which the Pope gave to it and his insistence on promoting brotherliness with other Christians. In 1960 a dramatic personal visit was paid to the Pope by Archbishop Geoffrey Fisher of Canterbury, an event which had far-reaching psychological results and was one of the most influential events in helping to prepare a better atmosphere. That one visit itself brought out into the open a surprisingly large number of Roman Catholic priests and theologians who were deeply convinced of the need for Christian unity, but who had hitherto been restrained from expressing it.

The Vatican Council itself, which continued for four long sessions from 1962 to 1965, was probably the most important event of Christian history since the Reformation, for it changed things in a way which any reasonable person would a short time before have said was quite impossible. It covered the whole field of church life and revealed an astonishing readiness to entertain new ideas and radically to re-examine many of the practices and much of the thinking which had been taken for granted for centuries. The ferment which it promoted has only begun and will continue for decades in the future. Its chief note was the need for renewal throughout the Church.

Pope John died in the middle of the Vatican Council and was succeeded by Paul VI, a man of very different temperament but committed to the same ideals as his predecessor, as he himself stated quite clearly before his election. His behavoiur towards other churches has been marked by a deep humility and love, and visits to Jerusalem and Istanbul were startling signs of his earnestness in the cause of better understanding.

At the beginning of the council observers from other churches were invited to be present. Not only were they formally welcomed but they were given better places than most of the bishops who were members of the council. Their wants were constantly met, and courtesies frequently paid to them. They were also consulted about the council and its procedure, and on more than one occasion their views resulted in an alteration of the agenda to satisfy them. This was an incredible reversal of all they had learnt to expect, and it betokened a genuine change of outlook on the part of the whole Roman Catholic Church. Certainly there were some who disliked the change, but they were shown to be in a surprisingly small minority at the council.

So many and so widespread were the changes as to leave a sense of bewilderment. They could perhaps be summed up by saying that the

Vatican Council brought about a complete reversal of the mentality and attitudes of the Counter-Reformation and substituted for them a loving regard for their fellow Christians instead of enmity. The council recognised other Christians not only as erring brethren but as fellow-workers in trying to win the world for Christ, and went so far as to accept their churches as real churches in the providence of God. The visit of Archbishop Michael Ramsey of Canterbury to the Pope in 1966 was undertaken as the visit of the head of one world-wide church to another.

All this did not mean that the Roman Catholic Church in one fell swoop abandoned the dogmas which it had hitherto maintained. They remain, and with them serious obstacles to complete agreement still exist. But it has become plain that many of these dogmas do not provide such serious obstacles as was once thought, that they can be re-interpreted in a more acceptable form than was usually understood. Two main lines of development in this respect can already be seen among Roman Catholics. One is a reinterpretation which is affecting both belief and morals. Some Roman Catholic theologians have abandoned the old way of explaining the presence of Christ in the sacrament as transubstantiation, one example which is chosen from many. In morals changes on the subject of contraception have already taken place, and others have been discussed. In these reinterpretations it is possible for Roman Catholics and members of other churches to find themselves much closer together than they thought. Official discussions with Anglicans, Lutherans and other theologians have begun to help towards such understanding, and Roman Catholics have more and more taken part in the deliberations of the great ecumenical bodies, of which they have become to all intents and purposes members, even though they do not always have the technical status belonging to membership.

The second line of development is the possibility of regarding certain Roman Catholic dogmas as applying to their own church rather than to all Christians. This has been suggested as a way of explaining the dogma of infallibility, that it could be regarded as a dogma for Roman Catholics, which need not hinder the growth of sacramental relations with Christians of other churches. As regards the Orthodox churches, Roman Catholics have already recognised the validity of their sacraments and permitted a certain freedom of inter-communion between the two. The Pope's position has already been modified by the council's acceptance of the doctrine of collegiality of all bishops.

It is not surprising that stresses have appeared within the Roman Church as a result of these remarkable developments. The problems which Christians face are basically the same, and they have begun to work together in meeting them. In such common cooperation Christians have learnt to understand each other better, and a new sense of unity has appeared.

At the end of the 1960s there was a large number of unity negotiations in train among churches in all parts of the world. Many of them, like those between Anglicans and Methodists in Britain, were concerned with the creation of new constitutional bodies either in stages or at once. The sudden whole-hearted entrance of Roman Catholics into the ecumenical field has changed the whole balance of relationships, and has required new thinking. The end of the Vatican Council inaugurated a new era in Christian life and unity. Theological views are in a state of flux, and churches have begun to recognise that it is only through facing theological, practical and liturgical problems together that they can make their full contribution to the world.

## Some Issues in Christian Unity

In conclusion, various alternatives face Christians when they try to find practical forms of expression for relations between them. It can hardly be denied that if Christians were intended by their master, Jesus, to live in loving fellowship with one another some outward forms are needed through which such fellowship can be shown. To give attention to the outward does not mean any diminishing of the truth that it is inward unity or unity of the spirit which is most important. An outward unity without the spirit of unity is nothing but an empty shell, but in grappling with the problems of men living together in a material world the external needs to be given its due importance. Although in the gospel of John, Jesus is reported as saying that unity is basically spiritual, he also added that all men would know that Christians were his followers by the love which they showed to one another, and this implies outward manifestation.

The attitudes which Christians take towards the subject of church unity fall into several roughly identifiable groups.

1. There are those who see no need of any organisational unity among churches to express the essence of Christian unity. All those

who sincerely profess faith in Jesus Christ should be free to form their own associations with one another and should be freely welcomed by other groups and accorded full privileges in receiving the sacraments and other spiritual benefits. There are numbers of Christian sects organised on this basis, and even within the more traditional churches there are many individuals who in practice share this view and are accustomed to act upon it. Among such groups the question of ministry has no importance, and there is little or no distinction between the layman and the ordained minister.

2. There are also Christians of the Independent or Congregationalist type who hold as a basic principle to the independence of the local congregation, but in practice have organised themselves into regional or national groups which have a recognised and ordered ministry. Nevertheless, in principle every congregation is independent, and the association of local congregations is wholly voluntary at the will of each.

3. There are large Protestant churches which are centrally organised, some of which have long traditions, with an ordered ministry carrying with it the authority of the whole church and organised and controlled by a central church authority. But no theological weight is given to the particular form of the ministry which such churches uphold. These churches justify their form of ministry by appealing to the New Testament, but differences of interpretation of what is to be found there are reflected in varieties of organisation.

4. There are churches like the Anglican or Old Catholic churches which maintain that bishops in the apostolic succession are a necessary part of church order for the fullness of the catholic tradition. The word 'necessary' perhaps begs the question, for there are differences of emphasis among Anglicans as to the need for episcopacy. Some hold that it is essential—of the *esse* of the Church; others maintain that it is desirable but not strictly essential—of the *bene esse* of the Church; yet others have held that it is of the *plene esse*, necessary to the Church's fullness, though in this case it is difficult to see much difference between *esse* and *plene esse*, for something necessary for the Church's fullness must surely be part of its essential nature. Anglicans have been able to hold differing views, and *non esse* is certainly one of them, because the formularies which they use do not attempt to explain why episcopacy is needed, but content themselves with asserting that it should be maintained.

5. The Orthodox churches consider episcopacy to be necessary to the ministry, and with this opinion they hold that the Orthodox themselves alone comprise the true Church. In this last view they take an attitude similar to that of the Roman Catholics about their own church, though there is no authoritative statement defining the church which binds the Orthodox, and there are signs that their exclusiveness in regarding others is gradually being modified.

6. Last, there is the Roman Catholic Church, whose principle of unity is submission to the authority of the Pope. It has often been stated that this means a rigid centralisation and uniformity, but this is not the case, and there is immense variety in custom and outlook, to which the Uniate churches bear impressive witness. Moreover, one effect of the second Vatican Council has been to encourage variety on subjects which hitherto have been sharply defined.

With these facts as background, efforts at reunion between churches have followed one of several patterns which in turn may be numbered.

(a) Those Christians who do not put any importance on outward relations do not think it important to enter into formal negotiations with others. They regard intercommunion with other Christians as a natural state of affairs which needs no particular organisational form.

(b) The Lambeth Quadrilateral (see p. 239) drew attention to the fact that for any union to have reality it must be based on some minimum agreement. The first three terms of the Quadrilateral— Bible, creeds and two main sacraments—are readily acceptable to most of the large churches of Christendom, and attention has been concentrated therefore on the problem of finding a mutually acceptable ministry.

(c) Unity can be reached through what is often known as a 'merger', that is, the abolishing of separate organisations and their replacement by one which takes over the administration and control of the two or more churches concerned. This pattern was followed by the United Church of Canada in 1925, which did not have to face the problem of an episcopal ministry.

(d) Another pattern is that adopted by the Anglican and Old Catholic churches, in which no attempt is made to join two separate organisations together, but each is left to continue in independence, the barriers to full intercommunion and interchange of ministries being done away. For this type of relationship full mutual recognition of one another's ministries is indispensable. In the case quoted both groups of churches possessed fully authenticated episcopal ministries, so that no difficulty arose.

(e) Between (c) and (d) are various intermediate possibilities. The Church of South India adopted episcopacy, but left its non-episcopal ministers to carry on without reordination. This made some awkward problems for relations with other churches which thought episcopacy necessary. It meant, for example, that the ministers who were not episcopally ordained, though full ministers of the Church of South India, could not minister to former Anglicans or in Anglican churches, where their lack of episcopal ordination was considered to be a barrier.

(f) As a result of such difficulties, most schemes involving episcopal and non-episcopal ministries aim at achieving the unification of ministries from the start by some ceremony, which can be regarded as episcopal ordination by those who think it necessary, and yet at the same time does not involve those taking part in any repudiation of the ministry to which they have already been ordained. The ambiguity of such a method seems to some to introduce a species of 'double talk' which is highly unsuitable to such a solemn event, but its supporters maintain that it is not for Christians to tell God exactly what he has to do in responding to the prayers of such a rite, and that the end result can be left to him.

(g) Both (e) and (f) are means of organisational unity, often wrongly and misleadingly called 'organic' unity. From a Christian point of view 'organic' unity is unity in spirit and sacramental fellowship and has no need to be associated with one form of organisation. In the case of plans for unity between the Church of England and the Methodist Church two stages have been proposed, the first to precede the second by a number of years. The first stage is to be a service of reconciliation to unite the ministries, and stage two a merging of organisations.

In 1946 Archbishop Fisher of Canterbury proposed in a sermon at Cambridge that a fresh approach to Christian unity would be for the non-episcopal churches to take episcopacy into their systems. To some this seemed to be a means by which the Church of England could achieve unity with other churches without the pain and trouble of renewing its own life and abandoning those features which are obnoxious to many Christians of the Free Churches. Others, in England at least, saw considerable danger in an organisational union between the Church of England and one or more of the Free Churches, for the latter might lose their freedom and diminish their particular contributions to the religious life of the country.

The recent history of Christian relationships has revealed a number of new factors, the significance of which has not yet fully appeared. But there can be little doubt that a new stage has begun with the conclusion of the second Vatican Council. That council may be seen as the climax of the twentieth-century movement which first brought together the Protestant Churches (Edinburgh Conference), then the Protestant and Orthodox traditions (World Council of Churches), and through the Vatican Council has brought the Roman Catholics into a movement which now embraces the vast majority of the Christian world. For the first time the main bodies of Christendom have begun to concentrate their attention on common action and common life, instead of on the promotion of the interests of their own separate institutions.

Another development of long-term importance has been the appearance of change in the attitude of Christians to non-Christian forces and organisations. Cooperation among Christians has been extended to include the Jews, with whom the Christian churches have recognised a special relationship. Attitudes since the Second World War have shown a reversal of Christian outlooks in the past: these often exhibited extreme hostility to the Jews, accusing them of being the enemies of God, and inflicting fearful persecution and suffering. Christians have begun to seek understanding with the Jews based on a common religious heritage.

Further, the outlook with regard to other great religions has shown significant change. No longer do the leaders of Christian thought adopt an attitude to other great religions which denies the validity of the insights which those religions contain and express. On the contrary there is recognition that the truth is revealed to men in many different ways, and that, even if the Christian gospel is the fullest expression of truth, other religions have their own contribution to make to the truth and they may emphasise aspects of it which Christians undervalue.

In their relations to the secular world Christian points of view have also begun to alter. Many of the best Christian thinkers have recognised that movements in the secular world of thought, marked by an anti-Christian character, have in many instances been a protest against the failure of Christians to meet the demands of their own religion. Dialogue has begun with Marxists and Humanists, in which Christians approach their erstwhile antagonists with a mind open to the insights which others can provide, and humble enough to recognise their own failures and limitations.

The Christian struggle may therefore be seen to be a part of the endeavour of men to find unity in the second half of the twentieth century. It is not for an historical study to predict the future, but those who study history may try to discern the signs of the times, so that men may learn from the mistakes and the achievements of the past. In this way history can be redeemed and may find hope for the future.

# Appendix 1.   A Note on Toleration

STRICTLY speaking, the word 'toleration' does not denote a condition of full religious liberty. It carries with it the suggestion that some ruling power has the opportunity and perhaps the right to inflict penalties or disabilities on others, but graciously refrains from doing so. The twentieth century has not yet seen the application everywhere of the principle of religious liberty, even though the right of men to liberty in religion has been publicly proclaimed and accepted by the majority of national authorities.

In the western world the toleration accorded to religion in the twentieth century has been put down to indifference, and there can be little doubt that a weakening of conviction as to the importance of religious beliefs has contributed to a general feeling that they do not much matter. The movement towards Christian unity, which has been so marked during the first half of the century, has owed some of its success to the enfeeblement of sectarian conviction, even though it has been accompanied by an increased awareness of the importance of charity in relations between Christian bodies and their members.

At the same time, in Communist countries there has been a distinct regression from toleration, and the power of the State has been freely used to try to extirpate religious belief and practice from its citizens. The formal constitutional 'guarantees' of freedom which are to be found in all these countries have not prevented their rulers from using their power to bring pressure against any who profess religious beliefs. It cannot therefore be claimed that there has been an uninterrupted advance in the acceptance of the practice of toleration, even though lip service may be paid to the principle for reasons of policy.

The pressures which have made for toleration in history have been varied. Christians have frequently fallen into the temptation to coerce those who disagreed with them, often other Christians, as our narrative has shown. It is a sad reflection that, when power is available to men, they often use it to stifle opponents and to advance their own ideas. Christians have been peculiarly liable to do this because of the depth of their conviction of the unique character of their faith and of the vital need for men to accept it. Among the Greeks and Romans toleration was common so long as the interests of the State were safeguarded.

Before their alliance with the State under Constantine, Christians maintained the desirability for tolerance, as it was clearly in the interests of their own survival. After Constantine the power of the State was more and more accepted as a proper means to implement Christian orthodoxy, though there were honourable exceptions among Christian writers who upheld the principle of toleration. In the later Middle Ages, when the struggle between Church and State in the West became largely a matter of power politics, and the Christian Church was one element in what was essentially a secular combat, toleration all but disappeared.

The re-establishment of toleration in western Europe came from a combination of many different elements, which took effect slowly and patchily in the various countries of Europe. The Renaissance was an important influence, bringing about toleration through the encouragement of an independent spirit of enquiry, which could not be exercised fully except in conditions of reasonable freedom. The break-up occasioned by the Reformation brought into play a new force for toleration in the shape of minority Protestant churches, who, like all religious minorities, needed toleration for the practice of their own forms of religion.

The events of the sixteenth and seventeenth centuries show that both civil and ecclesiastical authorities were persuaded to abandon a policy of coercion in religion only when it proved to be unworkable in practice. It was found impossible to force the new religious sects out of existence, and the interests of the State gradually forced rulers to give modest freedom to all who were prepared to support the civil establishment, and to confine intolerance to those who seemed to threaten civil security and peace. Security could not be assured without reasonable cooperation among those who made up society, and needless repression became a liability instead of an asset. During the succeeding centuries in England the interests of the State forced ecclesiastics to tolerate religious opinions and practices which they would otherwise have been ready enough to try to suppress.

Even in bad times there were far-seeing men who wrote publicly against intolerance and defended liberty and tolerance on grounds of principle, and Christians themselves gradually came to see that they could not promote a religion based on love by methods which denied it. The most famous writer and influential thinker on the subject in English was John Locke, whose first *Letter Concerning Toleration* appeared in the same year as the Toleration Act of 1689.

Recent developments make it plain that the establishment of religious freedom has by no means been firmly secured, even in Europe. Historical events seem to show that, to be universally accepted, religious liberty must rest on a basis of principle, accepted as binding on every nation throughout the world. It needs to be safeguarded by legal guarantees which can be tested by independent tribunals outside national control, as the minorities commission of the League of Nations began to show between the two world wars.

# Appendix 2. Main Groups of Christian Churches

**Under the Obedience of the Pope**

*Roman Catholics*

Once Christians of the Latin rite, but now using rites of their own language.

*Uniates*

Christians with their own customs and discipline and ancient rites deriving from sources other than Latin.

Maronites
Syrian Catholics
Malankarese
Armenian Catholics
Chaldaeans
Malabarese
Coptic Catholics
Ethiopian Catholics
Russian Catholics
Greek Catholics
Melkites
Rumanian Catholics
Bulgarian Catholics
Ruthenian Catholics
Ukrainian Catholics

**Eastern Orthodox Churches**

Oecumenical Patriarchate of Constantinople

Patriarchate of:
Alexandria
Antioch

Jerusalem
Moscow and all Russia
Rumania
Serb Orthodox Church
Bulgaria

Church of:

Cyprus
Poland
Czechoslovakia
Finland
Georgia (U.S.S.R.)
Albania
Mount Sinai

Synod of Russian Bishops Abroad
Russian Orthodox Greek Catholic Church of America
American Carpatho-Russian Orthodox Greek Catholic Diocese
Estonian Orthodox Church
Ukrainian Greek-Orthodox Church of Canada
Ukrainian Autocephalous Jurisdiction
Holy Ukrainian Autocephalic Orthodox Church in Exile

## Lesser Eastern Churches

Armenian Church (sometimes called Gregorian)
Syrian Orthodox Church (sometimes called Jacobite)
Coptic Church of Egypt
Ethiopian Church (Abyssinian)
Syrian Orthodox Church of Malabar
(The above belong to the so-called 'Monophysite' group)
The Church of the East (Assyrian Church, belonging to the so-called 'Nestorian' group: also called Holy Apostolic and Catholic Church of the East and the Assyrians)

## Old Catholic Churches

Old Catholic Churches
Netherlands
Germany
Austria
Czechoslovakia

Poland
Christian Catholic Church of Switzerland
Polish National Catholic Church of North America

## Anglican Churches

Church of England
Church of Ireland
Church of Wales
Episcopal Church of Scotland
Protestant Episcopal Church of the United States of America
Anglican Church of Canada
Church of England in Australia
Church of the Province of:

New Zealand
South Africa
West Africa
Central Africa
East Africa

Church of Uganda, Rwanda and Burundi
Church of India, Pakistan, Burma and Ceylon
Nippon Sei Ko Kai (Japan Holy Catholic Church)
Chung Hua Sheng Kung Hui (The Holy Catholic Church in China)
Church in the Province of the West Indies
Episcopal Church of Brazil

## Churches with which the Church of England has special relations

Spanish Reformed Episcopal Church
Lusitanian Church of Portugal
Philippine Independent Catholic Church
Mar Thoma Syrian Church

## Other Churches

*The Lutheran Churches*
*The Moravian Church* (Unitas Fratrum)
*The Reformed Churches*
(Presbyterian and Calvinist are also titles used for these churches)
*The Methodist Churches*

*The Congregational Churches*
*The Baptist Churches*
*The Disciples of Christ*
*The Church of South India*
*The Pentecostalist Churches*
*The Salvation Army*
*The Plymouth Brethren* (Darbyites)
*The New Church, the Church of the New Jerusalem* (Swedenborgians)
*The Adventists*
*The Society of Friends* (Quakers)
*The Catholic Apostolic Congregations* (Irvingites)

# Appendix 3   The World Council of Churches

The World Council of Churches was formally constituted at its first assembly in Amsterdam in 1948. It has more than 200 members, each of which is a separate church,[1] sending delegates in proportion to its size to the assemblies. The dates of assemblies subsequent to 1948—Evanston (U.S.A.) 1954; New Delhi (India) 1961; Uppsala (Sweden) 1968. The structure and main organisation of the World Council of Churches are illustrated on the diagram opposite. The member churches belong to the Orthodox, Anglican and Protestant traditions: Roman Catholics are closely associated with the Council, but their church is not at the time of writing (1968) a member of it.

The World Council of Churches is a means of common consultation and action for the churches which are members of it, but the council has no authority over the member churches. Decisions taken by the council, its assemblies or its various organs of action do not commit the member churches except in such cases as the churches themselves have specifically agreed to action through their own authoritative bodies.

The basis of membership of the World Council was amended at the Assembly of 1961, as follows:

'The World Council of Churches is a fellowship of Churches which confess the Lord Jesus Christ as God and Saviour according to the Scriptures, and therefore seek to fulfil together their common calling to the glory of the one God, Father, Son and Holy Spirit.'

In a number of countries the ecumenical work of the World Council is promoted through regional or national bodies such as the British Council of Churches or the National Council of Churches of the United States of America. There are also conferences of Churches held regionally from time to time in Africa, East Asia and Europe.

---

[1] Churches, not denominations, are members: thus Orthodox, Anglicans, Lutherans, and other confessional groups have each a number of member churches which are members in their capacity as independent church organisations.

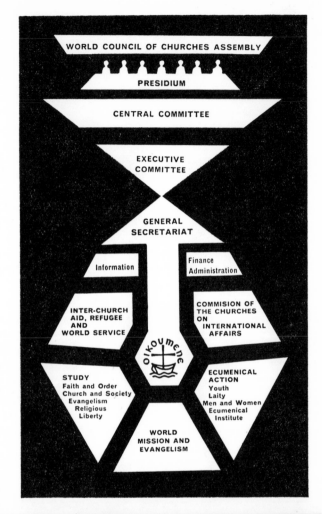

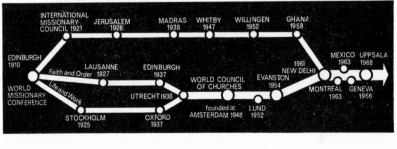

# Index

The following is mainly an index of names. Subjects should be sought through the 'Contents'. Certain names recur too frequently to be indexed, e.g. Orthodox, Anglican, Roman Catholic, etc. Only a few special references are given in these cases. The letter 'f.' following the page number means that further references are to be found on the following pages, and sometimes indicate a substantial section containing references. In cases where one name may cover several aspects of political and religious life, the basic name should be looked for, e.g. Russia will have references to the country, its church at home and abroad and other allied matters.

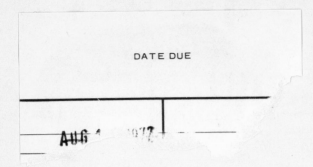